# Executive Etiquette
# in the New Workplace

# *Executive Etiquette in the New Workplace*

*Marjabelle Young Stewart*
*and Marian Faux*

St. Martin's Griffin
New York

This book is dedicated to my family: husband William E.
Stewart, Esq.; daughter Jacqueline Young Anderson, R.N.;
son William Cullen Bryant Stewart, Navy pilot; granddaughter Erin Marjabelle Anderson, teen model.

M.Y.S.

For my parents

M.G.F.

Library of Congress Cataloging-in-Publication Data

Stewart, Marjabelle Young.
    Executive etiquette in the new workplace / by Marjabelle Young
Stewart and Marian Faux.
        p.    cm.
    ISBN 0-312-14103-3
    1. Business etiquette.   2. Executives.   I. Faux, Marian.
II. Title.
HF5389.S74   1996
395'.52—dc20                                                95-41052
                                                           CIP

First published by St. Martin's Press

First St. Martin's Griffin Edition: January 1996
10  9  8  7  6  5  4  3  2  1

# Contents

v

*Too Hot • Catsup and Other Sauces • Jams, Jellies, and
Butter • Stirring and Mashing Food • Using Bread to Clean
the Plate • Drinking • Dropped Flatware or Food
• Removing Dishes • Food Spilled on the Table • Used
Flatware • Sharing Food • Smoking at the Table
• Tricky Foods*

CHAPTER 9

## THE ART OF EXECUTIVE GIFT GIVING 195

*When It Is Appropriate—and Inappropriate—to Give a Gift
• Choosing the Right Gift • Who Chooses Business Gifts?
• Who Pays for Business Gifts? • How Much to Spend
• Tipping Is Gift Giving, Too • Holiday Cards • Office
Collections • Office Showers • Gift Giving Among Colleagues
• Bad Gifts • Wedding Presents • Gifts to the Ill
• Birthday Gifts • Retirement Gifts • Acknowledging a Gift
• Presenting a Gift • Keeping Track of Gifts*

CHAPTER 10

## BUSINESS TRAVEL AND CONVENTIONS 210

*Airplane Etiquette • Expense Account Etiquette
• Conventions • International Travel • Travel Precautions
for Women • A Final Word*

CHAPTER 11

## ETIQUETTE IN THE GLOBAL ECONOMY 223

*Less Ethnocentricity, Please • Skip the Instant Friendship
• Gender Relations Around the World • The Power of Face
• Learning the Ways of Others • Greetings Around the
World • Visiting Customs Around the World*

# Introduction:
# THE NEW WORKPLACE

As we advance on a new century, two fundamental changes are occurring in the world of business. Many experts now agree that U.S. business is undergoing a major restructuring, one that promises to rattle the very bones of our system. This will leave us with a tauter, leaner workplace, one to which managers will be expected to bring a broad range of experience in contrast to the highly specialized skills that were often valued in the past.

The second change is an overdue expansion of our horizon into the global arena. No longer will U.S. executives working in foreign markets be able to get by on technological or intellectual prowess alone. For many years the United States was able by the sheer force of its industrial might to impose its business style on the rest of the world, which could, quite frankly, take it or leave it. Now, as Americans struggle for their place in the global economy, U.S. managers are learning that they must adapt to—and adopt—the manners and mores of other cultures in some instances.

The 1990s also do not look as if they will be an extension of the anything-goes 1980s. Manners may not have been a particularly important accessory for executives in the fiercely competitive, rough-and-tumble 1980s, but the same cannot be said for the cur-

1

rent business climate. If one major trend has already begun to emerge, it is that executives in the new workplace need a solid understanding of executive etiquette. They need to know how to get along in a work environment that is growing more cosmopolitan by the day.

Whether we conduct business at home or in the international arena, graciousness and good manners are important keys to success. Finesse and true sophistication are once again important, much-needed, and highly respected executive skills. Executives will continue to be hired because they have spectacular production records or are superb managers of people, but, in the 1990s, they will also be hired because they know how to dress and speak, how to plan a stylish evening entertainment for international customers, and how to conduct business in another country.

Executives have always been judged in part by their behavior, their ability to navigate the hierarchical and often ritualized structure that we call the American corporation. Everything an executive does, whether it's writing a memo, making an oral presentation, asking for a raise, or typing a letter, portrays an image. The person who aims for an executive-level position (or already has one) must display poise and self-confidence. One's success always depends in part on one's skills, but an equally important part of success comes from one's social skills.

Nothing builds an executive's successful image faster than the ability to handle colleagues, clients, and superiors with tact and style. A lack of social skills can put a damper on a career every bit as much as a lack of technical skills can—and sometimes more. No amount of technical expertise can fully compensate for the inability to get along with others. John D. Rockefeller recognized this decades ago when he said: "The ability to get along with people is as purchasable a commodity as sugar and coffee, and I pay more for that ability than any under the sun."

With the advent of the "me decade," however, top management began to lament the difficulty of finding outstanding people-handlers. One executive said, "Being able to work with others is the single most important characteristic a junior executive can have. I can always buy specialized knowledge, but it is sometimes a problem to find someone with good people sense, an ability to communicate well with others, to build their self-esteem." Another executive defined his personnel needs this way: "I don't care how intelligent my managers are; what I need most are people with people knowledge."

Good manners are essential in building good relationships with other people—and they can ensure that you have a steady supply of support and cooperation. Keeping the stress level high in an office may work for a while, but it rarely works in the long run. What does work over a long period of time is treating people tactfully and graciously, recognizing their work, making them feel comfortable—in short, using good manners to make your way to the top. And that's what this book is all about.

*Executive Etiquette in the New Workplace* was written for men and women on the rise in their professions, people who find themselves in business situations where they are expected to take the lead, whether in conducting a business meeting, entertaining an important client during a convention, or writing a well-planned business letter. It will show how to get ahead using business manners, but, most important, it presents manners realistically, showing what actually happens among people in real situations where good manners are called for and not what an ivory-tower expert thinks should happen. The art of afternoon tea will not be served up in this book, but good, solid business etiquette designed to promote careers will be.

All details of business manners are covered, from how to dress for various professions so the powers-that-be will know someone is serious about advancement, to how to eat tricky foods and order an appropriate wine. Also covered are such subjects as how to speak and write correctly and intelligently, how to apply the etiquette of business travel and convention etiquette, how to manage business entertaining in the home and in restaurants—in short, all aspects of business where one can put gracious manners to work. We discuss emerging business (and social/sexual) etiquette among male and female professionals. There are special chapters on the etiquette of hiring and firing and the etiquette of landing a job. But most important, *Executive Etiquette in the New Workplace* is a book about getting along with others—and how to use that ability to get to the top.

# 1

# Daily Goodwill
# in the Office

The degree of civility that exists in any corporate culture is fairly easy to detect in a short amount of time. Every office has an unwritten code of behavior that includes how employees treat one another. Of course, any etiquette book can list rules of etiquette toward coworkers, but a savvy employee needs to know how to balance this advice against the prevailing atmosphere. Too much formality in an office that does not call for it can make you look stuffy. And a lack of good manners toward fellow employees can make you dangerously unpopular.

Even the failure to promote goodwill in the office can hurt plenty. Executives are people who almost subconsciously take the pulse of relationships among their employees, and such readings do not always follow direct lines of authority. A manager may solicit a secretary's opinion of a junior executive; even if he or she does not do so directly, it may be offered, and the comments will be heard.

If a colleague or even a subordinate is disgruntled with a coworker, rest assured that he or she may well find a way to convey those views to top management. A wounded colleague may not even be out to get someone but may only be responding to a threat to his or her sphere of authority. And in the long run, it simply is not in the best interests

5

of management to promote someone who is disliked or who fails to command respect from coworkers. For this reason, goodwill among the people one works with can never be underestimated as a tool in upward mobility—and as a source of power.

Obviously, since business is basically a competitive operation, one will not always be able to keep a clear record with everyone. Fortunately, with good manners, one can handle even the awkward moments with grace.

## EXTENDING GREETINGS

The way people greet each other varies from office to office. In a large advertising agency occupying several floors of a highrise, coworkers may not even recognize each other on sight. In most companies, though, you do know most of your coworkers, and greeting them at least the first time you see them each day is the custom.

In some companies and regions of the country, particularly in the South, greetings are typically extended to an exchange of pleasantries. People not only greet each other, but they may even stop to chat each time they meet.

You can and must decipher the pattern in your company and in your region of the country. You should make a point of greeting everyone known to you with at least a nod or a spoken word. Many subordinates wait for executives to take the lead in greeting them, so, as an executive, you should be prepared to initiate greetings.

## MAKING INTRODUCTIONS

Introductions are far more casual these days, largely because everything about American life is more relaxed. A few general rules for making introductions do persist, though.

When introducing two peers to each other, it doesn't matter who is presented first to whom. Say: "Joan Porter, this is William Rathbone," or "Jack Jones, I would like you to meet Bill Bailey."

Generally a lower-ranking person is introduced to a higher-ranking person and a man is still presented to a woman; in business, this is definitely true if she holds a more prestigious position than he does. When a secretary or administrative assistant, male or female, is introduced to a superior, however, he or she is presented to the superior. This merely means you say the superior's name first, as follows: "Mr. Fox, I would like to introduce Joan Porter, my administrative assistant." In an informal office, the introduction might be: "Don Fox, I would like you to meet Joan Porter, my administrative assistant."

If you are introducing a new employee to fellow workers, it is nice to add a statement about the new person: "Dick Weber, I would like you to meet Sidney Smyth, who will be working with you in accounting."

Stuffy as it may sound, there is really only one appropriate way to acknowledge an introduction, and that is to say, very simply, "How do you do." Try not to say "Pleased to meet you," "My pleasure," or "Pleased to make your acquaintance," all statements that may not be true ten minutes after you meet someone.

## SHAKING HANDS

People shake hands less frequently today than they did twenty or thirty years ago, and the rule about waiting for a woman to extend her hand has fallen by the wayside, with good reason. A man who is interviewing a woman as a potential employee or serving as host to her if she is a client would naturally be the one to extend his hand first today, and this is often exactly what happens. On the other hand, a woman who wants to signal that she is to be treated the same way as her male contemporaries may show the initiative in shaking hands on occasions where she might not previously have extended her hand. What this means is that you should be prepared to shake hands with anyone you meet.

## USING FIRST NAMES

These days, almost everyone in every office feels free to call everyone else by his or her first name—with the possible exception of an aggressively powerful CEO or an elderly senior partner who has been around since the days of Queen Victoria. Furthermore, in our youth-oriented culture, it's easy to give offense two ways—by making a boss feel old by not using his or her first name and by not showing enough deference when you leap to use first names prematurely.

The best, and possibly only, strategy if you're new to a corporate culture is to not call anyone anything until you figure out what plays well in your particular office. With a superior, it rarely hurts to err on the side of respect.

And for those right out of college and brand new to the workplace, another tendency is to "sir" and "ma'am" superiors. New graduates report being struck with this syndrome even when they've never sirred or ma'amed anyone in their lives before.

Our advice is not to let yourself fall victim to this malady. It may be okay (and even required) with a headmaster, but it's stuffy and aging in the workplace. Better to resist the urge, particularly if there is only a ten- or fifteen-year difference between you and the person at whom you're directing this undue level of respect. It's hard to believe when you're only twenty-one, but thirty-five isn't really that old—certainly not old enough to be called "sir" or "ma'am."

## GREETING SOMEONE WHO ENTERS YOUR OFFICE

There used to be a long list of rules about when to stand to greet someone: Men stood to meet each other and to meet women, women remained seated, and so forth. Today the rules have shifted somewhat. Men still stand to meet each other, and they still stand to meet a woman. There is a growing tendency for women to stand when meeting another person these days. A woman who is greeting a client for a lunch she has planned may feel it is only appropriate to stand to greet that person, even if she is already seated at a table in a restaurant. On the other hand, many women retain the prerogative of remaining seated under these circumstances. Use whichever seems the more natural and gracious action toward the person whom you are greeting.

Younger people rise to greet older people, but, as with the custom of calling an older person Mr., Mrs., or Miss, this custom can have a cutting edge in one's professional life, and it is sometimes difficult to know when it is more tactful *not* to defer to a colleague on the basis of age. About the only honest answer is to play the situation by ear. If your company is very casual, or if a person with whom you deal has indicated anxiety about getting older or even seems vain about appearing young, it is probably more tactful not to stand. On the other hand, if yours is a company where young executives show a great deal of deference to old hands, it is smarter to extend courtesies of this nature.

It is gracious to stand to greet anyone who comes into your office, with the exception of a secretary, assistant, or coworker who comes in regularly. Always stand to greet a visitor to the office. Colleagues frequently shake hands when they have not seen one another for a while, such as when someone returns from vacation or an extended business trip.

As soon as you have finished the greetings, motion the person to a nearby chair if the visitor is obviously going to stay.

## DISMISSING OR ESCORTING SOMEONE LEAVING YOUR OFFICE

Usually the person to signal the end of a meeting is the one with greater power or prestige. A boss, for example, by gesture or word, dismisses an employee. Secretaries and clerical workers are especially accustomed to waiting for this gesture.

You can dismiss someone by simply nodding or thanking him or her for whatever information, material, or service just provided.

Dismissing a colleague requires more subtlety, and, of course, a colleague can also leave whenever he or she wants to. Standing up often signals the end of the meeting between two colleagues.

Important visitors require more diplomacy. If you have time, it is gracious to walk someone out of your office to the elevator or stairs. You can also simply walk him or her to the door of your office, or you can ask your secretary to show the person out. Never allow an important visitor to find the way out, especially if your office is in a maze of corridors.

There is, furthermore, an unspoken etiquette surrounding the order in which coworkers leave a room or go through a doorway. A young person always defers to a superior—in fact, observing a group of coworkers going through a door is a fairly good way to judge pecking order. Technically, a male boss can leave a room before a female secretary or administrative assistant, or even before a lower-ranking female executive, but in practice, men still often defer to women.

## Smoking and Eating in an Office

The etiquette of smoking and eating is basically one of consideration for others. Do not smoke in someone's office without first asking his or her permission; the absence of an ashtray can frequently be taken as a sign that smoking is not appreciated.

In your own office, particularly if it is private, you may smoke as you like, but it is always considerate to ask any visitors if they mind your smoking before you light up.

Increasingly these days smoking is an unacceptable activity. Rightly or wrongly, it is now banned in many work environments as people have become wary about the health risks of even secondary smoke. If yours is a workplace that bans smoking, it is only courteous to oblige—even when no one else is around to see you light up.

It is never polite to eat in front of another person. If someone enters your office while you are indulging in a snack, the only civilized thing to do is to offer the visitor some; an equally civilized person will refuse your offer or take only a small portion. There is one obvious exception to this rule: If you are eating lunch at your desk when someone comes in, you need stop eating only until the person leaves. No one expects you to share a corned beef on rye with mustard.

## ROLLING UP YOUR SLEEVES

There seems to be an unwritten code in each office about whether people shed their suit jackets, loosen their ties, and roll up their sleeves. You will have to decide for yourself whether any or all of these actions are appropriate, depending on the atmosphere in the office where you work.

If you do any or all of these things, it is generally appropriate to unroll your shirt sleeves, put on your jacket, and tighten your tie when you leave the office, even if only to go to lunch.

Now that female executives have settled on suits as appropriate dress for the office, the same is true of them, but to a lesser extent. If an office is really buttoned-down, female managers should take the hint and take off their jackets only when they are working in their own offices or departments. This custom is a funny remnant of a day when dress codes were more archaic, but for the moment, it's still with us.

## NURTURING YOUR COLLEAGUES

When life was simpler, colleagues had more in common and found it easier to be together. A group of young men hired right out of college to work as clerks in the billing department of a major accounting firm—in which they were sure to rise gradually to the top—found it relatively easy to relate to each other.

Relating to colleagues today is far more complex and fraught with opportunities for error. In part, this is because the competition is fiercer and the rewards are greater, but it is also because the workplace is more multicultural. Professional peers today tend to have widely disparate interests in and out of work, as well as a variety of levels of technical knowledge. Nevertheless, anyone who expects to climb the executive ladder cannot afford to ignore peer-group relationships. Maintaining good peer relationships is, in fact, an excellent way to earn the respect of top management.

There are three basic spheres in which you must learn to coexist with your peers—and there is an etiquette to each one. First, you must learn to be a gracious team player. Second, you must learn how to handle your rivals with tact. Third, it is important to show good manners and appreciation to corporate allies or friends.

## Using Team Play

The arrangement of workers—usually junior executives and middle-management people—into teams is a technique that has gained wide acceptance in well-managed companies. The underlying assumption of such organization is that the team players will subordinate their urges to compete for the sake of achieving collectively the task at hand. Teams are often used to implement long-term goals of a company or to solve especially difficult problems, so either the amount of time spent or the intensity of involvement with team players makes it necessary to cooperate, be gracious, and play the game with some degree of civility. Other books on business can provide information about the strategies of team organization. In this one, we are primarily interested in the etiquette of team play, which, quite frankly, consists of how to promote yourself graciously while remaining a good team player.

Sometimes your interests will coincide with those of the other team members. Occasionally they will not. In these instances, it is important to know how to look out for yourself while maintaining a veneer of good manners that will permit you to promote yourself even as you seem—and indeed, remain—a good team player. However important team play may appear in terms of the company's interests, you are never expected to submerge your self-interests for the sake of the team. You are expected only to depart graciously and according to a few rules of good manners.

Even on teams leaders emerge. There will be stars—and although all the team players may appear to function on an equal basis, it is a safe bet that the stars are more noticed—and more rewarded—than those who are strictly team players. It is also a safe bet that those stars make more money and are in line for bigger promotions than the nonstars.

The way to promote self-interest on a team is fairly simple: Play fair with teammates, but take action to make sure you stand out from the group. Call attention to yourself, but do it politely by using your own fine manners, and none of your cohorts will be able to fault you, at least not publicly.

Without upsetting the aura of cooperation, you can use a basic strategy of self-promotion by producing memos playing up your role on the team, speaking up and speaking well at meetings, and asking for rewards for yourself when you have won individual recognition.

Consider the case of John Q., who was part of a four-person team designed to reorganize the sales division of a major corporation. Because the sales force was located in five regions throughout the country, someone would have to begin the study by doing a field survey on current conditions. This necessitated traveling with, talking with, and studying the sales force in action over a period of several months. Since everyone on John's team had personal ties, and since all had responsibilities to other projects in the office, no one volunteered for this time-consuming task. Although the opportunity for glory was there, it seemed like a laborious way to achieve it. In addition, whoever volunteered for this task would be out of the office for two to three months—and that meant losing touch with the fast-paced political situation there. Three of the team members thought they could advance themselves more readily by staying in the office, letting someone else do what they viewed as tedious groundwork, and then moving in to play an integral role in the analytical process that would follow the information-gathering stage.

John, however, saw what he could do with such an assignment. For one thing, he had come up through the sales force, and with his contacts he knew he could do an excellent job of information gathering based on his previous experiences. So he graciously volunteered for the task.

Before leaving to do the fieldwork, John issued a long, detailed report to his manager, describing what he planned to do, how he planned to go about his task, what results he expected to bring in, and, incidentally, modestly pointing out why he was *the* most qualified person to do this job.

An added benefit that he had not anticipated was the closer relationship that resulted with his manager, who had also come up through the sales ranks and who consequently made the extra effort to talk more frequently by phone with John than he did during an average week in the office. The manager even flew out to join John one day in the field to show his support. His praises for John were widely sung in the staff meeting the following week.

Knowing a good thing when he saw one, John completed his assignment, waited ten days, and then went in to his manager to request a raise, based on his additional effort on behalf of the team. Of course, he got it.

John Q. did the correct thing by asking for a raise. Too often in teamwork, it is easy to think of oneself as belonging to the team and to think of rewards as coming to the entire team rather than to individuals. But all teams are made up of individuals. And, as we can see from the example of professional athletics, all the members of a team are not necessarily valued—or paid—equally.

The important aspect of team play is to cooperate only so long as you do not lose ground professionally and then, when you must depart from the team's collective interests, to do so as graciously and politely as possible. This is an easy business maneuver to master since it is a rare teammate who will challenge you *if* you depart fairly. It isn't that someone won't want to challenge you; it is just that to do so will look mean-spirited, hostile, and rude.

While undertaking such a self-promotion effort, it is important to be especially courteous to team members. This is the time (in front of your boss) to make a point of how well a colleague handled a project, to back up a team member's idea in a meeting, to listen with extreme attention to whatever other team members are discussing. Extra efforts such as planning a dinner meeting with a cantankerous colleague or offering to work out a special problem after work will pay dividends in goodwill.

Finally, you must learn to depart from the team effort in order to set yourself apart as someone with leadership potential. The small signs of creativity are often what separate leaders from followers. For example, while you would never deliberately sabotage a meeting of the team, if you have an important and presumably brilliant suggestion about an action the team is recommending, don't bring it up in a team-planning session—bring it up during the big meeting with management. If you bring it up during the team meeting, everyone may jump on the bandwagon and you will have lost a valuable chance to show off your analytical skills. On the other hand, it is polite—to say nothing of cagey—to pretend when you introduce the idea that you thought of it only the night before.

## Handling Rivals

It is a matter of survival to know how to handle a tough, overt competitor. Since you have already chosen to run a civilized race, it won't do any good to try to beat such a rival at his or her own game. You are probably not in top fighting form—not for the kind of fighting that jungle fighters engage in, anyway. There is, moreover, a way to handle treacherous rivals, and that is to beat them *at your own best game*—good manners and fair play. Almost any dirty tactic a rival uses, from starting rumors to antagonizing you in a meeting with a superior, can be countered with a round of polished manners.

In one Park Avenue law firm, where an associate was attempting to form compatible relations with her peers and with the partners who would judge the quality of her work, several problems arose.

The first problem involved a peer who also was Ms. Eaton's officemate. Mr. Addington was always at his desk when she arrived in the morning, and she felt that they held a nightly contest to see who would work latest at the end of the day. Eaton, having worked several years before attending law school, compared her experience in the world of work with that of Addington, who was newly arrived in the work world. She soon arrived at a very simple strategy that worked the first time she tried it: She asked Addington to join her in a quick drink after a particularly tense day. Over drinks they become good friends and their rivalry, while still existing, became an easier and friendlier one.

Eaton's other problem was not so successfully solved. Her other rival was a boy whiz, her age, who had earned partnership in the firm at a prodigiously early age—and who appeared to dislike her on sight for no apparent reason. Her first strategy—discussing their person-ality conflict with him openly—failed. It was like talking to a brick wall.

Once Eaton realized the degree of his inflexibility, she developed a less satisfying but alternate strategy, which was to enlist the aid and support of several other partners whom she subtly made aware of her problem in working with the man. In particular, she told one very senior partner of the constant stream of criticism she was receiving and asked if he would give her a progress report from time to time so she would know where her real strengths and weaknesses lay. She got the supportive feedback she needed and had at least a 50–50 chance of garnering some support if a showdown became necessary. In her day-to-day dealings with her rival, she maintained a polite but frosty relationship. This strategy hardly reduced what was a deadly serious rivalry, but it made life in that law firm slightly more bearable for everyone involved.

Handling overt and possibly malicious rivals requires a great deal of flexibility. On one level, you must show yourself to be an equally tough competitor—as Eaton did when she enlisted the aid of a partner with even more clout than her major rival had—and on another level, you have to handle the situation tactfully—again, as Eaton did by maintaining her veneer of good manners even though she was not receiving the same courtesy in return.

## Dealing with Others' Underhandedness

Never hesitate to rebuff someone if necessary, particularly someone who will eventually attempt to discredit you openly. If you show initial toughness, your rival may just give up and go on to easier prey.

Attacks by this kind of rival often take the form of a challenge, particularly when you are both in an important meeting. It may also take the form of criticism intended to shake your confidence.

If the criticism or challenge is public, change the battlefield to a more private one if at all possible. Stay calm, stay polite, and, what-ever you do, don't let the issue blow up. You might, for example, respond to a critical statement made during a meeting by saying

"That's an interesting point, Bill. Perhaps we should discuss it after the meeting." If your rival continues the attack, he or she will only appear hostile and may even run the risk of raising others' ire by prolonging the meeting, a real faux pas in most companies.

Avoid riling this kind of a competitor (or anyone, for that matter) with such statements as: "You're dead wrong about that," or "You don't know what you are talking about." This is arrogant and guaranteed to produce anger in anyone toward whom it is directed. On the other hand, it is polite and slightly unnerving to a rival to say, in your most gracious tone, "There are probably some facts about this situation that you don't know, and perhaps you would revise your thinking somewhat if you understood them fully."

If a challenger won't quit, you will have no choice but to rebuff him or her. Particularly in public, take care to do this in polite, articulate, measured tones that show you mean business. To withdraw at such a time, either in anger or with perfect grace, is liable to be taken as a sign of weakness on your part—not a good executive quality.

A dash of polite anger can even, on occasion, be put to work for you. Show anger, if you must, but do not let it disintegrate into rage. Most important, reserve displays of anger for moments when they will be truly effective; anger is not worth wasting on small things that do not matter to you.

When you must make a counterattack that shows a degree of anger, try to do it privately. Do not do it, however, over dinner or drinks; the issue is a professional matter and should be transacted in your office if at all possible.

Tell your rival you want to speak with him or her. Begin the meeting by pointing out that you have been angered by the unfairness of the person's actions. If he or she reiterates your errors again, be prepared to defend yourself, if necessary, to show that you know your strengths, but do not let the conversation sink to a nitpicking level.

The point in showing anger during a confrontation with a rival is to warn the person off, not to extend the battle over what either of you thinks is right or wrong. State flatly that you will not tolerate unfair or untrue comments, particularly when they are made in public places, such as in a conference with your supervisors. Be specific about what you will not tolerate. Do not add any "or elses." Let the other person worry about what they may be. Try to be the one to end the conversation.

The next time you see your rival, be polite, although this is not the time to gush or extend an olive branch that might be taken as a sign of weakness. Such an action could, in fact, undermine the element of threat in your previous meeting. A rival will undoubtedly be prepared for further hostility on your part and may likely be harboring some, so a show of good manners will serve to throw him or her further off balance and possibly make others wonder what the person's new level of hostility toward you is all about.

## Overcoming Malicious Gossip

Gossip is part of any office's informal channel of communication. There is one wise way to deal with it: Earn a reputation for not spreading gossip and keep alert to any gossip that is interesting or helpful to you. If someone is spreading malicious or damaging rumors about you, you will want to know about it, and one way of ensuring that you will hear about it is to be receptive.

Rumors may seem to be too petty a subject even to bother with, but, sadly, more than one career has been needlessly destroyed by a wily competitor who was all too willing to stoop to spreading them. Beware—and be prepared. The most damaging kinds of rumors are those that have to do with sex and how you do your work. A rival may also start a rumor that you are actively seeking another job or even that you have accepted one.

When a damaging rumor is started, confront its originator as soon as possible—in public. Since you are going to handle this situation in a calm, polite, up-front manner, and since there is little doubt about the motives of the person who has started the gossip, you have nothing to lose and everything to gain by making the confrontation a public one.

Even if the rumor contains a grain of truth, all is not lost. You still may be able to outwit a rival while not obviously denying the rumor. A well-mannered public confrontation might go like this:

J.: I understand that you have been telling people that I am having an affair with Jane in accounting.

M.: (*probably in a very flustered voice*) Well, I did hear something to that effect.

J.: And so you passed it on to a few people.

M.: (*very flustered*) I don't remember, I may have told someone.

J.: Where exactly did you hear this?

M.: Why, ah, Betty, the woman I ride home with, told me she heard it from someone in accounting.

J.: Well, I would really like to get to the bottom of this, so suppose you and I go talk with Betty to find out more about it.

Sometimes you don't even have to go this far to confront someone who has spread a rumor about you. You might simply say:

K.: I heard that you told our boss that I was planning to accept a new position with ABC Corporation.

S.: (*will probably just stutter*)

K.: Well, that's quite a piece of misinformation, isn't it?

S.: (*more stuttering, or*) I don't know. Is it?

K.: It certainly is. I've straightened it out with our boss, and I assume that you won't be repeating it anymore.

End of exchange and end of rumor, most likely. What is interesting about this exchange is that K. just might have been making a move to accept a new position. But if she does not yet know for sure that the new position will materialize, or even if she will be accepted if it does, then K. can honestly label the rumor as misinformation. And even if K. cannot honestly so label it, it might be better to do so anyway for the sake of self-preservation.

## Mending Fences with Rivals

Fortunately, most instances of competitiveness are small flare-ups that may irritate you momentarily but not truly jeopardize you professionally. Therefore, whenever possible, let meaningless gossip or malicious acts go past you. Always try to save ammunition for the big fights. And finally, it is just good manners always to be willing to make an ally of a former rival. It is better for you, your colleagues, and the morale of the company if you maintain an optimistic, open stance. A one-time confrontation with someone doesn't mean you're destined to be lifelong enemies. In fact, a person who thinks enough of you to make you a serious rival might do wonders working on your behalf. Always look for a chance to mend fences whenever you have had a run-in with a colleague—over lunch or with drinks after work, or work out your aggressions on the racquetball court.

## Learning the Importance of the Right Friends

If you are a young executive or a new employee in a company and trying to make your reputation, it is important to choose friends at work with great care. This does not mean selecting friends only for what they can do for you, nor does it mean choosing those people whom you would most enjoy socially. It does mean associating yourself with those of your peers who are earning reputations for themselves as serious, earnest comers within the company.

Often there is a social group within a company. Members will fraternize with each other during the day (often to the detriment of their work) and they may see a lot of each other outside work. This group may or may not consist of the real comers in the company; often, particularly if they are young, members are more involved in their social lives than in their professional lives. Groups like this are most often formed by young executives just out of school who miss the informal camaraderie of their school days and want to continue it in an office atmosphere. If you want to make an impression on the top brass, it is better not to be too closely associated with these social groups, unless they're also very serious about their work.

On the other hand, it is always wise to maintain good relations with all your peers. One way to be friends with such a group is to socialize with them occasionally—but only occasionally—outside work. Do this by occasionally participating in fairly structured activities—dinner or a round of golf or tennis.

## Building Allies

As important as genuine friends are at work, it is also important to have allies—those business associates with whom you see eye to eye and with whom you can strike mutual agreements to help each other from time to time, either in terms of actual time spent working together on a project or in less defined ways, such as supporting each other's ideas in a meeting or speaking well of each other when the opportunity arises. Allies and friends are not necessarily the same thing. As relationships go, alliances are fairly subtle, and there may be no discussion at all about such a tie. But if you have performed a favor for someone, you can expect that he or she will repay you when possible—and vice versa.

## Helping Out a Colleague

It is considerate to offer help to a troubled or overworked colleague. Offer one of your workers if a colleague needs extra hands on a project, or offer to help out yourself with some important planning that needs to be done in a short amount of time. Whatever you do, do not become a do-gooder about offering your services. Offer only when help is truly needed, and keep your assistance quiet. If the colleague you have helped is at all knowledgeable about the etiquette of business, he or she will give you due credit at an appropriate moment or make sure word of your generosity gets around.

## Handling Your Promotion

Sometimes office relationships are temporarily thrown off balance when one member of a peer group—preferably you—is promoted. Graciousness to those who were not promoted this time around can help to ease the situation. Be ready with little amenities—extra praise, help on a project—to soothe any wounded feelings. Take the initiative by asking your previous peers to lunch or to some other social activity. As you move up the ranks ahead of peers, the friendships may indeed change, but you can at least ease the transition by your gracious consideration of others.

## YOUR RELATIONSHIP WITH YOUR SECRETARY

A few years ago, office etiquette was far more formal than it is today. Even after working together for twenty years, a secretary and supervisor used "Mr.," "Miss," or "Mrs." and surnames with each other. Today office life is far more informal—and harder to keep under control. First names are frequently used throughout a company—the only one who seems to be able to command the respect of "Mr." or "Ms." these days is the company president or chairperson of the board, and even he or she does not always manage to do so. Such informality is not a cause for complaint; after all, coworkers spend eight or more hours a day together year after year. In retrospect, it seems ridiculous that people could be so closely associated with one another for so long and maintain so much formality.

A manager or executive is the one to make the decision whether to call a secretary by his or her first name; just keep in mind that if you decide to do so, he or she may well respond by calling you by your first name.

Since you will see your secretary frequently throughout the day, there is no need to rise when he or she comes into the room. It is polite to gesture for a secretary to sit down whenever he or she has obviously come in to talk with you at any length, particularly if your working relationship is new and your secretary is not sure what to expect from you.

Managers today do take their secretaries for lunch—and these are not necessarily working lunches. It is simply a gracious gesture to ask a secretary or assistant—or any other subordinate, for that matter—to be your guest at lunch on occasion. Birthdays and secretaries' appreciation days offer excellent opportunities to show your appreciation in this way.

When appropriate, introduce a secretary or assistant to visitors to the office. If you are in conference with a client, and your secretary brings you sandwiches or coffee, for example, it is only gracious to make introductions when you thank him or her.

A good rule of thumb when making the introduction is to use whatever form of the names you think the persons involved will use later. For example, if a very senior and older executive is in your office, it is only gracious to say: "Mr. Riley, I would like you to meet Ms. Baden, my secretary." If the person in your office is a peer and your office is informal about using first names, you could say: "Bob Jones, I'd like you to meet Sandra Locke."

Take care not to monopolize a secretary's time. It is a secretary's right to have lunch with whomever he or she pleases, so while an occasional working lunch may be acceptable, asking for working lunches on a regular basis is rude. The same thing applies to asking a secretary to work overtime; it may be necessary occasionally, but to do so on a regular basis infringes on his or her privacy. If a great deal of overtime is expected, say, at particular times of the year, this is something you should discuss when you are describing the job to a potential employee.

Above all, show respect for the work a secretary or assistant does for you. Secretaries' work is important and in many ways eases your workload. Although secretaries today have become vocal about their demands, a good supervisor can do a lot to ease relationships by offering fair and gracious treatment before it is demanded.

Any number of important and not-so-important tasks belong to a secretary or assistant. He or she will handle your correspondence, book appointments, make travel plans, do filing and typing, and carry messages and memos to others; a bright secretary may correct your spelling or do some slight editing of an obviously ungrammatical sentence.

A secretary should not be expected to wait on you or perform personal services. Personal services include such chores as bringing coffee (unless the secretary is going to get some for himself or herself or you are in an important meeting with someone), balancing your checkbook, babysitting, or lying about your whereabouts. Your secretary may, of course, answer your phone, and he or she may well protect you from unwanted callers by saying that you can't take a call or are in conference. Just do not ask him or her to tell obvious lies, particularly those that relate to your private life.

## Managing Relationships with Superiors

In day-to-day office relations, the tone is set by top management. They may see their junior executives socially—over dinner, lunch, or drinks or for a round of golf or tennis at the country club—but they will probably not be seeking an intimate friendship.

Since top management is what you want to be part of, it is wise to handle yourself as if you already were. For example, never refer to or even start thinking of superiors as "they." Try to look and think as if you were one. If your superiors work long, hard hours, take a cue that this will be expected of you if you want to advance. Note the way managers dress, and pattern your dress accordingly. (See Chapters 12 and 13.) Take note of the amount of formality and informality in the office from what the top people do, as opposed to what your peers do.

## Handling Confidential Information

Finally, while discretion is important in all phases of business, it is never more so than when you are privy to confidential information. Learn to keep confidential information quiet. Several executives interviewed for this book even admitted to "setting up" an employee as a means of testing how well he or she could keep important confidences. So beware the tidbit that seems too unimportant to keep secret even though you have been requested to do so. Besides, it is simply good manners to keep confidential anything that someone indicates is private.

## ACCEPTING CRITICISM GRACIOUSLY

It is also important to learn to accept criticism from superiors graciously. First, never lose your poise when criticized. Do not offer excuses, and, above all, do not take the criticism personally. It is usually intended to help. Thank the person who offers criticism. One very wise executive said he always counters with: "Is there anything else I should know that would help me in my work?" It is a mistake to meet criticism with a flip response, a joke, laughter, and, most certainly, a defensive or sharp reply. These are rude ways to treat anyone who is trying to help you.

## MANAGING SUBORDINATES

Type A personalities may have been the rage in the roaring, obsessively aggressive 1980s, but they are out of fashion in the 1990s. Now calmer, cooler personalities prevail. All signs are that management styles will be subdued and smart—smart, that is, about handling subordinates. If the desire to be current isn't motivation enough to keep you low key, then remember that even though you are a manager or executive, you still need the cooperation, support, and loyalty of those who work for you. Never underestimate the power of a subordinate—even the least important filing clerk—to sabotage your work if disgruntled.

Many executives who are first given responsibility for other employees are unsure of the etiquette of working with their new subordinates. For starters, temper your expectations. This isn't a personality contest. Be friendly, but do not be a pal. Intimacy and friendliness are not the same thing; with the former you may find yourself leaned upon in a way that can be detrimental to your ambition.

Remember that a truly good leader motivates others to do their best. As a new manager, you might begin by asking your employees for written job descriptions. This will help you analyze how they see themselves and to plan a corresponding strategy for treating them.

Be open with those who work for you. Explain what you will and will not tolerate and also explain decisions about work that will affect them. Leave subordinates room to differ with you, but remember that you are the leader and it is you who must eventually make the decisions.

Sooner or later, you will have to handle a dispute among subordinates. There is an art to doing this. First, do not play favorites. Insist that the feuding employees treat each other politely and with respect; then treat both of them with respect in turn. One good ploy is to ask each person for a written memo detailing the aspects of the dispute. This will give you some breathing room and will force the arguing employees to confront the issue more directly.

## WHEN YOU NEED PRIVACY

Now that you have learned how to get along with your colleagues, it may be necessary to learn how to avoid them when you have important things to do. One sign of a good executive is the ability to manage time well. The Harvard Business School is rumored to routinely assign its students more reading than they can possibly handle as a means of teaching them to be selective about their reading—just as a good executive must be selective about using his or her time.

Some of the tips that follow are matters of etiquette (how to discourage a pest from talking too long), and others are simply tips on how to get the time you need.

Every office has its yakker. Someone really should estimate how many millions of dollars are lost every year to routine but unnecessary office chitchat. When you are cornered by one of these people, the way you handle the situation depends on the rank of the person. If your superior likes to come in to talk at length, obviously you tolerate it, work late to compensate—and get another job if the problem becomes too serious.

Rarely, though, will an excessive talker be a top power; executives do not get to the top by wasting time—a fact to keep in mind. If it is a colleague who is overstaying his or her welcome, start fidgeting with the papers on your desk or cast wistful looks at your "In" box. If this doesn't work, say firmly: "What you are saying is very interesting, and I wish I could talk about it longer, but I am feeling pressure to finish this memo I'm preparing." Another technique is to stand up, put an arm around the pest, and walk him or her out of your office. If the person still doesn't take the hint, you are stuck—unless you want to be rude, which isn't a bad idea if someone is too boorish to know when to leave. Finally, a sure way to get rid of someone is to get up and leave the room yourself.

A subordinate who talks too much—to you or to anyone else—can be reined in by a polite but firm talk about not wasting time in the office.

As for guarding your time for important work, the first step is to rank work according to its urgency. One very successful executive admits that for years she has done only the urgent work and that no one has ever pressed her for any other work. Another executive says that he escapes to an unused office or a conference room when he has pressing work to do. Several executives report having their calls held or even limiting them to one specific time of day. One junior executive keeps a small timer on his desk and tries not to spend more than five minutes on any phone call.

The important thing to remember in office relationships is to treat others with the same respect you would like to receive. Assume that all kinds of work are important, as indeed they are. Earn a reputation for polite, fair dealings with your coworkers of all ranks, and you will find yourself rewarded immensely at appropriate moments—moments that could well prove to be crucial to your career.

# 2

# Tricky Relationships— Professional and Otherwise

The sexual revolution of the 1960s brought sex into the open, and the feminist revolution of the 1970s brought women into the workplace in positions of power. These two events collided in the 1980s and changed office life forever, in ways that most of us would say are both good and bad. Most workplaces are much more relaxed and open than the offices of even twenty years ago, but office relationships are also vastly more complicated today.

In the 1990s, it seems, our tasks will be to sort out the results of these social revolutions—the office courtships, coworker marriages, collegial cohabitations, gay partnerings, spouses who work together (and sometimes even for one another), births and adoptions (as well as miscarriages and abortions), and the separations and divorces as well. In all these situations, we need to devise new etiquette guidelines that make us all comfortable.

## OFFICE AFFAIRS

Only a few decades ago, office romances, even ones that ended in marriage, were considered scandalous and typically resulted in someone—usually the woman—getting fired or being asked to leave.

Today everything has changed, and men and women who work together as colleagues expect to date their coworkers—and to marry them as well. And virtually no coworkers get married without first conducting an office courtship. The idea of finding a mate at work is no longer unusual, and all but the stuffiest employers have learned to adjust to office life that often includes one or more ongoing courtships.

Playing out a personal life publicly at work calls for discretion and tact, above all else. In fact, the first rule of office romances is not to flaunt them. After all, the relationship may not last, or may not result in marriage, and, if it doesn't, you will still have to work with someone who was once a lover. Not only will you have to work with him or her, but you will have to do so in a civilized fashion that doesn't make those around you uncomfortable. Because of this, the most savvy lover-colleagues don't go public until they know they have something to go public about. If you have a few casual dates with a coworker, consider it your private business and keep it quiet.

The degree of discretion required to conduct an office romance also depends on the corporate culture where you work. And keep in mind that corporate cultures—and the attitudes they engender toward love affairs—vary not only from company to company but also from geographic region to region. Midwesterners and those who live in small towns and cities tend to be conservative while urban easterners and westerners are more open about any kind of relationship.

If you report to someone who is casual about sexual relationships or about personal friendships at work, you will probably encounter little resistance to an office affair. If you report to someone who is straitlaced, resistance may be so high that you will find you must keep an affair entirely under wraps. People's feelings vary widely—some executives, for example, object to married people playing around but are more tolerant of affairs between single employees.

Total indiscretion is about the only thing you cannot get away with. Being caught in flagrante delicto in the office can and probably will get you fired. One young Wall Street lawyer finally managed (on a Saturday afternoon) to indulge his fantasy of putting the boardroom to his idea of good use only to discover that his romantic activities led directly to his being fired a few weeks later.

Most bosses and coworkers are justifiably irked at public displays of affection—long conversations during work, lunch taken for too long and at irregular hours for what might be deemed irregular purposes, and in some offices, lovers who are indiscreet enough to walk in together in the morning.

In other offices, however, where two people are known to be having a relationship or even living together, bosses and coworkers think it is silly for them not to walk in together if they have in fact spent the night together.

Coworkers and top brass alike will be more tolerant of the relationship if they are not made to feel awkward over it. Longing looks or lovers' spats, even insiders' comments that have meaning only to the two of you, are best avoided.

It is a matter of courtesy to make an extra effort to be discreet when you are at work, and the less you bring your personal relationship to work, the less chance that it will harm your career.

Two lovers may find that they work better when they are separated. In that case, there is no reason why one of you cannot request a transfer to another department of a large company. If one of you decides to seek another job outside the company, that is another matter that should be conducted as discreetly and quietly as any job hunt would be.

Finally, the amount of discretion necessary for interoffice relationships can vary within a single office from year to year. One astute observer of a publishing firm that had seen more than its share of office romances in the past few years, most of which had culminated in a flurry of divorces, marriages, and cohabitation relationships, noted, "A year ago when office romances were the big thing, there was a lot of sexual talk in the office during the day. The talk was split between those who dropped hints about their own sexual lives and those who dropped comments about the sexual lives of others. At the moment there are no office romances going on—at least, none that I know about—and there is almost no sexual banter either. The subject of sex just never comes up during working hours anymore. And although there has been no change in top management, I think everyone senses that playing around obviously with someone in the office would not be accepted very readily today. For some strange reason, the mood is straighter now."

## Asking Top People to Dinner When You Cohabit

In these days of routine cohabitation, the question of whether to expose your personal life to the top people in your company often arises. Again, an executive's reaction to this situation is likely to be highly personal. Some managers or executives have no second thoughts about socializing with an employee who is unmarried and living with someone, while others do not want to know anything about your living habits. You have to take a reading and decide how open you can be.

The answer, if you have a live-in roommate, is not to invite top people to dinner with the idea that they had better accept your values—or else. If you are friendly with the person to whom you report, chances are he or she is aware of your lifestyle and has no complaints. You can feel free to socialize without hiding anything.

If you do not socialize with your manager, and you sense that your actions would only earn disapproval, do not invite your manager to dinner—or do anything so overt that he or she will have to face the fact that you are living with someone. At company parties or on other social occasions, take your partner if you are invited to bring someone, but do not make an obvious point of letting people know you are roommates unless you are sure it won't matter.

If you know that the place where you work is generally stuffy, it is best to be discreet about your relationship with all your coworkers and not just your direct manager. Being discreet, unfortunately, often means telling white lies about the nature of the relationship and the living arrangements. While no one enjoys having to lie about so major a part of one's life, remember that your career is also a major part of your life—and that you want to control the direction it takes. The white lie is usually worth it if you sense that you will meet with severe disapproval.

Such a white lie is usually successful, since the people in this kind of office are less likely to fraternize with one another than those who work in more easygoing offices.

## Gays and Office Life

Gays and lesbians are often unsure of how much about their private lives to reveal at work—and rightfully so, we note with regret. In many respects, they are in the same position as cohabiting couples in that their lifestyles may be accepted in some places and not in others.

It would be easy to say that each of us should always live a totally open life and stand up for what we believe, but people also have to earn a living, and, unfortunately, in our society these two facets of our lives are still sometimes in conflict.

For the gay or lesbian who wants and needs to be secure in his or her job, discretion may be necessary. Again, the best way to know how to behave is to assess the corporate culture. If it's liberal and accepting, you can probably be open about your private life. This means you can bring your partner to office parties and other gatherings, and can freely discuss him or her as an important part of your life.

If the culture is not open and accepting, and you want to keep your job—or your upwardly mobile career path—it may be best to keep your private life private, even though you may have to go through the pain of attending office parties alone and not talking about someone who is very important to you.

We hasten to add that we don't think this latter course of action is a healthy way to live, and we would love to see a world where people are accepted for what they are and where stereotypes are erased, but until this day arrives, some people will have to exercise discretion in order to protect their livelihoods.

A third course of action also may be open to you: Once you have earned a reputation as a good employee and become a known commodity, you may introduce your partner to your colleagues. Presumably once you have proven yourself, you should be liked and respected well enough so that your personal life won't matter—and probably also won't shock anyone. Note: We can't promise this will work in a homophobic work environment, and we all know that these still exist.

## MINORITIES IN THE WORKPLACE

The past ten years have seen an explosion of minority workers in executive positions, where, to no one's surprise, they encounter the same kinds of problems that they confront in society at large.

Obviously your color or religion has nothing to do with your ability to do your job, and in a perfect world, these would not even be a factor. Unfortunately, this is rarely the case. Minorities still encounter prejudice and have to decide how to deal with it.

When faced with a blatantly racist comment, a withering stare is utterly appropriate and may well be your first line of defense. While the object of good manners is to treat the others (even ignorant others) with kindness, there are lines with all of us that should not be crossed.

Another approach is to laugh off the offender and, if possible, turn the comment back with a light touch, letting the person know how silly such thinking is and perhaps making him or her more aware of what he or she has said. When one Ivy League–educated black advertising executive heard a client comment on how blacks were "natural" athletes, he merely laughed and said, "Right, that's how I got where I am." Enough said; point made.

When someone asks a question that you consider inappropriate about your personal life, your color, your race, your age, or your religion, there is a response that our friend Ann Landers has been recommending for years. Look at the offender with wonderment and ask: "Now, why would you want to know a thing like that?"

When you come up against the more insidious kind of ongoing prejudice that many people unknowingly harbor, and especially when the person works for you, with you, or above you, educating him or her may be your best course of action. When it comes to race and religious relations, familiarity often erases contempt. And even though it's difficult to hammer away at another person's stereotypes, none of us has to stand by politely while others make disparaging and false comments about our fellow humans. Feel free to state that you do not agree with what the person is saying.

## Working with Minority People

As the workplace becomes more diverse and business more global, many of us find ourselves working alongside people whose race, religion, or culture may be unfamiliar to us. And while we may be eager to get to know these people, we are also curious to learn more about them.

The first rule in getting along with others is to treat everyone alike. And to make no assumptions. An otherwise sophisticated New Yorker who was giving a benefit cocktail party for a posh private school not only made a social blunder but cost the school a huge donation when she greeted three white women and a black man who arrived at the same time by shaking hands with the women only. But it was the black man who had the means to contribute to the school, and he obviously wasn't interested in doing so after being greeted in such a fashion. But then, who would be?

Although you may be curious to know about a coworker's religion, culture, or customs, stifle your curiosity. Let the other person bring up these topics if and when he or she feels comfortable doing so. Once the other person raises the subject, then you can ask questions and begin the process of getting to know one another better and eventually becoming friends.

Try not to make assumptions about someone else's world based on what you believe or on popular cultural stereotypes. Comments that start with "You people don't eat . . . " "You people really like . . . " or "You people are good at . . . " are offensive and the mark of an unsophisticated person. Actually, comments that start with "You people" are highly inflammatory, as one would-be presidential contender found out during the 1992 campaign.

And what if, despite your best efforts, something stereotypical and rude pops out of your mouth? The only solution is to apologize—immediately. Be brief, though, and don't mention the incident again, because neither the offender nor the offendee will have any desire to replay or prolong the moment.

As an employer you have a role to play in creating a culture in which minorities feel comfortable. An employee who is heard making derogatory comments should be told not to say such things, not least because they are not good for business in a world where races, cultures, and religions have begun to mix as never before.

## SPECIAL PROBLEMS OF WOMEN IN THE WORKPLACE

In many offices a certain amount of sexual banter is part of the daily routine. After all, these are adult human beings with whom you spend a large chunk of every day year after year. Never to discuss sex—either directly or indirectly—would be unrealistic.

Sexual banter in an office is no more serious than any other kind of light joking about any other subject, and in many instances, responding the right way to a light pass can help you ward off a more serious one.

One professional woman who works with many lawyers has developed her own method of dealing with sexual banter she encounters and the occasional serious pass. If someone with less-than-innocent motives asks "How about a drink after work?" she replies "Actually, I've wanted you for a long time. Why don't you leave your wife and run away with me?" She carries on in this vein until the other person realizes he won't be taken seriously and goes away. She swears her technique has kept her out of serious trouble. She gets away with her outrageous comments in part because she has a reputation for no nonsense in the office about work or personal matters and in part because her banter calls the other person's bluff.

## Saying No

Occasionally the sexual banter does turn into a serious pass. This can happen to men and women, and each individual must decide how to handle the situation.

If you find the person attractive and want to follow up on the relationship, that is fine. You are on your own, since this section deals with how to say no and minimize the damage to your career and another person's ego.

Usually signals are sent back and forth before a serious overture is made, and if you are not interested, make this clear from the beginning. The easiest way to ward off a pass is to be busy with someone else who occupies a lot of your free time outside work. When you sense that an overture is in the offing, start making regular mention of "the person I go with."

If the situation is still fairly light, and you sense that this is a serious but nonmanipulative pass, you can be more relaxed about it. You might even say "You know, I really do find you attractive, but I'm seriously involved with someone at the moment" or the more honest "I do think you're attractive and I'm flattered, but I just don't get involved with the people I work with."

One man reported that dropping hints of an earlier and very sad and unsuccessful office relationship—in another office, of course— was enough to cool things off.

If you know you are not willing to engage in anything sexual with a coworker, be ready with a firm statement about your feelings. There is, however, no reason to snarl or unnecessarily hurt another person, so smile and use a pleasant voice. One stockbroker reported stopping all suggestions for office romance dead by saying with a smile "I'm sorry, but I am just not interested in that. I know you will under-stand." If badgered, she repeated her message and left the room as soon as possible.

You need have only one reservation about using the "I'm sorry, I don't do that with my coworkers" excuse, and that is that someday you might find you *want* to become involved with a coworker, which could cause bitter feelings on the part of the person you turned down earlier. Of course, it would be rude of him or her to remind you of this, but you may find it easier in the long run not to use this excuse unless you mean it.

## DEALING WITH SEXUAL HARASSMENT

Sometimes a pass crosses the line into sexual harassment. This is not a time to be polite. If the harassment is truly severe, and you feel you cannot control it yourself, go to the manager of the person who is harassing you. Such complaints are taken very seriously these days.

We have as a society become much more sophisticated about sexual harassment in the past few years. We now realize, for example, that it is a far more complicated issue than most of us ever imagined. We know that the vast majority of incidents of harassment involve women, although occasionally men are harassed as well. We know that not everyone feels she or he can report an incident or is strong enough to carry out a threat to do so. We know that sexual harassment is an enormously undermining experience that can leave some persons feeling drained and demoralized. Having said all this, though, we encourage anyone who is seriously harassed to report the incident immediately, as this is one of the most effective ways of halting harassment.

About the only etiquette involved in doing this, and it is merely a last-ditch attempt to save face for all involved, is to warn the person politely that if you are not left alone, you will talk to someone with the power to do something to stop the harassment.

One of the trickiest and most painful situations a person can encounter is when the harassment comes from her or his immediate superior. We can only repeat that every person is entitled to do her or his job without sexual harassment. If you find yourself being harassed, start by saying no very firmly and unequivocally. If this does not work, we suggest that you go to your manager's superior for support.

## MENTOR RELATIONSHIPS

For years men have had mentors who promoted their careers, and this has never been cause for comment. But since women have begun to occupy positions of power, many are finding that they must cope with the ramifications of maintaining a close and often platonic relationship with a boss-mentor or an older, more powerful male executive who has taken a personal interest in their career. And increasingly often young men are finding themselves with female mentors.

In some offices, these relationships are accepted and there is no cause for comment from one's coworkers. In other offices, such a relationship may be mistaken for an office romance or may cause resentments among coworkers who misunderstand the nature of the relationship, or who understand it perfectly and still resent it.

About the best you can do with this situation is to weather it through. Obviously, a mentor relationship is beneficial to anyone's career and is not something to be dismissed lightly. You can play down the relationship and take care not to flaunt it among your peers. Try to ignore any particularly gossipy comments, although one good thing about this kind of gossip is that it rarely reaches the ears of the person who is its subject. If you work in an office where your relationship is resented, no one will believe your denials anyway, so it is best to say nothing and be as discreet as possible about the relationship.

## PEER FRIENDSHIPS

Genuine friendships among coworkers often are struck up these days, since men and women work together in positions of equality and, in many cases, travel together for business. How peer friendships are handled is a personal decision on the part of those involved.

If you work in a very conservative office, there is no point in adding grist to the gossip mill. If you enjoy a coworker's company and a friendship develops, skip the long lunches or other activities that normally give rise to gossip in the office, and meet after work—

unless, of course, you do not care and you are sure the gossips will not be able to harm your career.

There is no particular reason to explain such a relationship, even if one or both friends are married to other people. Simply enjoy the friendship as discreetly as possible and say little to anyone about it.

## COWORKER MARRIAGES

Along with office courtships have come office marriages, which in turn have led to married couples working together or for competing companies and the slew of conflicts and tricky situations that ensue. These pioneer couples and their employers have been busy forging a new etiquette for coworker relationships.

For the record, it is legal for a company to have nepotism policies that forbid the hiring of family members or married couples. But the trend is away from such policies, and today's employers are more interested in finding ways to let partners work together. Some employers even go out of their way to hire couples together, especially when they want them to relocate to a new city.

The first rule for married couples working together is the same as for coworkers who date: Don't flaunt the relationship. Even though you are married, keep everything low key and, of course, totally professional. Don't expect any less of each other because you work together than you would if you were unrelated. The reverse is also true, especially if you want to protect your marriage: Don't expect any more of each other just because you happen to be married.

Not only will you need to make each other comfortable, but you also will need to put your superiors and your coworkers at ease. How you do this will depend to a large extent on your corporate culture. If it is open and easygoing, you can be the same way about working with your spouse. No one will mind if you huddle to make plans to get little Ned to his soccer game or leave each other voice mail shopping lists of dinner ingredients.

But if the work environment is fairly formal, then you'll probably have to be equally circumspect. Don't huddle more than a minute or two about the soccer game, and don't leave a voice mail or paper trail about your personal life.

Sometimes the situations that married coworkers encounter are so new that the couples themselves must come up with their own solutions, but there are a few situations that all couples must handle. For instance, all couples must decide how much time they will or should spend together during the day.

Some couples arrive and depart from work together, while others take separate cars—not so much for the sake of appearance, many couples report, but because their work schedules are so different. She may have to stay late for a meeting, while he goes home to cook dinner.

Whether to have lunch together is another issue. Married couples should go to great lengths to avoid giving the appearance that they are a special or, worse, an inclusive unit that excludes others. If your work draws you together and you would ordinarily lunch together, then go ahead and do it, taking care to include others on a regular basis. If your work does not throw you together in this way, then perhaps it is better not to lunch together—lest you be seen as clinging unduly to one another.

One female bank president says she regularly schedules lunch with her husband-lawyer (along with other bank lawyers, she is quick to add) because it's the most convenient time to meet with him about bank business. At NASA, several married spouses eat lunch with one another regularly because, as they readily admit, they discuss nothing but work all during their lunch hour. In this and other similar situations, you have to take the temperature of your particular workplace and then act accordingly.

Another problem married couples encounter is that their coworkers often hold them to a higher standard of conduct than they do other workers. Two coworkers can go out after work for drinks and hash over their day, but a married couple is supposed to act as if they never discuss work at home. Similarly two nonmarried coworkers can have a disagreement at work, and their argument does not echo though silent hallways that are all ears. But married couples' spats at work (about work) are seen as something more serious. In general, your coworkers will want you to present a more unified front than would ever be required of other, unrelated coworkers.

Whether you can do this, it is still up to you to allay coworkers' anxieties. A tactful, well-timed comment often can do wonders to put your colleagues at ease. One female executive reports that she makes a point of letting her coworkers know she is as surprised as they are by some upper-management decisions in which her husband has played a role. Another woman, who is a partner in a law firm where her husband is also a partner, is frequently heard to comment: "We don't discuss work at home. It's our time to be with each other."

As for the inevitable disagreement, first, make sure that it is about work and not a personal issue. Couples must learn not to bring their personal issues into the workplace, but no one can expect them not to have the occasional professional disagreement.

One television producer says she has never minded her public professional battles with her husband, a network executive, but she's aware that it makes everyone around them uneasy. Her tack, and that of many married couples, is to treat the spat as if it were with any other coworker. In other words, act as if you aren't married. Disagree when you must, smooth ruffled feathers to the extent that you would for any other coworker, and get on with daily life.

## THE END OF AN AFFAIR
## OR A MARRIAGE

Occasionally an office romance or marriage will go sour, and, just as often, an outside romance or marriage will break up and you will find that your personal life weighs heavily on your professional life.

However torn up you may be, your coworkers are not necessarily the people who should have to bear the brunt of your pain. It is neither professional nor polite to bring such problems to work. If life is really unbearable, take a few days off—and give a reason other than a broken heart unless you report to someone who is very understanding.

If you must continue working with an ex, try to be civil, at least during the times you spend around others. Spare coworkers the gory details, if at all possible, and above all, don't take potshots at him or her. This is not for his or her sake, but for yours. Unrequited love only makes everyone feel ill at ease, and people may well start to avoid you just at a time when you need them most.

If your ex takes shots at you, your best bet is to ignore them. Most people will see what is going on and also observe your good behavior.

## Pregnant Executives

The idea of a pregnant executive was unheard of only a few years ago but is common today.

Although it's currently fashionable to announce a pregnancy very early these days, you might want to think about whether you want to do this at work. Especially if you're an older mother as so many women executives are, you might find it more convenient to announce your pregnancy as late as possible. On the other hand, don't keep people guessing so long that your Is-she-or-isn't-she? status becomes the only thing coworkers can talk about.

You should continue to dress like an executive even when you are pregnant. Choose maternity clothes that are businesslike, preferably suits and dresses in conservative colors. Use jewelry and scarves to divert attention from your growing body and toward your face.

While your announcement is certainly a joyous one, after making it, play down the pregnancy as much as possible. Save the long discussions about your changing form and the very real complaints for your family and personal friends. Remember, your goal is to preserve your status as a valued executive in a world where there is still a fair amount of prejudice against pregnant working women. Some companies still are reluctant to let themselves be represented by a pregnant woman, so the more low key you manage to play the pregnancy, the better off you'll be professionally.

### Treatment of Pregnant Executives

People are still curious about pregnant executives. Specifically, they want to know how she will carry out her responsibilities, how much maternity leave she'll take, whether she'll travel less, and even whether she'll perhaps quit altogether (and thus open up a good job for a coworker, to get right down to the hidden agenda).

You can think these thoughts, but it's rude to ask a pregnant colleague about them. Let the woman tell you her plans when she's ready, including the announcement that she's pregnant. It's even rude to ask a coworker if she is pregnant. No matter how obviously *enceinte* a fellow worker appears to be, ignore that fact until she makes the announcement.

Also let her take the lead in deciding how much she'll curtail her workload. These days few women expect to work any less during pregnancy. If a woman does encounter a medical problem, she should discuss this with the person she reports to, and together they can work out whatever arrangement will best accommodate her health needs.

## Pregnant, Unmarried Executives

Although single mothers are no longer rare, a certain amount of speculation and gossip surrounds the woman who decides to have a child on her own. If you are an executive who makes this decision, you can take some steps to minimize the discomfort of the awkward situation.

Much as you would if you were married, time your announcement to suit yourself. Don't make it prematurely, but also don't wait until the office sets up a betting pool on your delivery date.

Coworkers, for their part, should ignore the pregnancy until it is announced. Once an unmarried woman has announced her pregnancy, though, it is a kindness to make her feel as comfortable as possible. Deciding to be a single mother is never an easy or lightly made decision, and support from coworkers is always welcome.

For example, you might inquire about the woman's condition more than you would for another pregnant coworker, particularly if you know she is going through her pregnancy alone. It is appropriate, as her delivery date approaches, to ask about any arrangements she has made and to offer any assistance you can.

## The Birth of a Child

The birth of a child to any coworker (or for that matter, a client) is always a joyous occasion. You may send a personal note, a card, flowers, or a gift or even plan a visit—whatever you are comfortable with and whatever seems appropriate to your relationship.

It is also kind to offer to take on some of a colleague's workload or otherwise help out while the new parent is out on parental leave.

Although women still take 90 percent of the parental leaves, a growing number of men are interested in them. Prejudice against leaves for men is the only reason more men do not take them. (Men who take parental leave are viewed as less ambitious than their peers.) Coworkers can help out by being supportive and tactful to either parent who takes a parental leave. Sometimes the support is physical, as when, for example, you offer to drop off an important report to the person on leave, but more often the support is emotional and takes the form of a kind word or a note sent to let the person know that you applaud what he or she is doing.

## The Adoption of a Child

The news of an adoption should be treated just as joyously as the news that a colleague has given birth. If you know the mother or father well enough to send flowers or a gift, do so. A note or card is also welcome. In whatever form, be sure to extend your congratulations.

It is neither polite nor kind to ask too many questions about an adoption. No matter how curious you may be, it is not your business to know (a) where the child is from; (b) why it was put up for adoption; and (c) what its race, religion, or ethnic background is.

## Breast-Feeding and the Female Executive

Murphy Brown wasn't being outlandish when she arrived for her first day of work after having her baby toting a breast pump. Increasing numbers of working mothers, many of them executives, are tucking these devices into their briefcases. One enterprising company has built a business around supplying corporations with pumps, on-site rooms, *and* a lactation consultant, but most women are on their own when they breast-feed at work—and many find they are pioneers.

One high-powered executive at a pharmaceutical company was surprised to find her decision regarded as cause for suspicion. Twice a day, she retired to her office for thirty minutes, closed the door, and used the pump. Initially, her secretary guarded her privacy, but her coworkers soon learned what her closed door meant.

Although she knew she was no less efficient for taking those thirty minutes twice a day, others were not so sure. When one male executive asked her secretary how long it took and whether she did any "real" work while she pumped, her secretary grinned and replied, "Oh, she only averages ten letters and twenty memos every time she's in there. Frankly, my day would be easier if she didn't do this."

## Baby Showers

A shower may be given whether a baby is biological or adopted, but these are personal events and should not be given at work. Nor should coworkers be asked to contribute to a fund to buy a gift for the newcomer. Although these collections can be a hardship, many offices still take them. Ironically, they are more common among clerical than executive staffs. (See "Showers" in Chapter 9, page 203.)

## Baby Talk

Once you've returned to work after giving birth, try to get your work life back to normal as quickly as possible. Rightly or wrongly, you'll be watched to see if you can still do the job. You'll want a picture of your little one on your desk, of course. This is perfectly acceptable and even expected today, but don't wallpaper the room . with baby pictures and other memorabilia.

Also avoid sprinkling your conversation with too much talk about the baby, lest you be perceived as a stereotype—the one where the woman has a baby and no longer cares about her work. You can mention the baby and, when someone asks, enthusiastically give a brief report, but as you can well imagine, nonstop talk about the baby doesn't play well at work.

## Dealing with a Miscarriage or an Abortion

Because pregnant women work, they also sometimes must cope with a miscarriage at work as well. The days are long gone when anyone would ignore such an event in a woman's life if she chooses to share it.

If the miscarriage occurs very early in a pregnancy and you have not yet announced your pregnancy, you need not mention it unless you want to. When it occurs after you have announced your pregnancy, then some sort of announcement will be called for.

This is a time to be kind to yourself, and the kindest thing you can do sometimes is to let someone else—a friend, an assistant, or a secretary—pass the word about what has happened to you while you are out of the office recuperating. Alternately, you may of course tell people yourself if you feel up to it.

Upon learning that someone has had a miscarriage, you should offer your support and sympathy. Ignoring such an event is callous and rude. Send the woman flowers or a note expressing your sadness over hearing her unhappy news. You can also offer your support in person.

Often the best way to show support is to simply be there for the person, asking her out for coffee or a drink after work or taking her to lunch to cheer her up.

Far rarer these days are instances where a pregnancy ends in stillbirth or a woman decides to undergo an abortion after announcing her pregnancy, usually as the result of information she has obtained through prenatal testing. A loss at this late stage of pregnancy is extremely painful, and coworkers would do well to take their cue from the woman. A note of support is always welcome, and other gestures are good as well, but it's important to realize that a woman who has suffered this kind of loss may not feel much like talking about it.

## CHILDREN AND OFFICE LIFE

As any two-career couple or single mother knows, there are times when office life and parenting clash, and the parent has to figure out what to do with the children while still preserving his or her professional status. Children have become much more a part of executive life than they were when only fathers were executives. Today, when your child has a school holiday that you don't have, it's expected that you might bring him or her to the office for all or part of a day.

When you must do this, however, be sure to bring along toys and games to keep him or her occupied. Explain that this is a place of business and that he or she will have to play quietly for a few hours while Mommy or Daddy (and everyone else) works.

Don't expect others, including your secretary or assistant, to entertain your child except in the direst emergency. And while your coworkers will enjoy an occasional visit from a child, clients who are paying for your time usually will not. Children have no place in meetings with clients either on or off your premises or at top-level meetings with your superiors.

For that matter, visits from children should be kept to a minimum and should be made only if it is obvious that people generally don't mind having a child around the office for a few hours. Even in an office that encourages such relaxed arrangements, it's easy to wear out a child's welcome. Some bosses who say it's okay to bring children to work really mean it's okay once in a blue moon and so long as the children don't do anything to alter the pace of work.

Although ill children pose special and very real problems for parents who work, they have no place in an office or, for that matter, at a day care center. It is extremely bad manners to impose your children (or yourself) on others when you are ill.

\*　　\*　　\*

Some people think that office life is worse for all the changes that have come about, but most of us are enjoying the open and relaxed atmosphere. Just as we have always maintained that etiquette is really about kindness toward our fellow humans, we also believe that manners can be used to accommodate social change and, more important, to make our lives easier.

# 3

# The Etiquette of Handling the Person to Whom You Report

The most important relationship you must develop—and you must develop it in every single job you ever have—is with the person to whom you report. And make no mistake about it, *you* must be the one to nurture and develop the relationship. A manager has the power to hire and fire and does not have to mend his or her ways to fit the attitudes and values of employees. You, on the other hand, have to make an extra effort to work with the manager or be prepared to end up on the street.

Peter F. Drucker, a fountain of wisdom on manager-employee relations, has pointed out in his books that overrating a superior carries no stigma. You win an ally and show loyalty to someone whom you respect. Underrating a superior, on the other hand, can be insulting if he or she is sensitive enough to notice and can eventually result in your being unable to work together.

From a practical standpoint, you should be doing everything possible to help your superior succeed. The sooner he or she is promoted, the sooner another door is opened to you.

Then, too, the way you handle the relationship with your superior is a matter of concern to everyone in the company. The top executives will be watching your manner, particularly if they know you are working with a notoriously unpleasant person. The ability to develop a working relationship with someone who is known as being tough to get along with does win points in the long run. The way an employee manages his or her manager tells a lot about the person's executive potential.

## UNDERSTANDING THE CHIEF

Perhaps the best way to begin to understand your manager is to realize that he or she is human, has weaknesses and strengths, and may from time to time be beset with the same financial and personal problems that plague the rest of us.

Realize, too, that you are on this person's team. A manager does not owe an employee anything, whereas an employee owes his or her job to an employer. Therefore, your task is to fit into the manager's working habits, time schedule, and plans and goals for the future.

The rules for getting along with a supervisor are fairly short and simple. First decide whether you have a reader or a listener. Since a large part of your time must be spent communicating with your supervisor, it is important to find the best way to do so right off the bat. Readers prefer to get their information in written form—via memos and reports. Try always to give them something to read before going in to talk to them.

Listeners, usually people who issue statements such as "My door is always open" and "I always want to talk to you if there is any kind of problem," prefer that you come in directly and chat. They may even find a written communication slightly cold.

Still, appearances can be deceptive. A manager may have read a management book recently that advocated being more accessible to employees when, in fact, he or she still personally prefers little contact and lots of memos and reports. Look under the surface before you typecast someone. A manager who says the door is always open but then proceeds to issue two written memos a day is not someone who truly wants to chat with employees any more than is absolutely necessary. A manager who expresses a desire always to be available to talk with employees but is always rushing off to do something else does not really want this kind of contact. Stick with written memos when you have this kind of supervisor.

Deciding whether to approach a supervisor in writing or in person is part of the art of managing that person's time. While deciding what kind of manager you have, look for clues as to how he or she manages time and then do everything you can to help him or her use it efficiently. Does the manager like to chat for a few minutes about the day's business just at quitting time? Be willing to hang around and oblige. Does the manager like to be left alone in the morning to work on his or her own projects? Wait until afternoon to confer about your projects.

Another important guideline in getting along with a supervisor is never to confuse or surprise him or her. In other words, never make your boss appear stupid. Oliver Spencer, president of Graphic Alliance, Inc., a midwestern graphic arts company, commented: "You never want your boss to appear stupid to his boss. He should always have a file, a memo, something—somewhere—on a project you've been working on. This is very important, this face-saving thing. In a big company, especially, nothing is more embarrassing for a boss than to be asked something by the top brass and not even to be aware of what they are talking about."

Keep a manager abreast of your work—the work you are currently handling as well as the projects that you are going to tackle later and why you have put them off. If a problem arises that is your responsibility, make it known and discuss your plans for dealing with it.

Along with keeping your supervisor informed and helping him or her to manage time, always go to the supervisor's office prepared. You don't need to have every fact or detail on hand—to do so even could make you appear a bit too detail-oriented—but always be prepared to discuss the topic at hand.

Follow up on all assignments. Managers who make trivial assignments are often the very ones who remember to ask about them at the most inopportune times, and they rarely forget them entirely.

If a manager has promised to do something for you, remind him or her politely if necessary. Offer the supervisor a chance to do what was promised.

Excuses for projects that have gone awry or work that simply has not been done on time can really hurt you. If you sense that you are going to need extra help with a project, discuss this with your supervisor, long before the deadline approaches. If you will require an extension, this, too, should be worked out in advance rather than at the last minute.

## THREATENING A MANAGER—THE ULTIMATE MISTAKE

A lot of ego is involved in being an executive. The higher one climbs, the less involved one is with actual products and the more involved one is with intangible products, such as the talents and skills of other coworkers.

It is hard for an up-and-coming executive with some ego involvement of his or her own not to threaten the person he or she works for. Yet business survival demands that you not do so. Many young executives could use a course in nonassertiveness training, and some management programs are now offering seminars in this very subject. Assertiveness, which has its place in the competitive work world, too often looks like arrogance or presumptuousness to a manager or to a conservative, old-school member of the board. Nonassertiveness, on the other hand, sometimes is a recognition of the fact that there are situations when a restrained style works best.

Remember that your manager usually has more information than you do about the company and may or may not be able to share it with you. Keeping a relaxed attitude when you sense that you are confronted with this situation will do a lot to keep you out of trouble. If your manager suddenly insists that a project be done a certain way, acquiesce.

There are several good nonassertive techniques to keep in mind when dealing with a manager. First, remember empathic listening. Give a manager time to tell you about *his* or *her* other plans and objectives rather than always pushing yours.

Second, develop the skill of delivering facts to your supervisor in a noncritical way. Occasionally you may be asked to do some research on a touchy project—closing out part of the manager's domain, for example. This is not the time to assert yourself. Instead, just give the facts and let him or her worry about their interpretation. To come up with a finding that makes your manager unhappy, even if you do so innocently, may be threatening.

Third, learn the art of selective passivity. You will do better to remain aloof from some issues. If your manager has been ordered from above to cut back on staff because the company had a bad year, and you have some dynamic new management techniques that could save the situation, this is not the time to mention them. Again, it just threatens a manager who is losing some power. Try to remain aloof from the situation, as far as your manager is concerned.

If you want to challenge your manager, and there is no reason not to do so occasionally, do it privately. Prepare your argument in advance and make sure it is well thought out. Public power plays with a manager are invariably seen as a threat to the manager's power base, and a smart manager won't let anyone get away with them very often.

If you sense that, despite efforts to the contrary, you are threatening your manager, some nonassertiveness training or a few sessions with a good counselor may help to smooth the relationship. Then, too, there are those managers who just cannot tolerate bright young people; it is best to give up on them and look elsewhere for a job where you can shine. Truly poor managers also should be abandoned, as should ones who are corrupt, unfair, overly critical, and incompetent, and those who want only yes-people working for them. While you usually can arrive at some kind of compromises in such working situations with most managers a young executive is never really allowed to shine, and it is better to advance your career in another company or another department, if possible.

## BEING THE ONE IN CHARGE

The other side of the coin occurs when you, the manager, have responsibility for a number of people. It is sometimes harder, just because of the power that goes along with being in charge, to treat employees in a nonassertive, gracious manner. Yet doing so can lower employee defenses, improve interpersonal relationships, and motivate young executives—in short, it can make everyone on your team pull that much harder for you, and this is what management is all about.

Milton Wood, president of Wood Computer Associates, Inc., a well-known executive placement company, drew on his own experience of running a company and his experience in counseling the numerous executives his company has placed to comment: "Management is a science in itself. A truthful managerial style develops around an executive's personality. Many executives are poor managers. They are either self-concerned with their own ego and position, or they do not take time to learn to delegate and manage properly. The success or failure of any manager is a direct product of the people he can hire, fire, manage, motivate and retain. If you're the type of man who has to do everything yourself, you're doomed to fail. The hard-nosed SOB-type manager who doesn't develop some type of personal relationship with his key people is also doomed to fail, because it's only through esprit de corps that you can accomplish things. That does not mean you're a divorce counselor or a financial manager or any kind of dumping ground for an employee's emotional problems, but there has to be some kind of relationship where employees feel you are personally concerned with their professional growth."

A good manager needs to remember to use the same nonassertiveness techniques that he or she used or uses with his own superior, plus a few others. The art of procrastination has some benefits when you are motivating others, for example.

Let employees work out their interpersonal squabbles. As long as no one is getting hurt, let an employee work out a project on his or her own time. Mature adults generally work well by themselves. They don't need a mother hen clucking over them every minute, nor should a manager assume that he or she has a captive audience whenever an employee comes looking for advice or a suggestion.

If possible, help someone seeking advice to think through the problem and to find his or her own solution. Above all, when giving advice, avoid the tendency to expound. The person who constantly expounds on various subjects to his or her employees often knows little about what truly goes on in the office and thus has little control over the people he or she manages.

## EXPRESSING DISSATISFACTION

However much loyalty is owed to a manager, there are times when an executive wants to take on more authority or simply wants the opportunity to shine more within the company than a superior will permit. There are ways to manage this. When you want to express dissatisfaction with a manager over the amount of authority you don't have—or about any other problem, for that matter—try to do so diplomatically. Let your manager know that you are unhappy about something and would like to talk it over as soon as possible.

Prepare carefully for the meeting. Go into it with a calm attitude; be very organized and know exactly what you hope to accomplish. If you seek more authority, know why it should be given to you and how the company will benefit from it. Wood said: "You get a lot more mileage by selling a function and by trying to understand a boss's reactions—why he is the way he is—and by then trying to work a solution around that than by producing a threatening situation. The person who goes in to see his manager to gripe without having a remedy is wrong. Why is the boss reluctant to give up some of his authority? Was he stung by a subordinate who took advantage of him? If this is the case, try to develop a level of trust so that the boss will give you a shot at what you want to do."

If you have to back off the first couple of times you try for more authority, do so rather than threaten a manager. Gradually a bond of trust will build and you will probably get the authority or anything else you seek.

## GOING AROUND A MANAGER

Sometimes you have no choice but to work around a manager. There is, however, an etiquette to doing this. You can go around your manager to his or her superiors if you keep your manager fully informed of what you are doing. Write a memo to your supervisor detailing any contact with a superior. When you have gone around your supervisor, say so and then add, "I got an OK from (*your manager's superior*) on that," or "(*Your manager's superior*) said to go ahead with the project as soon as possible."

Actually, the only time you should go around a manager this way is when you truly believe that he or she is not doing the job as well as it could be done and you are convinced that you can do it better. Such managers usually know they aren't performing adequately and will rarely give a young executive a fight when he or she starts to work around them.

If you are reprimanded for going over a manager's head (and someone who understands power will not waste a moment in doing this), back off, claim innocence, and don't repeat the offense. You have warned your supervisor that you need more authority, and he or she will either give it to you or not.

A more subtle way to go around a manager is to get exposure for yourself. A bright young man who worked for a Louisville manufacturer but felt held down by his supervisor, the division sales manager, came up with the idea of taping sales messages that salespeople could carry around with them and play while they drove from appointment to appointment. He went right over his supervisor's head to sell the idea, won the recognition he deserved, and eventually went out on his own to sell his product.

Along the same line, you could give slide presentations and talks, organize seminars, or do anything that gets you known around the company. Your supervisor won't be able to do anything as you direct your energies in new directions, as long as you are still doing the job you were hired to do. And you will be making valuable allies and contacts.

## COPING WITH TOO MUCH AMBITION

Be careful, however, not to overexpose yourself or get a reputation for being too ambitious. Ambition that is too obvious can hurt. It usually earns one the reputation of being "too hot to handle." Usually such men and women burn out early in their careers. In effect, what happens is that no one will take them on, since no one wants a worker who is so obviously promoting only himself or herself at the expense of everyone else.

Even when getting exposure for yourself, it is important to give the appearance that you are doing this for the company's benefit. As one executive at IBM said, "Why should I give a break to a guy who, however bright and talented, weighs every work project in terms of how it will look on his résumé?"

Executives who get too hot to handle rarely get fired. Instead, they get a lot of lateral promotions and wake up one day to find themselves on dead-end career paths. This happens most often in large corporations. Here, one does not threaten a manager. There are so many jobs that one can simply be shoved aside or moved from place to place because no one wants to advance the career of someone who is busy advancing himself or herself every minute.

## COMPLAINING ABOUT A COLLEAGUE

You can always go to a superior to complain about a coworker who is not doing his or her job properly, but there is an etiquette to doing this. First, you must know what you can legitimately complain about. As one executive noted, "You can only lose face if you go in to complain because the secretarial pool doesn't get your letters out fast enough." Then, too, it is wiser not to complain about anyone on a level higher than you; it may threaten your manager, who will undoubtedly have his or her own peer loyalties.

Most managers advise that you go first to the colleague who is not doing his or her job satisfactorily. Since you still need to work with this person, it is more tactful to try to work things out with him or her before going to management. If this fails and you feel you have to go higher, you can do it, but as one man noted, "It's important to couch the complaint in diplomatic terms. For instance, if you need to work with that colleague, you almost have to go to your boss and suggest another method of getting the job done, one that takes the burden off the person who is not carrying his load. You can't ever go in and bad-mouth a colleague. You really can't gossip, either. You mostly have to go in and describe the work situation to the boss—often without using names—and hope that he gets the message."

Most executives get the message. They know when they have someone working for them who is not pulling his or her weight, and they take a complaint from a colleague, however subtly it may be worded, as a sign that the time has come for action.

When a general air of dissatisfaction prevails in an office, a direct confrontation with top management often works. It has worked so well at Dean, Witter in Chicago that Thomas Clark, branch office manager, regularly schedules "beer and bitch" sessions at which employees can open up in an informal session with their superiors. Clark said, "Everyone gets a couple of beers in him and then lets off as much steam as he wants to. There's no pressure because we're in a group. There aren't any hard feelings the next day, and I learn a lot."

The key to these sessions is their collective nature and the fact that the employees can really open up to their manager. After all, managers are not mind readers. There are times when they simply have not yet caught the vibrations that all is not well in the offices.

## DEALING WITH A MANAGER WHO ERRS

Sometimes your superior will make an embarrassing blunder, and you, as the subordinate trying your hardest to advance your career and the manager's, will find that you must react. There are three things you can do tactfully when this happens. First, you can ignore the error if it is minor enough.

Second, you can defend it. Do this by pointing out the wisdom of your supervisor's decision. Pointing out the long-term value of the decision is an especially good tactic. Few people will remember the mistake when the future finally arrives and the decision has been proven right or wrong, and few people know what will happen in the future anyway, so who can say whether your supervisor has erred or not if you put the mistake in this light?

Finally, if you feel strongly about a manager's error, you can privately and tactfully express your views to the manager. If you feel that the error could harm your career, express your dissatisfaction in a memo for the manager's eyes only—and keep a copy for future reference.

## DISPENSING CRITICISM

One of the functions of being a manager is to evaluate the work of your employees. Some companies have procedures for critical evaluation while other companies let each executive handle this in his or her own way. All executives interviewed felt that it was essential to talk over an employee's performance from time to time. Doing so, however, calls for a great deal of tact and graciousness on the part of the person proffering the criticism.

Milton Wood expressed his philosophy on evaluating people this way: "You do have to be tactful, but a boss does an individual a big injustice by not exposing specifically what problems exist. For example, if someone who worked for me didn't speak well, it would be my responsibility to let that person know right up front. I try to tell the person that I want him or her to succeed and that I am confident that he or she will, but that there are a few factors that are not necessarily hurting at the moment, but which should be remedied if the person wants to grow with this organization or professionally.

"I always try to be diplomatic and I always try to have a solution. A person who doesn't speak well, for example, is offered the opportunity to take a course—at company expense—to improve his or her speech. I also try to sell the reason that the person needs to improve. Most important, I think, is to offer a solution whenever criticism is offered. It makes the criticism seem less ominous."

People work well only when they think they are good at what they do, and to undermine confidence is also to undermine the company, so criticism always should be couched in the most tactful terms. One way to do this is to minimize your authority when giving criticism. Let an employee know that you want to talk about his or her work, and ask the person to prepare any notes or thoughts he or she may have.

Evaluative sessions should always be a two-way street. If possible, get out from behind your desk when giving criticism and sit in a chair beside the employee or across a table. Let the employee begin. Ask "How do you think things are going? Do you have any specific problems?"

Focus on just one or two issues and save anything else for another meeting. One executive said, "Not only does a boss have to be diplomatic in giving criticism, but also he has to understand that people aren't perfect. Don't take people to task for something that doesn't amount to a hill of beans. Ignore the minor stuff and go on to the major problems."

Listen carefully to any complaints an employee has, and avoid giving the impression that you are biding your time until he or she gets done speaking so you can get down to the real business at hand: criticism. When you do get down to specific areas that could be improved, it is important to phrase comments in plain language.

One executive reported that a friend at a major oil company had been told he needed to work on motivating those who worked for him, but the suggestion was written in pure corporate jargon, so the person just laughed it off. The executive said, "I could tell that this was a problem with my friend and that, had the suggestion been put to him plainly, he would have responded. But as it was, he entirely missed the point because he found the corporate jargon so funny, and in a way, I could see his point, too."

Major corporations usually have forms that are used in employee evaluation. One oil company executive said he knows just what to do with the forms. He begins every employee-evaluation interview by tearing up the forms and saying "These don't matter to me. What I want to do is discuss with you seriously what you are doing well and what areas need improvement." He continued, "The employee always responds and we have a good, open talk. Of course, I have to go back later and fill in the forms, but the employee doesn't have to submit to this grading process. Unless something is really wrong with an employee, everyone gets good ratings on those forms, anyway."

Wrap up a critical session by soliciting the employee's goals for the future, by outlining his or her accomplishments, and by discussing what he or she will be doing on current projects. Reassure employees that you value their work, and always try to end the session by complimenting an employee on a strong point.

## ACCEPTING CRITICISM

No one loves to hear criticism, but everyone wants reinforcement for a job well done. In most companies, one comes with the other, or at least, you cannot escape hearing an evaluation of your work. How you respond to criticism depends in part on the personality of the person giving it and on your relationship with him or her. Never laugh off criticism—always treat it very seriously. Ask for specific examples of situations you have handled poorly. Ask for ideas on how you might better handle yourself.

When the session is drawing to a close, tell your supervisor that you appreciate his or her honesty and suggestions. Thank the manager for giving you such a fair report, especially if you got one.

Should you find yourself constantly subjected to what you feel is unfair criticism, it may be time to look for another job. You may need a lower-key job or a better employer. In either case, accept the criticism graciously while you work your way to another job or department. Don't give a former supervisor a reason to tell a prospective supervisor that you don't take criticism well.

## ACCEPTING PUBLIC CRITICISM

Criticism should be given privately. Offering public criticism is invariably an underhanded power play. If someone suggests a truly rotten idea, it will fall of its own accord without another person's cynical prompting. Avoid such demeaning actions.

Should you find yourself being criticized publicly, stay calm—and stay polite. Attention, fairly or not, has been focused on you, and everyone will be watching to see how you handle the situation. Say as little as possible and treat the person who offers the criticism civilly. You could say something vague such as "You may be right," or you could offer to discuss the matter later.

## ASKING FOR A PROMOTION OR RAISE

Asking for a promotion or a raise is torture for the timid and downright hard work even for the assertive. Most managers feel that a good employee should not have to ask for a raise, that it should be offered before the employee has a chance to ask for it.

Ironically, there are times when asking for a raise before it is offered is good strategy. Sometimes the biggest raises go to the people who dare to ask for them. If, for example, the rumor is circulating that raises will be held to 5 percent for management, and you feel that you have done outstanding work, it's appropriate for you to talk with your supervisor about your work and the fact that you would like a raise of 15 percent for your efforts. Usually a compromise will be achieved—the manager won't be able to get the 15 percent for you, but because you have made it known tactfully that you won't be happy with 5 percent, he or she may fight for you and probably win slightly more than the 5 percent that everyone who doesn't speak up will be getting.

On the other hand, if you know your supervisor's hands are tied, you can still let it be known that you feel you deserve a raise, but don't take too hard a line about something that can't be changed. To do so only creates unnecessary tension. Giving someone a raise makes a manager feel powerful, but stressing someone's inability to give a raise at a certain time can be threatening.

### When Not to Ask for a Raise

Some moments are poor ones for requesting a raise. Even a star employee is unlikely to get a big boost in salary if he or she asks at the end of the company's fiscal year during a year when profits are down. Then, too, if business is in a slump, large raises might be less readily granted.

## How to Build Your Case

The only way to ask for a raise is to build a case for why you should be given one. This case, if at all possible, should be built in round dollar figures. Point out the profits of your department or how it has grown over the last year; show how you have contributed to the company's growth. Never ask for a raise because you need the money personally or because you have just bought a new house or car and must make payments.

Raises and promotions are almost never based on performance charts but are instead based on personal evaluation. Even a company that appears to have a tight salary schedule is almost always more flexible than you would imagine, so never let this stop you from asking for whatever amount you think you are worth, which in most companies in relatively good economic times is about 5 to 10 percent above your salary. Even if you are sure raises are set in the company you work for, see your current supervisor and let him or her know that you want more before the supervisor meets with superiors to determine your raise.

## ASKING FOR ADDITIONAL BENEFITS

You can request benefits or privileges in lieu of a raise if you want to. Take care to request only those privileges that are truly business-related. Asking to take a client to the boss's ski lodge in Aspen when, in fact, the boss always controls who is invited there is just plain gutsy and may hurt you. On the other hand, if the lodge is clearly meant to be used as company property, and you want to take a very important client there, the risk of asking might pay off. One executive said he would admire an employee who had the nerve to make such a request.

Requesting something such as a club membership, a car, a credit card, or an increase in life insurance coverage is more acceptable. The awarding of privileges, either in lieu of or in addition to salary, is anticipated by top management. In fact, those who ask are usually the only ones who get.

## REFUSING PRIVILEGES, RESPONSIBILITY, AND RAISES

Once in a while it will be to your benefit to assert yourself and decline a promotion or raise that you deem unsatisfactory. This happened a few years ago at a major airline to a woman who had paid her dues for many years and was finally, upon the resignation of her boss, asked to assume responsibility for his job—at considerably less money than he had been making.

Rather than throwing a tantrum or lecturing the vice president who offered her the new job—who was himself totally out of touch with what women wanted in business—she simply said that while she was flattered and would like the job very much, it simply was not worth it to her to take on the extra responsibility for so little extra money.

She flatly but graciously declined the offer, whereupon the vice president made a trip to personnel to see what they could make of this strange refusal. Fortunately the vice president of personnel was more in tune with the times and suggested that his colleague offer the woman $10,000 more than her predecessor had been making.

The matter was settled to the woman's satisfaction and no one's ego was wounded. A similar strategy can be applied to promotions and perks that are not exactly what you wanted.

On the other hand, an executive has to be careful not to assume more responsibility than he or she can handle. Some managers even try to keep their employees a little overburdened, knowing that a person will have difficulty asking for a raise when he or she is barely getting through each day. Young executives frequently think the most direct route to success lies in being the person who is willing to do anything and everything. Older and wiser executives are rarely caught taking on more than they think they can handle.

If your supervisor pushes you to do too much, use the opportunity to ask for more help, thus expanding your power base. If this is not feasible, request a meeting at which you explain that you fear your work will suffer if you take on too much and that you are at your limit. In one form or another you will most likely be given some help.

## A FINAL WORD

Too many people are afraid to ask for what they want, especially in a work situation. Almost everyone interviewed for this book expressed fear of one or another manager. With age and experience most successful executives overcome this. Oliver Spencer probably summed up this universal fear by saying: "When you start working, you tend to think your boss is brighter, more special, and that's why he is where he is. You respect him just because he is your boss. It didn't occur to me until I was in my thirties that my boss got where he was because two guys ahead of him died, and there wasn't anyone else to replace them with. That's when I lost my reverence for my boss and started asking—and getting—things I wanted and had earned. Today young executives lose this reverence really young. That's probably good."

# 4

# *Executive Communications*

Every letter you write, every telephone call you make (or fail to make), even the warmth of the message that your voice mail delivers reflect not only on you but also on the company you work for—or own. How we communicate with one another is one of the most important ingredients of business not only for legal purposes, as most of us already know, but also for its human relations value.

Most modern business communications are brusque and impersonal even though little time or effort would be required to soften them. It's easy and quick to add a line of New Year's greetings or ask after someone's welfare, and such personal touches often work to give you a competitive edge in a fast-moving, impersonal world.

We are also undergoing an explosion in communications technology that is still so new we are just now figuring out polite methods of dealing with it. This chapter presents ways to help you cope politely with such new technologies as voice mail, cellular phones, and, of course, the ubiquitous fax machine.

## BUSINESS LETTERS

Until recently, business letters were written in a stuffy jargon that was a language unto itself. Today, fortunately, the trend is toward more personal expression, and most of the formal, stuffy idioms are no longer used. There is still an art, as well as an etiquette, to writing an excellent business letter.

Although a secretary will undoubtedly bear much of the responsibility for the actual preparation of a letter, never forget that your signature goes on it and that the message it carries is a reflection of your business skills. Without looking over someone's shoulder, any executive should routinely read some of the finished letters and all the memos and reports that emerge from his or her office.

There is a right and a wrong way to set up a business letter. This is the right way:

|  |  |
|---|---|
| 342 High Street<br>Knaw Bone, Indiana 46208<br>February 28, 1994 | **Heading** |
| Mr. John Walsh<br>Vice President, Sales<br>ABC Wholesalers Association<br>32671 North Street<br>Lexington, Kentucky 40505 | **Inside<br>Address** |
| Dear Mr. Walsh: | **Greeting** |
| I was delighted to receive your letter last week<br>informing me of the new insurance plan being<br>set up for the growers. It is something cotton<br>growers have sought for years, and I shall be<br>pleased to be one of the first to join.<br>Please do call on me, as you suggested, with<br>additional details. My secretary, Ms. Irma<br>Smithfield, will be pleased to make an appoint- | **Body** |

ment for you, and I shall look forward to seeing you again.

Sincerely,                                        **Closing**


Jack Randolph                                    **Signature**
President, Randolph Farms, Inc.

## The Parts of a Business Letter

A business letter has six distinct parts: heading, inside address,
greeting, body, closing, and signature.


### Heading

In business, and even for personal business correspondence, you
will most likely have printed stationery, so the heading often consists
of only the date, an important detail that should never be omitted.


### Greeting

Acceptable greetings for business letters include:

Dear Joan: (*or* less formally, Ma'am)
Gentlemen: (*or* Ladies: *or* Gentlemen and Ladies:)
Dear Sir or Madam:
Dear Ms. Hindsmith:
     (*or* Miss *or* Mrs.)
Dear Mr. Jackson:

The greeting "My Dear Mr. Trent," once considered more intimate than "Dear Mr. Trent," is not used much today and has become
the more formal of the two greetings. Whenever possible, use the
name and complete title of the person to whom you are writing.

"Mr.," "Mrs.," and "Dr." were for many years the main abbreviations used in greetings, but "Ms." has gained popularity, because it serves to take away the distinctions between married and unmarried women in business. It has become common as a greeting and is perfectly acceptable in a letter today—and even desirable on occasions when you do not know whether you are addressing a single or a married woman.

It is tactful—and often a savvy business move as well—to use an egalitarian greeting when writing to someone you do not know. Instead of writing "Dear Sir," you could write "Dear Sir or Ma'am." Alternately, some people are opting for an equally acceptable greeting that uses the name of the company. If you were writing the Lands' End Company, you would say "Dear Lands' End." This latter greeting is a little less formal than the first one. You would not use it, for example, if you were writing the Human Relations Department of a company to which you were submitting your résumé. Then it is better to write "Dear Sir or Ma'am"—and best of all, of course, in communications like this is to get the name of the real person.

It goes without saying that whenever you are writing to someone who has an important business tie to you (as in: you are hoping she will give you a job or become your client), the only acceptable greeting is the one that uses the correct name of the person to whom the communication is directed. If computers can generate our names in mass mailings, now there is no excuse for our not tracking down an important name—if there ever was.

### Body

The body of the letter is where the business is conducted. Most business letters today are quite brief. They rarely run longer than one page, and many run only one paragraph. When a business letter becomes long and complicated, it is time to consider picking up the phone and calling someone.

Another reason for the brevity of business letters today is that they are often used only to transmit a report, memo, or some other enclosed piece of information. Years ago, such materials were rewritten in letter form; today, memos and reports are often simply forwarded to someone outside the company with a short transmittal note.

Some people have also adopted the practice of writing a return response on the bottom of a letter they have received, especially when only a line or two is required. This is not a particularly gracious practice, as it seems to be saying to the other person "Although you showed me the courtesy of a letter, I am too busy to reply in the same manner." There is one time when such a reply might be acceptable, and that is when the sender of the initial letter has indicated that it would be fine for you to reply on the bottom of the page. Even then, the truly gracious gesture is to respond with a short letter on your own letterhead.

In these fast-paced times, it is gracious to resist a telegraphic style when writing business letters. Be sure every sentence is complete and logical, and avoid dropping necessary articles and pronouns.

For example, the following response unintentionally borders on rudeness:

"Received letter December 8. Will advise no later than one week."

Consider how much more gracious is the following:

"I received your letter last week. I do need a couple of days to consider your proposal, but I'll be getting back to you no later than next week."

Whenever possible, in a business letter, use the first person, which is friendlier and more polite. If you are truly using a corporate "we," that is one thing, but when you are the one responding, use "I" whenever possible.

Simple effective language highlights most business letters today. For example:

| Avoid these phrases | And use instead |
|---|---|
| I beg to enclose | I enclose |
| Please find enclosed | I enclose |
| Will send same | I shall send you |
| Yours of the second | Your letter of July 2 |
| Hoping to hear from you | I hope to hear from you |
| Thanking you | Thank you again *or* I want to thank you again |

*Avoid these phrases entirely*
And oblige
Beg to advise
In reply I would say

It is appropriate and well mannered to include some personal greeting or closing in a business letter, such as "Hope you have a very nice weekend," or "I want to wish you and your family a very happy Fourth of July." This is not the same as getting chatty in a business letter, which is an unprofessional thing to do—business letters should be kept as brief as possible—but since the trend is toward conveying the message as quickly as possible, all the more reason to sign off with a cordial line or two.

## Closing

About the most formal closing ever used today is "Very truly yours," or "Very sincerely." More often, a closing is less formal: "Cordially," "Sincerely," and "Best regards" are frequently used, particularly among people who regularly correspond.

## Signature

The signature consists of the full name and title of the sender, although it is acceptable to sign only your first name when writing to someone who knows you well. The name and title are always typed, and the signature is always handwritten.

## Correct Forms of Address

You may have occasion to write to people of official importance, and there is an etiquette to using their titles both in writing and in speaking. The list that follows shows how to address dignitaries when writing to them and when meeting them.

*Titles and Forms of Address*

THE PRESIDENT

*Address:* The President
The White House
Washington, D.C. 20500

*Letter opening:* Dear Mr. President:
*or*
Mr. President:

*Closing:* Respectfully,

*Speak of him as:* the President

*Call him:* Mr. President
*or* Sir

*Introduce people
to him as:* "Mr. President,
may I present ... "

*Say:* "How do you do,
Mr. President."

THE PRESIDENT'S
WIFE

*Address:* Mrs. John Adams
The White House
Washington, D.C. 20500

*Letter opening:* Dear Mrs. Adams:

*Closing:* Sincerely,

*Speak of her as:* Mrs. Adams

*Call her:* Mrs. Adams

*Introduce people
to her as:* "Mrs. Adams, may
I present ... "

*Say:* "How do you do,
Mrs. Adams."

UNITED STATES
AND
STATE SENATORS

*To address
them both:* The President and
Mrs. Adams

*Address:* The Honorable
Judith W. Johnson
United States Senate
Washington, D.C. 20510
*or*
The Honorable
John J. Carlson
State Capitol
Springfield,
Illinois 62701

*Letter opening:* Dear Senator
Johnson:

*Closing:* Respectfully,

*Speak of her as:* the Senator *or*
Senator Johnson

*Call her:* Senator Johnson

*Introduce people
to her as:* "Senator Johnson,
may I present ... "

*Say:* "How do you do,
Senator Johnson,"
*or* "How do you do,
Senator."

*To address
Senator Michaels
and her husband:* The Honorable
Judith Johnson
and Mr. Johnson

MEMBERS OF
CONGRESS OR
STATE
LEGISLATURE

*Address:* The Honorable
Elizabeth A. Scott
House of
Representatives
Washington, D.C. 20515
*or*
The Honorable
John A. O'Reilly
State Capitol
Des Moines, Iowa 50300

*Letter opening:* Dear Ms. Scott:
*Closing:* Respectfully,
*Speak of her as:* Ms. Scott
*Call her:* Ms. Scott
*Introduce people
to her as:* "Ms. Scott, may I
present . . . "
*Say:* "How do you do,
Ms. Scott."

*To address
Ms. Scott
and her
husband:* The Honorable
Elizabeth A. Scott
and Mr. Scott

THE CHIEF JUSTICE
OF THE
UNITED STATES

*Address:* The Chief Justice
The Supreme Court
Washington, D.C. 20543
*Letter opening:* Dear Chief Justice:
*Closing:* Sincerely yours,
*Speak of him as:* Mr. Chief Justice
*or* Mr. Douglas
*Call him:* Mr. Douglas *or*
Mr. Chief Justice

|  |  |  |
|---|---|---|
| | *Introduce people* | |
| | *to him as:* | "Mr. Chief Justice may I present ... " |
| | | *or* "Mr. Douglas, may I present ... " |
| | *Say:* | "How do you do, Justice," *or* |
| | | "How do you do, Mr. Chief Justice." |
| | *To address the Chief Justice and his wife:* | Chief Justice and Mrs. Douglas |
| GOVERNORS | *Address:* | The Honorable Carol E. Neely Governor of California The Governor's Mansion Sacramento, California 95800 |
| | *Letter opening:* | Dear Governor Neely: |
| | *Closing:* | Respectfully, |
| | *Speak of her as:* | the Governor |
| | *Call her:* | Governor Neely *or* Ma'am (Sir) |
| | *Introduce people to her as:* | "Governor Neely, may I present ... " |
| | *Say:* | "How do you do, Governor Neely." |

To address the
governor
and her
husband: The Honorable
Carol E. Neely
and Mr. Neely

## THE MAYOR

Address: The Honorable
David Lindbeck
Mayor of Kewanee
City Hall
Kewanee, Illinois
61443

Letter opening: Dear Mayor Lindbeck:

Closing: Respectfully,

Speak of
him as: the Mayor or
Mayor Lindbeck

Call him: Mayor Lindbeck
or Sir

Introduce people
to him as: "Mayor Lindbeck,
may
I present ... "

Say: "How do you do, Mr.
Mayor," or "How do
you do, Mayor
Lindbeck."

To address the
Mayor and his wife: The Honorable
David Lindbeck
and Mrs. Lindbeck

MINISTER

*Address:* The Reverend Samuel
George
*or* The Reverend
Dr. Samuel George

*Letter opening:* Dear Mr. George:
*or*
Dear Dr. George:

*Closing:* Sincerely,

*Speak of him as:* Mr. (*or* Dr.) George

*Call him:* Mr. (*or* Dr.) George

*Introduce people
to him as:* "Dr. George, may I
present . . . "

*To address a
clergyman
and his
wife:* The Reverend
Samuel George
and Mrs. George
*or*
The Right Reverend
Samuel George and
Mrs. George

PRIEST

*Address:* The Reverend Daniel
W. Williams (*or* other
initials indicating
his order, if he
belongs to one)
Pastor, St. Peter's
Church
Chicago, Illinois
60657

*Letter opening:* Dear Father Williams:

*Closing:* Sincerely,

> *Speak of him as:* Father Williams
> *Call him:* Father Williams
> *Introduce people*
> *to him as:* "Father Williams,
> may I present . . . "
> *Say:* "How do you do,
> Father Williams,"
> *or* "How do you do,
> Father."

RABBI

> *Address:* Rabbi David
> Rosenberg
> *Letter opening:* Dear Rabbi
> Rosenberg:
> *Closing:* Sincerely,
> *Speak of him as:* Rabbi Rosenberg
> *Call him:* Rabbi Rosenberg
> *Introduce people*
> *to him as:* "Rabbi Rosenberg,
> may I present . . . "
> *Say:* "How do you do,
> Rabbi Rosenberg," *or*
> "How do you do,
> Rabbi."

## Forms of Address for Executive Women

As always in the M.E. (Modern Era), we have recommended and continue to recommend that you call people by whatever titles and names they prefer. It costs you nothing in psychic energy and satisfies them enormously.

An excellent case in point has been the use of "Ms." for executive (and other) women. It is a title of respect that makes no judgments about whether a woman is married, and this more than anything probably accounts for its rapid rise in popularity. The *New York Times,* that last bastion of unchanging, traditional language, finally yielded in the mid-1980s and began to use "Ms."

Another, more recent case in point is First Lady Hillary Clinton's request that she be referred to as Hillary Rodham Clinton. Like many women of her generation who marry, she chose to keep her own name, and bowed to the pressure of using Clinton only when her husband became governor of Arkansas. Letters to her (and to other women who have kept their own names) should be addressed as follows:

Ms. Hillary Rodham Clinton

Alternately, you may follow the other trend and drop the use of any title in an address, making her simply:

Hillary Rodham Clinton

Whenever any woman decides to keep her own name upon marrying (whether she does this professionally or socially as well), she should be addressed accordingly in making introductions and in correspondence.

In theory, Hillary Rodham Clinton could be addressed as "Mrs." since she is using her husband's name. A woman who does not choose to use her husband's name cannot properly be addressed as "Mrs." She is indeed these days most correctly addressed as "Ms."—unless of course we want to reinstate the old colonial custom of addressing any woman over a certain age as "Mrs." But who would want to be in charge of deciding what constitutes a "certain age"?

## BUSINESS STATIONERY

When you go to work for a company, you will be supplied with printed stationery with the company name and logo and your name and title. Along with stationery invariably come business cards. In many companies, stationery and business cards are supplied automatically, and you have little to say about their quality. When you do have a hand in their selection, order something conservative. The most impressive business stationery is white or buff-colored, is printed in black or another conservative color, and is generally 8½ by 11 inches in size, with matching envelopes.

Business cards should also be conservative. The most tasteful ones show your name and title and the company's name and are printed in black on white or off-white stock. If you have a choice, select a plain typeface.

When you need to order stationery on a new job, simply ask your secretary or the office manager how to go about placing an order.

### Personal Versus Business Stationery

It is generally a good idea also to keep your personal letterhead in stock; it should follow the guidelines just discussed. The letterhead should contain your name, home address, city, state, and zip code.

No reference should be made to your company affiliation on personal stationery, but appropriate titles, such as attorney-at-law, LL.B., PH.D., or M.D., may be printed after your name.

In some professions, it is common practice to print one or more professional affiliations, but in general, omit any but the barest details on personal business stationery. If you have a professional reputation, it will precede your letters. You need not advertise it.

## The Personal Touch in Business Correspondence

Business correspondence offers a wonderful opportunity for networking. In a world that is rapidly losing many of its gracious touches, you can be the person who still writes the personal note—and, more important, who takes time to offer congratulations and condolences.

What are some occasions for note-writing? Send brief handwritten (or typed) notes to congratulate someone on a promotion, to congratulate an associate whose child graduates from college, to wish someone a good year, or to extend condolences. These letters, with the possible exception of a condolence note, may be typed. It is more gracious if they deliver only their special message and do not contain any business. Better to send the condolence note and then pick up the phone and suggest that a bereaved colleague take her time with a report she's working on than to mix business and pleasure. The same thing holds for personal notes of congratulation. Tell the new father how happy you are for him in a note, and then discuss any business over the phone or in a fax.

A note to express condolences always seems more personal when it is handwritten, although it may be typed if that is your strong preference. It may be composed on the company letterhead.

Only a few lines expressing your sorrow are necessary, particularly if the person who died was not known to you personally. The following is an example of a condolence note to a business associate:

Dear Ben,
I was saddened and shocked to learn of the sudden death of your father last Tuesday. Please accept my sympathy for you and your family. If there is anything I can do, please feel free to call.

Sincerely,


Joe Perez

A congratulatory note can be equally brief:

Dear Janet:

Congratulations on becoming division vice president. I know you'll be an asset to the company in your new position, and I wish you all the luck in the world with your new responsibilities.

Cordially,


Fred Burns

## Sending and Receiving Faxes

The newest and perhaps most popular form of communication of the past decade is the fax machine, which is now as ubiquitous in offices as microwaves have become in homes.

Documents and letters are now routinely (and instantaneously) transmitted by fax. These documents should simply follow the format that would be used for any contract, letter of agreement, or letter.

Since fax machines are often located in mailrooms, you will need to attach a "cover sheet." This designates to whom the fax should be directed. Many companies have begun to provide their employees with standardized fax cover sheets, but, lacking this, you can always type your own.

If you are preparing a fax cover sheet, a good format to use is that of an interoffice memo. Include the date, a "To:" and a "From:" and possibly an "RE" as well so you can add a line or two about the purpose of the fax.

Faxes are more public than letters and even interoffice memos, so it's not a good idea to include anything personal in one. In fact, there are times when it is better not to send a fax at all. They should not be used for thank-you letters after job interviews, résumés (unless a fax communication was specifically requested), rejections of proposals (or of anything else, for that matter), and certain personal communications, such as congratulatory letters. There is nothing wrong with sending the latter communication by fax, but a personal letter just isn't as elegant a gesture when it falls from a machine as when it arrives by post.

A growing and distasteful phenomenon is the use of the fax machine for advertising. Literally thousands of sheets of paper (to say nothing of the time required for mailroom personnel to sort out these "junk" faxes) are wasted every day with nonessential, unsolicited information—usually advertisements. In many offices these communications are treated as junk mail and left unread, even undistributed, so you may want to think twice before using this medium to transmit advertising messages.

## Memos and Reports—When to Use Them

Memos and reports are the other two forms of written communication used in most offices. It is especially important to know when to use each channel of communication. As a rule, talking to someone in person results in the greatest degree of mutual understanding, but it can be time-consuming, and, unless notes are taken, a conversation can be distorted over time. Written communication is the next most effective method of communicating with someone. When you need to explain something quickly, calling a meeting or writing a memo are the two most effective ways of doing it, although a memo is more considerate of the other person's time. Often when an immediate response is required, phone calls to the individuals involved are the most effective method.

Writing a memo is perhaps the most challenging form of business communication. It is also the form of communication that is most critically read by others. The memo must be brief, to the point, and, in many cases, persuasive.

The golden rule in memo and report writing, as in letter writing, is to present a low-key, friendly image. Especially in a memo, in which the main purpose is to convey information, do not talk down to an audience. Avoid discussing annoying or irritating subjects, and do not lecture. Avoid, for example, such condescending expressions as "of course," "as you know," and "as I was saying."

Conciseness is the key to effective memo and report writing. Go right to the heart of the matter being discussed, which means starting with a heading that accurately describes what you are going to talk about.

Organize your thoughts before starting to write. One way to do this is to use an old journalist's tip. Divide the information into the following categories: who, what, when, where, why, and how. Then select the most important category and begin with that, working your way through to lesser categories and omitting any category that is plainly not relevant.

Often the line between a memo and a report is unclear. A memo that was passed around to one's coworkers, for example, might well be dressed up as a report and passed on to top management.

In either form of writing, always keep your purpose in mind and make sure it is absolutely clear to those who read the material. Furthermore, if you want something, be sure to ask for it—in plain language. Nothing is more exasperating to a busy executive than to waste twenty minutes reading a report outlining a specific problem in the company and then to find no recommendation for solving the problem.

Don't write anything unnecessary. If it is at all possible to call someone with a request, make that your first option. People who turn out memos on a too-regular basis soon find that their masterpieces are rarely read. A memo or a report is a form of personal ammunition, something to be hoarded and used only at the right moment.

Try to avoid emotional overtones in a memo or report or, for that matter, in any form of business communication. Words such as "threat," "hate," "love," "punish"—even the word "should"—used in place of words that suggest rather than demand action sometimes read like rude demands.

It is especially polite when preparing a memo or report to give credit to coworkers when possible.

Before releasing a memo, a report, or even a letter, make it a practice to read it carefully in its final form. You are, after all, the person whose ideas it represents, who knows best what you wanted to say, and who will ultimately be responsible for its contents.

## YOUR WRITING STYLE

Any form of written business communication should contain the best English you know how to write. The proper choice of words, grammar, and sentence structure are all vitally important in written materials, and errors or carelessness are permanently there for all to see. Substandard English—even a simple word that was accidentally mistyped—may cause the reader to question the writer's ability to communicate and even to think logically.

On the other hand, you should try to avoid writing in a style that is excessively formal or stuffy since this can also put off the reader.

Long, involved sentences displaying several levels of meaning may have impressed college professors, but they are unimpressive and even damaging in business. While creative writing attempts to convey moods or ideas or to describe characters, almost all business writing is meant to convey facts. There is no place in business writing for convoluted sentences or for words that the reader may have to look up.

The object of business writing is to save people, mostly managers, time. It is rude to write something that attempts to show off what you perceive as your writing skills, with no consideration for the audience to whom the material is directed. Allen Weiss, author of a series of articles on business writing, succinctly summed up what not to do: "For the business writer, self-expression is secondary; self-indulgence is embarrassing, and self-amusement is merely a waste of time."*

Finally, in writing, as in other areas of getting along with people, avoid negativism. Even when writing about something unpleasant, use positive expressions to convey the meaning.

Writing can sometimes be too transparent in exposing a writer's feelings, so carefully check what you have written to be sure it does not show off areas of insecurity or defensiveness.

The most important thing to remember in using written communication is to be considerate of others' time and talent. Always take the audience into account when writing business material, and you will be on the road to success.

## TELEPHONE MANNERS

The way in which you answer a phone is often enough to determine whether the conversation will go well or badly. If you answer abruptly, you convey the image of an unfriendly, slightly rude person. While it is professional to sound businesslike on the telephone, remember that what you are saying may indeed be held against you if it is not said in a courteous way.

---

* Allen Weiss, "The Audience Comes First," *Supervisory Management* 22 (April 1977): 2–11.

Clarity on the phone is especially important, but rather than asking someone if he or she understands something, adopt such devices as repeating a figure, a statistic, or a key sentence or spelling a name just to be sure that both parties have gotten the facts straight. Also helpful is the practice of keeping a notebook or tape recorder handy to record what you thought a conversation was all about, particularly if there may be ramifications later. Sending a letter of confirmation after an important business call is another way to be sure the matter was understood by all concerned and is a courtesy to the receiver.

How you sound on a telephone is very important. Speak softly out of consideration for others around you, but also speak clearly and slowly so you are understood by the listener.

A cold, expressionless voice does more damage on a phone than it does in person, where your body can show animation even if your voice is less pleasant than it might be, so learn to show interest and liveliness over the telephone.

## Answering the Phone

If your calls are screened, you can simply answer by saying "Hello." If a secretary does not intercept your calls, say something to identify yourself and the company. For example: "Nelson Wade speaking," or "Accounting department, Susy Jones speaking."

If the caller asks for someone in the department or for someone you don't know, try to be helpful. Don't say "Who's this?" or, worse still, "You've got the wrong department," followed by a click of the receiver as you hang up. Make an effort to locate the person even if it means giving up a few minutes of your time.

If you are, for some reason, screening a call, ask "May I say who is calling?" or "May I tell Mr. Smith who is calling?" And remember that the caller has the right to respond "No, thank you."

If your calls are not screened, answer this way: "This is Frank Ellis." Avoid answering "This is Mrs. Dean," or "Dean speaking." The latter is merely rude, and the former answers avoid giving your full name, which may be exactly what the caller is hoping to hear.

## *Making a Call*

If a secretary places your calls, as is customary in many companies today, do not waste anyone's time by keeping the person you called on the line waiting for you to pick up the phone. This is rude and tactless and invariably a sign of a very big ego.

As a matter of fact, many of the companies interviewed for this book reported that they encouraged executives to place their own phone calls, because this saves time and is more considerate of others—secretaries as well as those who are called. But if you must ask someone to place a call for you, be right there to pick up the phone when the person you are calling is on the line.

If you reach a switchboard operator when placing a call, say "Is Mr. MacAllister there, please?" or simply "Mr. MacAllister, please."

Identify yourself immediately to the person who next answers, saying: "This is Allen Burke of ABC Company. May I speak to Mark MacAllister, please?"

If you are a frequent caller, say: "This is Al Burke. May I speak to Bill Jones, please?" If you have met the secretary or assistant who answers the phone, a line of greeting to him or her is especially considerate.

Don't say to the person who answers: "Hello, Mr. Dean, please," "Let me talk to Dean," "Dean there?" or "Is Mr. Dean in?" The person who answers the phone should not have to ask who is calling.

If you think the person you are calling may not remember you or recognize your name immediately, repeat it again when he or she comes on the phone, saying: "Hello, Mr. Jones, this is Allen Burke of ABC Corporation. I met you last week during lunch with Bill Jacobson."

If you are calling someone in a specific position, but you do not know the person's name, it is permissible to request this information of the operator or the person who answers the phone. Say something like this: "Hello. My name is Allen Burke and I am with the ABC Corporation. I am trying to get in touch with your sales manager and wondered if you would be kind enough to give me his name and then ring his phone for me."

If you reach a wrong number when calling someone, do not hang up but instead say "Is this 348-6192?" The party who answered will say "No, it isn't," and you can then apologize and hang up quietly.

If you are connected directly to the person you are calling (one perk for a top executive is a private phone list) or the person answers the phone because a secretary or assistant is absent, do not say: "Is this Mr. Burke?" or "Mr. Burke?" even if you recognize the voice. Instead say "This is John Smith; is Allen Burke there?" If Allen Burke is polite and sensible, he will not attempt to deny the obvious.

Do not talk to anyone else while you are speaking on the phone, and do not do other work at the same time. If you are unavoidably interrupted, say "Excuse me a minute, please. I have to handle something." Then cover the mouthpiece or use the mute button and quickly handle the problem. Apologize briefly when you resume the conversation.

Apply the same rules on the phone that you would during any conversation. Listen attentively and do not interrupt, although you may toss in phrases indicating agreement or disagreement just as is done in personal conversation, especially since silences are difficult to interpret over the phone. If you must interrupt someone on the phone, do so graciously.

On the other hand, there is no need to be a captive audience. In a social situation you are expected to wait until the caller signs off. Your business hours, however, are too valuable to always permit this formality, so if your time is being wasted, sign off gracefully, even if you did not initiate the call. If you are interrupted or are too busy to talk, say so and ask if you may call back, indicating approximately when you will return the call. A particularly gracious way to get rid of a long-winded talker is to say: "I really don't want to take any more of your time so I'll say good-bye now."

End phone calls by saying "Good-bye." Do not say "Bye-bye" or even "Good-bye now." Avoid the rude habit of hanging up without saying good-bye.

## Speaker Phones

Speaker phones are in widespread use these days, although they aren't much improved in quality from when they first came on the market several decades ago. Be aware when you use one that you will sound far away and distracted unless the quality is very good. Also be aware that the person to whom you are speaking will probably assume that you are sorting papers or engaged in some other activity in addition to speaking on the phone—and that's not very flattering to the caller.

There are times, however, when speaker phones are invaluable. When two people are reviewing a contract or other important papers or taking notes on a conversation, a speaker phone can be helpful in freeing up your hands.

Truly courteous executives use them only when necessary, and always tell the other caller when a speaker phone will be in use. Especially courteous is to apologize for using one.

## Directing an Assistant or Secretary to Handle Your Calls

Since your assistant or secretary represents you, it is important to make sure that this person handles your calls graciously and efficiently.

Instruct someone taking your calls about whether you want to know who is calling before you answer the phone. If you do, tell the person how this information is best obtained, namely by asking "May I say who is calling, please?"

If possible, do not ask the person who takes your calls to lie for you. If you cannot come to the phone, your assistant or secretary can say that you are in conference or unavailable, rather than saying you are out of the office when you aren't.

Finally, tell your secretary or assistant politely what you expect your phone messages to contain: accurately spelled first and last names, company name, nature of business, and phone number where you can return the call.

## Call Waiting

Many home-based or small businesses have taken advantage of call waiting, a telephone connection that permits incoming calls to break into a current telephone call. You (and often the person you are talking to as well) hear a blip on the line. The advent of call waiting has led to a new kind of rudeness, which consists of a breathless call recipient immediately (if only momentarily) dumping the person to whom he or she is speaking in order to announce equally breathlessly to the incoming caller "I'm on another call. Call you right back." The kindest thing we can say about call waiting is that it promotes impatience. On the other hand, it is invaluable to the person who needs to take all of his or her calls and doesn't want the expense of a multiline telephone system.

So we suggest that the cure be human. Don't rush when you hear the call-waiting click. Take a deep breath and remind yourself that you've got time to handle everything. Then politely ask the person you're talking to if he or she would mind waiting a minute and reassure him or her that you'll be right back.

Then click into the incoming call. Say hello and let the person identify himself or herself. You may have to interrupt your caller (as gently as possible) to say that you're on another line and could you call right back. Then say good-bye.

Then go back to the first call.

Of course, many of us protest that this is exactly what we do. But it isn't, or, rather, we do this, but we do it breathlessly and with great impatience as if the person on call waiting had done something wrong. Take a deep breath and try to do it slowly and with patience. Kindly.

In addition to using the standard desk telephone, executives are now often supplied with a panoply of voice mail, portable or cellular telephones, and beepers, all of which serve the desired or maybe-not-so-desired purpose of extending the range of telecommunications far beyond what any of us imagined even a few years ago.

## Voice Mail

The newest office innovation is an electronic device (or at least something less personal than a human) that answers the phone and takes messages for you. Some voice mail systems let you record your message in your own voice. These are definitely the friendliest kind of voice mail to have, since they offer reassurance that you do actually exist.

In a growing number of offices these days, you encounter voice mail first and a human receptionist only if voice mail does not for some reason work for you. And increasingly, it's all done digitally.

Voice mail is in effect an answering machine, so anyone using it should keep messages short and to the point. Voice mail messages are also more public than you might imagine, so it's wise to skip anything personal, pornographic, or even flip in favor of simply leaving your name, number, and a brief businesslike message.

How you set up your voice mail can affect how user-friendly you appear to be. It's reassuring to your caller if you can say when you might be back in your office or when you expect to return calls, for example. If you are out of your office for several days, leave a message to this effect. In an office, this offers none of the security problems that doing so with a home phone answering machine might.

## Beepers, Cellulars, Portables

These three devices manage to keep busy (and not so busy) executives in continuous contact with the world, although not perhaps in a way that the world finds comfortable. Here are some things to keep in mind when trying to use one of these technological wonders without giving offense:

- People are generally more annoyed than pleased to receive a call from you as you are flying down the freeway if the alternative is to see you in person in the office in another five minutes.
- Resist the urge to use these devices at off-hours. Just because you can call your administrative assistant, who always gets to work at 7:30 A.M. so he can catch up with his paperwork, doesn't mean you should. It's polite to stick to regular business hours unless you know a call will be welcome.

Even though they serve a valuable purpose, beepers are one of the more annoying new gadgets, not least because they are being used by many people who don't really need them. They are especially irritating when they go off during public performances, at dinner parties, or even during a movie.

Perhaps the best and most polite approach is to ask yourself any time you are headed out to a social event whether you truly need a beeper attached to your person. (We can't prove this, but we suspect that some people actually believe that a beeper going off in public gives them a kind of cachet. Take it from us and others who must endure these little gadgets: They are merely an annoyance.)

A beeper may not be necessary if (a) someone else is covering for you or (b) you could be reached by phone. Besides, they're ugly. Why would you want to wear one of these strapped to the waist of an expertly tailored suit or dress?

In summary, if you truly need one of these devices, then get one. If you simply love the gadgetry, then think twice, or get it and think twice about how you use it.

## A FINAL WORD

Telephone manners are fairly easy to cultivate. Writing skills may prove more troublesome, but in either case, the ability to communicate is an important—perhaps *the* most important—skill a manager needs. If you sense that you have problems in this area, look for help.

Weak written communication skills can be improved with a good self-help book. In addition, any serious communicator should have on hand several good style books that will guide him or her in preparing written materials. Among such reference books, the most concise and elegant is *The Elements of Style* by William Strunk and E. B. White. This small volume should be required reading for anyone who ever has to put pen to paper. Another helpful book is *The Careful Writer: A Modern Guide to English Usage* by Theodore M. Bernstein. Because punctuation seems to be a weak area for many business writers, a good book to own is *Punctuate It Right!* by Harry Shaw.

All these books assume a degree of literacy and sophistication on the part of their readers. They are in no way guides to better secretarial skills or textbooks on grammar but rather are intended for use by people who have already acquired the basic skills of communication and who need to add the polishing touches. Other books on specialized areas of business writing are available in a library or bookstore.

# 5

# *Talking Your Way to the Top*

Not speaking well can stop a career in midstream. Poor speech habits, though, like bad breath, are not something your supervisor will call you in to talk about improving. Young executives are frequently given guidance on how to manage a project or write a report, but even your closest friend will not suggest that you leave something to be desired because of the way you speak. Speaking poorly may grate on the ears of others, but well-mannered people won't tell you about it.

On one level, speaking is idiosyncratic; it is a reflection of learned patterns of talking and personality. On a deeper and more important level, it is indicative of the ability to communicate, and communication is what much of business is all about. A manager who is able to tolerate too much slang for his or her personal taste will find it difficult to overlook the kind of speaking that reflects a confused, illogical mind. Some people even go so far as to assume, erroneously, that someone who does not have educated speaking patterns is not bright.

Your posture, gestures, and facial expressions can be put to work for you in a powerful way, because body language is just as important as what comes out of your mouth. For proof, turn on your television and watch without the sound. You will be surprised at how well another person's feelings can be detected through gesture and posture. These same signals work when you are with others. They tell your peers that you lack confidence; they tell a manager that you will always be comfortable as his or her subordinate; they say that you want your supervisor's job. Body language shows when you are pleased, dissatisfied, guarded.

By now you have surmised that speech is not merely what comes out of your mouth when you open it. It is also a subtle interaction of body language and facial expressions, what you actually say, and, perhaps surprisingly, how you listen.

## SPEAKING SKILLS

The first rule of speaking is: If you don't do it well, do something to remedy the situation. There are numerous books and self-help courses designed to help improve speech. If you suspect that you have a truly bad problem (and get a friend to tell you honestly), take private or group speech lessons, or take acting lessons—but do something.

A good way to know when you have a speech or communication problem is to watch others react to you. Your speech flaws frequently show up in others' responses to you. A long-winded person soon makes everyone in the room uncomfortable. Such people are frequently interrupted, and rarely are they listened to with much attention. If you talk too fast or too slow or in an accent that is hard to understand, others will give clues, either by asking you to repeat something several times or by admitting later that they missed "that part of what you said."

Poor grammar or misuse of a word is more difficult to detect since polite people are trained not to show any reaction to such errors. Try to listen to the speech of others to see how yours differs. At any rate, analyze the effect you have on others, and if you find yourself getting negative signals, take them as a warning that a little self-improvement is in order.

## Listening Skills

There is an art and an etiquette to being a good listener. Listening is a supreme compliment to others that never fails to reap benefits for the listener. More than one person has been considered a brilliant speaker who was actually a brilliant listener. Listening well means listening raptly. Direct all attention to the person who is speaking. Do not interrupt. Look the speaker directly in the eye most of the time; lean slightly forward and, if possible, sit close to him or her.

Good listeners often have some device—albeit a subconscious one—that shows when their attention has been caught unequivocally. It may be taking off a pair of glasses when the conversation takes a particularly fascinating turn, moving one arm closer to the speaker, or cupping a hand over one ear. (Usually, this is more likely to be a sign of slight deafness on the part of the listener, but is nonetheless flattering.)

Above all, when you are listening to someone else, do not look as if you are mentally planning what you want to say next. Obviously, if you are in an important business meeting or listening to someone speak to an audience, you may have to take a note or two, but in small conversational groups or in one-to-one situations, it is rude to the speaker to appear to be on the verge of breaking into the conversation with your own thoughts.

As a listener, you are expected to react to what you are hearing. This is done largely through body language and a few code sentences or words that have almost symbolic meaning. Such signals stop a speaker from going on about a subject the listener has no interest in or with which he or she does not agree. They reinforce a speaker the listener agrees with. As someone talks to you, be prepared to give signals indicating a reaction to the conversation. Nod yes or no frequently. Slip in such statements as "I agree completely," "You are absolutely right on that point," or "I can see our thinking is alike on that subject."

If you disagree with the point being made, you might say "We'll have to talk more about that later," "I'll have to give that some more thought," or even simply "I'm not sure I agree with you on that point." Perhaps the subtlest statement ever heard along these lines is "You may be right." Spoken in just the right tone, this statement carries the silent implication "But I doubt it."

Be careful that your body language projects what you are actually thinking as you listen to someone, or you will have a misunderstanding to clear up later on in the conversation. For example, do not nod agreement when you do not agree with someone, merely as a means of encouraging the speaker to go on. At worst, the person may leave the room thinking you agree when nothing could be farther from the truth.

## THE ART OF FLATTERY

There is an art to flattering someone, and, in business, when compliments are often directly related to performance, it is particularly important to make flattery work for you.

Flattery has several definitions, two of which are of use in this discussion:

It can mean excessive and often insincere compliments, especially in order to win someone's favor; or it can mean portraying favorably, showing off.

When going about the business of flattering someone, make very sure that the latter definition is your motive. Otherwise your actions may backfire. False flattery rarely sounds like anything but what it is unless you are complimenting an excessively egotistic person who is enormously unsure of himself or herself. And even such a person, when the chips are down, can probably recognize a false compliment.

Two levels of compliments are generally heard in business circles. Level 1 we shall call simple flattery. You like a tie someone is wearing, and you tell him so simply and briefly. A colleague is carrying an especially handsome leather purse; again, you tell her so pleasantly and briefly. These little ego boosts make others feel good, and you need only be careful not to overdo the amount or length of the compliments in this category, lest your power to impress wear thin.

Level 2 compliments, which we shall call serious flattery, should still be honest but can have a definite motive. If, for example, you thought a colleague made an especially good point at a meeting, a well-thought-out compliment can work in your favor in two ways: It flatters the other person, and, equally important, it shows you off.

Serious flattery takes a bit more forethought than does simple flattery. It is not acceptable to say (or, worse, to gush): "That speech you gave Tuesday was really dynamite. Just marvelous! How do you do it!" Instead, with a little thought, something like this might better emerge: "I've been giving a lot of thought to the comments you made about reorganizing the order department. Your point about reviewing everyone's workload was especially impressive. I would really like to talk more about it with you sometime."

With this compliment, you have shown that you truly listened to and thought about the other person's comments. You have made some very specific and honest flattering comments about what he or she said, and you have shown an ability to analyze what others say. If the person you are complimenting is a superior with whom you would not normally initiate a meeting, just omit the last statement of this compliment. The person complimented is sure to remember what you have said and invariably will think more highly of you.

## JARGON, CLICHÉS, AND SLANG

Somewhat sadly for the state of the language these days, business jargon has become as common (and offensive to the ears) as the too-frequent use of clichés. Still, its use may be necessary at work. Try not to overuse the jargon of your profession. Many older executives complain about the lack of good communications skills in young men and women, and your use of jargon could easily be mistaken for confused thinking. Besides, being the nonjargon-using speaker on a staff of jargon-loving junior executives could be the factor that sets you apart from the crowd. Examples of business jargon that have crept into the language today and are still best avoided include:

*utilize* for *use*
*dialoguing* for *talking* or *conversing*

*directive* for *memo* or *report*
*impact on* for *affect*
*media opportunity* for *press conference*

The list could go on endlessly. The problem is what to do with such expressions. For example, if the term "memo" in your company has been entirely replaced by the word "directive," it is probably more graceful to yield to its use. Perhaps the most useful advice that can be given on the subject is to try to keep the truly insidious expressions out of your speech (and writing) and to yield to jargon only when *not* using it would label you as out of it.

The same rules apply to clichés and slang. It's impossible to eliminate these from your vocabulary, but use them sparingly, for they may work to convince a superior that you are not an original thinker.

Slang is mostly a way of talking with a peer group. Your manager and other superiors are rarely members of your peer group. They are undoubtedly older, and casual talk among young executives may make them feel older still. Furthermore, the purpose of slang is to display a sense of belonging, to define who is out and who is in—and it just does not make sense to do anything to put one's superiors in such a position. Taken to extremes, this is rude behavior.

## Your Working Humor

Humor in conversation can be deadly at work if you do not understand its place. The greater success you achieve, the more serious work becomes. Unless you are the president of a company or a chairperson of the board, in which case everyone has to laugh at your jokes, it is not appropriate to open a presentation at a business meeting with an anecdote or joke. In the same vein, don't wisecrack during a meeting or when you are with your superiors, unless you know them very well and can predict that your comments will be well received. Once top management has formed an impression of you as the office joker, it will be almost impossible to get rid of it, and you may be overlooked for the important, serious assignments.

## TALKING TO AN AUDIENCE

Talking to a group, whether as a postdinner speaker or a television talk show guest, frightens many people, perhaps because few of us do it on a regular enough basis to truly master the technique. Nevertheless, there will be times when you will be asked to represent your firm in these ways.

The key to successful public speaking is to prepare yourself and your materials well. As for preparing yourself, attend a speech class or consult a specialist who will teach you how to speak well in public. Buy a good book on the subject. There are numerous ones that help speakers learn how to show themselves off.

Equally important is to prepare what you plan to say. Sometimes your topic is obvious—you are asked to be a guest on a talk show because of something you have written or invented, for example. At other times, such as when you are asked to be a guest speaker at a dinner or lecture, your topic may not be so obvious. In that case, ask. Find out what your topic should be and also what topics anyone else may be speaking on so you do not overlap with other speakers and run the risk of boring your audience.

Research the topic thoroughly, but keep in mind the fact that you are giving a talk, not a term paper or a lecture. However serious your subject, there should be some entertaining moments. On the other hand, too many speakers—even practiced ones—feel the need to open with the obligatory, and usually corny, joke. Add humor only where it is appropriate, and make sure it is sincere and not dated. The best anecdotal materials come from news magazines and newspapers rather than toastmaster's books listing 1,000 of everyone's favorite jokes.

Once you have prepared your material, practice it—over and over and over again. It is better to be so familiar with your material that you cannot go wrong with it than to memorize a speech and run the risk of having a mental block at the last minute.

When the day of the big event arrives, half the battle is won if you have prepared your material and practiced it thoroughly. Do everything possible to make yourself comfortable before you speak. Start by arriving on time. If you are a speaker at a dinner, eat lightly and be careful not to drink too much.

This is one occasion when you will want to be appropriately dressed. Call the chairperson or the person who asked you to speak to find out what to wear. It is also a good idea to find out what color the backdrop is, so you can avoid wearing a color that will clash. Although there are times when you may not mind wearing a dark suit when the dress is black tie, the night when you stand up to speak almost certainly will not be one of them, so plan to dress appropriately for the occasion.

Once you become comfortable speaking before a crowd, a radio appearance should not pose much of a problem. Television makes many people nervous, but there are a few simple guidelines to help.

Both television and radio are far more intimate mediums than the speaker's dais. When speaking to an audience, while a degree of informality is helpful, you have no reason to seek intimacy. Yet intimacy with the audience is exactly what is required on television. This can be achieved partly by talking to the camera (the one with the red light on is the one focused on you) and partly by talking with the talk show host or other persons on the show. Really talk to them, as if you were having an intimate tête-à-tête. Balancing your attention between these two makes the audience feel like part of the presentation and creates a mood of intimacy.

Wear a pastel shirt of any color other than yellow, which photographs as white and is too stark. If you can possibly go without glasses, do so, since their glare is often unflattering. (If you appear on television a lot, it might be worthwhile to purchase a pair of glasses specially treated for television wear.)

Every habit you have will be magnified on television, so be careful not to slump in your chair, jiggle one foot, or exhibit whatever your personal idiosyncrasy happens to be. If at all possible, ask to check your appearance in a monitor before the show begins; this way you will see if you are wearing too much makeup or if your hair is out of place.

## MODULATING YOUR VOICE

Modulation refers to the rhythm and tonal quality of your voice. It is especially important not to talk too loudly. No one wants to be caught in the middle of what was meant to be an intimate business lunch with a voice so loud that the entire restaurant knows your company is about to be bought out by a conglomerate.

On the other hand, a voice that is too soft can hurt in a business situation, the most obvious disadvantage being that what you are saying—we shall assume it is something important—simply cannot be heard. Worse still for one's image, a soft voice can make one appear weak and ineffective.

Both men and women who want to be respected and listened to should make an effort to maintain a well-modulated voice most of the time. The modifier "most of the time" is important, because there are times when a lowered or raised voice can be used to make a point especially effectively. This only works, however, when someone normally speaks in a well-modulated voice.

Make sure that your voice is pleasant, loud enough to be understood but not so loud that it booms—most of the time.

## CHOOSING THE RIGHT WORD

Although diction may be a word you have not heard since grammar school, it refers to the choice of words a person makes. Using the wrong word at the wrong time or, for that matter, at the right time, can hurt or even be downright hilarious. A business acquaintance who frequently overextended her vocabulary without first checking definitions once admitted to having had a highly erotic evening when in fact she meant to say she had enjoyed a highly exotic evening. The laugh, unfortunately, was at her expense.

Although there seems to be no reason for many of the distinctions in usage and pronunciation of certain words, knowing how to use words correctly is the mark of an educated person. It is also the mark of a promotable person.

Good English is available to everyone. You may have learned it later than people whose parents corrected their every word, but there is simply no reason not to catch up. The following list consists of words that are frequently misused, to the social detriment of the user.

*allow* and *allow me*   This means "Permit me," not "I allowed as how he was right," an expression that should be banished by a well-intentioned speaker.

*all the farther*   When this means "I am going," say "This is as far as I am going," not "This is all the farther I'm going."

*an invite*   The word is "invitation," and nothing else will do.

*anywheres, somewheres*   It seems like such a little thing to attach an "s" to these words, and it is part of the everyday dialect in some cities. Still, try to say "anywhere" and "somewhere."

*aunt*   The broad "a" pronunciation is used on the East Coast, and some people from other areas of the country may feel illiterate not using this pronunciation; however, the short "a," as in "ant," is perfectly acceptable and nothing to apologize for. Say whatever is comfortable for you.

*bad, badly*   Adverbs, which generally take an "ly" ending, are another example of overdoing it in the name of literacy. The correct answer to "How do you feel?" is "I feel bad." "Feel," a copulative verb, is the equivalent of "am" and takes an adjective. On the other hand, someone does "perform badly." Adverbs can cause problems, but you will do well if you banish such awkward and pompous expressions as "importantly" and "firstly."

*between* and *among*   Between refers to an exchange involving two people; if there are three or more, use "among."

*between you and I*   People who are trying hard to sound literate often use this expression; the correct one is "between you and me."

*can't hardly*   This is a double negative; say "I can hardly."

*congratulate*   Do not pronounce this "congradulate." Do not shorten the word in any way unless you are among old high school buddies and talking about old slang expressions.

*consensus*   This means "agreement of opinion," so it's incorrect to add "of opinion" when you use the word.

*dais*   The platform you stand or sit on at a banquet; pronounce it with a long "a" sound: "da-is," not "di-as."

*dialogue*   Help fight fancy English. Why use this when the word "talk" will do just as well?

*egoism, egotism*   An egoist is someone who tends to see things in terms of how they affect him or her; an egotist is someone who cannot stop talking about himself or herself.

*either*   Either an "e" or an "i" pronunciation is fine.

*end result*   A result *is* the end. Use one or the other.

*federal, national*   "Federal" refers to the government of the United States; "national" conveys a sense of the spirit or patriotism that the citizens feel for their homeland.

*fifth*   Be careful to sound all the letters.

*fine, splendid, excellent*   Do not say finely, splendidly, or excellently, when talking about how you feel. Also see *bad*.

*folks*   Avoid using this term to describe your family. "Folk" is correctly used to refer to a people, a nation.

*gent*   This and other cute nicknames or terms such as "dearie," "honey," "tootsie," "hubby," "little woman," and "girls" (when referring to women) should be avoided; they make most literate persons wince, as well they should.

*give me, get me, let me*   Be sure to pronounce these as two separate words, not as "gimme" or "lemme."

*guesstimate*   This word seems to be worming its way into the language. However, it's more accurate to use "estimate" or "guess," depending on which one you mean.

*high class* and other similar expressions   Try to avoid saying people are high class, well-to-do, or wealthy. They are rich. Even if they are not rich, they may be of high quality, but not of high class. Such expressions suggest that you have a sense of inferiority and lack contact with the rich.

*hopefully*   In most sentences "hopefully" is not correctly used, and you can test this by trying to find the word it modifies. Consider: "Hopefully the sales deficit can be made up in the third quarter." Now see who is hopeful. The sales deficit? Whenever you have the urge to use "hopefully," bite your tongue and instead say "I hope," which is correct.

*house, home*   This pair is a lot like "national" and "federal." A house is the building. A home is the spiritual place. The correct answer to the question "Where are you?" is "at home," but you are physically in your house or apartment.

*itch, scratch*   An itch is the sensation that calls for the act of scratching.

*kudos*   This always takes a singular verb. There is no such thing as a kudo.

*lady, woman*   These are two words that have taken on new significance in the wake of the feminist movement. They seem to be reversing their meanings, with lady now being used disparagingly: "Look, lady, that's your problem!" Women today—particularly women seeking equality with men in the professional sphere—frequently resent being referred to as girls, as well they should, since their colleagues would not be overjoyed to be referred to as boys. "Ladies" seems to offend less, but men and women who want to show respect for their colleagues will try to use the word "women." Also see *person.*

*leave, let*   Do not confuse these two words. You leave a room. When someone is detaining you, you may want them to let you go. Do not say "Leave me go."

*lend, borrow*   You lend something to friends or acquaintances. They borrow something from you.

*like*   This may be the most abused word in the English language at the moment. Many people drop it into conversation, like, every minute, like, do you know what we mean, like, it's too much. If you have developed the habit of overusing "like," try to give it a rest.

*manufacture*   Pronounce the "*u*" distinctly and do not slip into "man*a*facture."

*myself*   This has come into common usage as a substitute for the correct form of "me" or "I." Just say "I am fine" rather than "I myself am fine" and "as for me" rather than "As for myself."

*neither*   See *either*. This word always goes with "nor," not "or."

*off*   Never use this in place of "from." "I got it off of (*from*) Jane" is illiterate.

*person*   Terms such as salesperson and chairperson have gained wide usage today, despite their seeming awkwardness. Few women object, and many men and women are now using the terms with ease. There is really no etiquette on this subject, except that each person should do what is comfortable for him or her and, more important, for those to whom the terms will be applied.

*personal friend*   Just the word "friend" will do. Friends are always personal.

*the reason why, the reason is because*   "Reason" means "why" and "because"; therefore, say "The reason is that . . . "

*rest room, bathroom*   Rest room is generally used to refer to public bathrooms, at work, in hotels, and anywhere outside the home; bathroom is used at home.

*second*   Be sure to pronounce the "d."

*sore*   This is how you feel when something hurts. It is not a substitute for "angry."

*strength*   Pronounce every letter, taking special care not to omit the "g."

*tomato*   See *aunt,* and stick to saying tomato the way you learned to in the old neighborhood.

*yeah*   You take your chances when you use this word in the business world; it is a sign of sloppy thinking.

*you know*   This has filtered into the language to an incredible degree; and while there is nothing grammatically wrong with it, it irritates a lot of people who were born before it came into common usage. Along with the word "like," this is a very overused expression these days, one that is best avoided as much as possible.

## (Almost) Everything You Need to Know About Foreign Languages

Familiarity with some foreign expressions has long been considered the mark of an educated person. It behooves you to know what your supervisor is talking about when she says something is strictly *entre nous* (a French expression for "between us") or *sotto voce* (an Italian term for "softly," which also means, very loosely translated, "between us"). But—and here's the catch—a truly sophisticated person uses his or her knowledge of other languages with great discretion. Nothing marks you faster as an overeager upstart than dropping *too* many foreign phrases into a conversation.

In addition, knowing a few foreign expressions is a world apart from knowing a foreign language fluently. In today's global marketplace, the ability to speak a foreign language is an invaluable skill and one that will increasingly be expected of those who work in the international arena. When the United States bought from the entire world, it could expect the world to speak English, but now that the United States is trying to sell to the rest of the world, Americans are discovering that they are expected to speak the language of their customers. Even if others did not expect this of us, it would be in our best interests to do so in today's highly competitive business climate.

Apart from mastering a foreign language (or two or three), the sophisticated executive should also have at least a passing knowledge of some other tongues as well. There are many good phrase books that can help you acquire this cursory knowledge. Memorizing a few expressions and words will give you the skills you need to work your way through a Japanese, Italian, French, or Swahili menu.

## A Final Word

The key to improving your speaking skills is practice. Watch others, and when you see something you like that you think will work for you, adapt it to your speech. If you know you have a serious problem communicating—you are too shy to speak in front of an audience, yet your work demands that you do so several times a year; you know you talk too long whenever you make a presentation, or you simply never had the opportunity to learn correct English—take private speech lessons, acting lessons, or any other speech class that might help you.

It *is* true that speech is a sign of good manners. But it is one of the signs that anyone can acquire without too much effort.

# 6

# *Power Eating and Other Entertainments*

The wheeling and dealing that goes on over meals these days has reached mythic proportions. Such meals—always paid for with "plastic"—typically last two or three hours and the tab may run to $200 or more for two, but then multibillion-dollar business mergers, million-dollar book deals, and even million-dollar raids by one corporation of another's top executives are often the goal of such meetings.

Regardless of whether you are involved in such high-level eating, don't underestimate the value of sitting down over a meal to hammer out a business deal—or even merely to build a relationship prior to talking business—and never underestimate how devastating not being able to handle the rituals of eating can be. Power dining has become so important that, at this writing, one Ivy League school teaches a two-semester, three-credit course called "The Dynamics and Management of the Business Lunch"—and it's required for the master's program.

The business meal—or any other business entertainment, for that matter—is where all your social skills and graces come together: table manners, your abilities as a host or hostess, your ability to speak well, your ability to handle others—all must be in peak working order. In

Japan, many centuries ago, a man could be executed for exhibiting poor table manners. Although none of the executives we have talked with have gone quite that far, many have noted with dismay the lack of finesse their young executives display in this all-important area.

## POWER LUNCH

The most popular business meal is lunch, although in some cities power breakfasts run a close second in popularity. Business lunches are for business, and often one or the other party to such a lunch makes it clear that this will be a working meal. Usually, though, the business conducted is minor, or the lunch is merely a prelude to business that will be conducted later. The point is that because any business could be accomplished with the accoutrements of a meal, there is an underlying reason for planning to share a meal with a client or employee. That underlying reason is camaraderie. In the case of the business lunch, the term does not necessarily refer to a strong, personal, social relationship but, rather, to the kind of relationship that enhances whatever business is involved.

One executive, in describing his long-standing relationship as a consultant to Oscar Meyer, put his finger on the role of business lunches in fostering good work relationships: "For twenty-odd years, I've been a consultant to the Oscar Meyer Company. There is no question in my mind that I would not have had that continuing relationship if the executive committee of that company were not very comfortable with me in the executive dining room. I'm so easy to replace; I'm here in Chicago, they're in Madison. I don't have a personal relationship, but I have a very comfortable business relationship. I think if there were *anything* about me that irritated them in the executive dining room, they would have terminated our relationship."

There are two kinds of business lunch. First, there is the lunch that, on the surface, appears to be purely social. Its purpose, nevertheless, is to establish or strengthen the informal business bonds just described or even to woo a client so he or she will lean a little bit more toward your company or product when making a decision.

Second, there is the working lunch, at which the participants have agreed, usually in advance, that business will be discussed. This kind of lunch may even have an agenda, and when an invitation is extended, the host or guest might say "Fine, then, we'll have lunch Tuesday to discuss those details of the contract that need working out."

Business lunches are also used to evaluate prospective employees and woo unhappy executives. Among employees, they are used to celebrate a raise or promotion, or to talk over a new position within a company. Some managers have even used the business lunch to fire, but this has never been recognized as being particularly good for anyone's digestion.

## Planning the Lunch

Setting up a business lunch is relatively easy to do. Invariably it is done by phone. If you are planning the lunch, make it clear that you expect to be the host, possibly by saying "How about having lunch with me next week?" or "I've been hoping we could get together over lunch to discuss our new project. How does Tuesday of next week sound?" Since it is presumed that all parties involved share an interest in getting together, a business lunch invitation is typically left more open than a purely social invitation with regard to time. Suggesting a lunch "next week" lets the person invited check his or her calendar and come up with an appropriate date. If the date suggested is not open for you, come up with an alternate day. Remember that the purpose is to find a mutually agreeable time and that business lunches among busy people are often scheduled far in advance.

Once you have settled on the day, another way to make it clear that you will be the host is to say "How about The Four Seasons?" or "How about the Town Club? They have excellent food there."

Confirm the time and place and repeat the details of the invitation later in the conversation. At the end of the call, you might say "Fine, then I'll see you next Tuesday, the fifteenth, at 1 P.M. at the Town Club—let's meet in the downstairs lobby."

Local custom will generally dictate the time of the lunch. In large cities, lunches are often planned at 1 P.M., and a 2 P.M. lunch date is not unheard of; in smaller communities, where people are less likely to linger even over an important business lunch, 12 noon or even 11:45 A.M. may be more common.

The choice of the restaurant is important, although it may be fairly obvious. An important business lunch calls for an elegant restaurant. In a small town or city, there may be only one or two such restaurants. In large cities, certain restaurants are frequently the "in" places for lunch for people in certain professions.

If possible, pick one restaurant and frequent it. This will pay special rewards in terms of your being recognized when you walk in, and it will probably result in better service. Of course, recognition and service are not necessarily automatic—you will have to cultivate (and tip) the headwaiter (also called the maître d'hôtel) to make yourself known. But for making a subtle impression on a client, nothing beats having the headwaiter ask if you will have your usual drink or your usual lunch.

In addition, always make reservations. If a restaurant is good, they are absolutely necessary; even if a restaurant is not busy, as happens in small towns, a call ahead still alerts the staff that you are planning a special lunch.

## Arriving at the Lunch

Since you are presumably the host, it is polite to arrive before your guests. If you are late, apologize briefly. If you have reserved a table, you can meet at the table, or you can meet at some prearranged place, such as the door or in the lobby.

Guests who arrive alone can check their coats if they want to. Since you will be with them when you leave, you can retrieve the coats and pay the coat-check person for your guests.

If you meet at the front of the restaurant, ask your guests if they want to check their coats. When this is done, give the headwaiter your name if you are not known, and let your guests precede you into the dining room.

## Amenities to Guests: Male and Female

The trend is away from treating a woman any differently from how you would treat a man when you are meeting over a meal. If you are the host and have taken your seat, you should stand to greet your guests regardless of their sex. The only exception is when you are seated at a banquette and can't get up. Then you should apologize.

By the way, banquettes are awkward at a business lunch, regardless of whether you are lunching with a man or a woman. It's sometimes better to avoid restaurants where you must sit on one, or where you don't have the clout to get a table.

Don't take guests' coats or hold a chair for them—that is the headwaiter's job. Do give your guests the best seats, unless for some reason you want to arrange the seating so a client is between you and a colleague. As the host you may open doors and indicate that your guests should precede you.

## Organizing the Seating

As the planner of a business lunch, you can suggest where the guests may sit. If two people are lunching at a table for four and you know you will need some space to spread out papers, you may have a very specific reason for wanting the other person to sit to your right or across from you.

## Smoking and Not Smoking

Smoking is a touchy subject today, as growing numbers of non-smokers have become less willing to endure the risks of secondary smoke. If you are a nonsmoking host, the solution is simple: You can simply make a reservation at a nonsmoking table. The general rule of thumb seems to be that smokers yield to nonsmokers, but then, a smoking host can also always book a table in the smoking section. And of course, if you are a nonsmoker courting a smoker for a client, then you may be more willing to endure the secondhand smoke.

When a group of coworkers, smokers and nonsmokers, eat out

together, the nonsmokers usually prevail if they are in the majority, and the smokers leave the table when they need to smoke.

## Ordering Drinks

As soon as you are seated, the waiter will probably take your drink order. Don't put a guest on the spot with regard to deciding whether to order a drink. Drinking has become a totally accepted part of business lunches, and even if someone does not drink, there is no reason to make anyone else at the table feel uncomfortable about this. When the waiter asks whether you would like drinks, look at your guest and say "Yes, I would, what will you have?" The guest can then order his or her usual drink, and you can order your usual drink— even if it is nonalcoholic.

If you are a nondrinking guest and drinks appear to be the order of the day, order something—sparkling water with lemon or lime, ginger ale, a virgin mary—and make no comment about the fact that it is nonalcoholic. The host should still feel at ease enough to order whatever he or she usually drinks.

What isn't accepted at lunch in most professions and companies is heavy drinking. While the drink before lunch may be a formality that leads to an air of informality, ordering two or three drinks—whether you are the guest or the host—can spell disaster.

If you are the host trying to impress a prospective client, it may be in your best interests to curtail your drinking at lunch. Your guest may blanch at the prospect of working with an overindulgent drinker. And if you are an overindulgent guest, your host may be annoyed at having paid for a wasted lunch—one where no business was conducted because the client was too tipsy to think. Fortunately these situations are increasingly rare as more and more people drink moderately or abstain totally.

## Ordering Food

While it has always been slightly gauche to eat as if you were going to your execution right after lunch, in these days of physical fitness and diet consciousness, business lunches often become contests between the eaters to see who can eat the least. Dessert is rarely ordered today; sauces are passé at lunch; and salads, fish platters, and pasta are de rigueur. But a word of warning: If you're on a diet, keep quiet about it. Everyone has talked the subject to death, and no one really wants to hear about anyone's diet over lunch.

## The Host's Role

As a host at a business lunch, you should show the same concern for guests in a restaurant as you would at home. If necessary, ask the waiter to fill the water glasses, empty the ashtrays, or do whatever appears to be needed. If a guest is displeased with the food—it is too hot or too cold or too rare or too well done—be sure it is sent back to the kitchen, unless the guest protests strongly against it.

When the meal (and your business) is finished, ask the waiter for the check. If you are at a favorite haunt, the waiter will have no doubt about bringing the check to you. In an unfamiliar restaurant, the person who asks for the check is the person who gets it.

Sometimes a waiter will automatically bring the check to a man when a woman is present. If you are a woman and the host, simply reach over and take the check—don't grab, but make a firm gesture. If necessary, reassure your lunch guest that "It's all on my company, anyway."

You can go to elaborate lengths to ensure that you do indeed pay the check. Pretending to go to the rest room and then paying the maître d'hôtel or arranging to pay in advance are two of the more common ploys, but these should hardly be necessary today. Most men, when they have been invited to a business lunch, have no qualms about letting a woman who is representing her company pick up the check. If a man is really Old School and you sense that he would be ill at ease sitting by while a woman pays, then acquiesce after minimal fuss and let him pay.

A host of either sex should look the bill over quickly and carefully. Figure out the tip and place your credit card or money, on the tray, with the check turned facedown. Don't leave pennies, nickels, or dimes as part of the tip, except when the waiter brings change near the amount of the tip. Then leave all the change. If you pay a cashier and do not have change for the tip when you leave the table, ask the cashier for change and walk back to the table to put it down. Even if a guest offers to pay all or part of a tip when it is obvious that you don't have the needed change, do not accept. The chart on pages 116–117 shows guidelines for tipping. In expensive restaurants and in places you frequent for business, 15 to 20 percent is the usual tip; 25 percent is showing off, and 10 percent is not enough.

## The Guest's Role

As the guest at a business lunch or other entertainment, you take no notice of the check, but you do thank your host when you are saying good-bye.

If you are invited to lunch at one of the fancier private corporate dining rooms, all you need to do to get through the occasion—aside from displaying your most perfect manners—is to stay cool. Act as if you are used to dining this way, even if your company's corporate dining room looks like the marines' mess. Do not permit yourself to be impressed—or if you are, do not let it show. Act as if this were the most routine of lunches. Of course, if your host has just spent the last six months of his or her work life redecorating the dining room or interviewing for just the right French chef, there is nothing wrong with showing your appreciation—in a reasonable, low-key way.

## Talking Business

Don't be misled by a festive atmosphere at a meal when you have agreed to discuss business. Most executives, however congenial or mellow they may become during lunch, still have an agenda. Not discussing business at a business lunch is not necessarily congenial; it is a waste of time and may put off a busy, organized person.

Generally the host initiates the business discussion, and a smart host takes the opportunity to do so before a busy guest gets impatient and beats him or her to the draw. Business, if not urgent, is often discussed more toward the end of the meal or over coffee. Don't wait

## Guidelines for Tipping

| Person | Service | Amount |
| --- | --- | --- |
| Headwaiter (maître d'hôtel) | Checks your reservation and shows you to your table. | No tip |
| | If he arranges tables to accommodate a large group or seats you without a reservation when one would normally be needed or performs any other special service | $2 to $5 |
| Waiter, waitress | Takes drink order, explains dishes on menu, recommends dishes, carves rack of lamb or any special food, flambées a food. Serves food. | 15–20 percent of bill, depending on quality of service and number of persons who attend you. |
| Bartender | Serves drinks at a bar. | 10 to 15 percent, minimum 50 cents |
| Busboy | Clears dishes, pours water, refills coffee. | No tip (he shares with waiters) |
| Strolling musicians —To get rid of them | | $1 |
| —To request a medley or song | | $2 or more |
| Rest-room attendant | | 50 cents minimum, if any service is provided |

| Person | Service | Amount |
| --- | --- | --- |
| Checkroom attendant | | 50 cents minimum per coat |
| Doorman | Opening door. | No tip |
| | Parking car. | 50 cents minimum |
| | Hailing cab. | 50 cents minimum |
| | Hailing cab in bad weather. | 50 cents to $1 |
| Taxi drivers | | Rarely is less than 50 cents given today for any length of ride. When fare is less than $1.25, give 50 cents. When fare is over that, give 15 percent. |
| Skycap | Handles bags in airport. | $1 per bag; more for large bags or trunks |
| Redcap | Handles bags in train station | There is usually a set fee of about $1; add 50 cents or more in addition if service is greater. |

too long, though, or you won't have time to accomplish your objective. If you have both agreed that this will be a working lunch, the direct approach is the best way to settle down to the work at hand. Simply say "Well, shall we talk about the new contract?"

If the agenda is more subtle, you would be more likely to ease into the discussion, saying something such as "Well, what do you think about the proposed merger?" or "While it's on my mind, I've been meaning to ask you about the new product line."

## Ending the Lunch

If you are discussing business, the lunch may continue long into the afternoon, although this is rare. As a rule, the person who is hosting the lunch is the first to lay his or her napkin back on the table or to stand, thereby signaling the end of the meal. Asking the waiter for the check is also a gesture that the lunch is about to end.

One good rule about ending a business lunch is to assume that the other person has other things to do that afternoon. Even if you are wooing a client to close a very big deal, you may lose his or her respect—and the account—if you act too casual about prolonging a lunch.

## POWER BREAKFAST

On both coasts, the power breakfast is the newest incarnation of a "working" meal. So far, the custom of breaking early-morning bread over business has not stretched beyond the continental United States, and in some cultures (France, for example), a working breakfast is frowned upon as bad for the digestion. It's wise to think twice before scheduling a power breakfast with international customers.

In terms of etiquette, a power breakfast is much like a power lunch. Whoever makes the date is the host. Since most restaurants are not open, hotels are of necessity the hot spots for breakfast. They're also a good choice if you are hosting international visitors because many hotels now offer multicultural breakfasts.

Although there is no hard-and-fast rule, it's difficult to imagine anyone conducting business before everyone present has had time to absorb some caffeine, so talk is generally delayed until coffee is served. Unlike other meals where coffee comes last, it is served first at breakfast.

Finally, if you simply are not a morning person and know there is no way you can sound intelligent (or even intelligible) at 7 or 8 A.M., then it is better to decline an invitation to breakfast. It's okay, that is, so long as your supervisor isn't doing the asking.

## TEA: THE BEGINNING OF RECIVILIZATION AS WE USED TO KNOW IT

Tea has made a comeback for business entertaining. It's the ideal way to entertain, some executives say, coming as it does when the hard work of the day is over, and you can relax and enjoy one another's company—even if your purpose is to conduct some business.

Any time between 4 and 6 P.M. is perfect for tea. In most major cities, one or more hotels now serve low tea—that being the tea that comes with small sandwiches and sweets rather than the full supper that is high tea.

Tea is incredibly civilized. Enter a hot steaming pot of tea, some light nibbles, and your brain and body seem both energized and relaxed. It's more casual, too. You can discuss business anytime you want to—for example, before the tea is served, during tea, or afterward.

To be a truly gracious host, consider ordering (for the table since you would never presume to order for anyone individually) and pouring. Alternately, people can place their own orders and, especially if the tea is brought in individual pots, each person may pour his or her own.

## ENTERTAINING ON PREMISES

Since major corporations have established corporate headquarters outside major cities, on-premises entertaining has become increasingly popular. It began as a means of feeding employees lunch when they had nowhere else to go, but it has emerged into full-blown, elaborate, and luxurious executive dining rooms, and some companies have even hired specially trained chefs who can prepare elaborate meals for their clients and customers on their own premises.

While an order-in lunch for a company's executives can be handled by a secretary, the kind of elaborate, carefully planned, on-premises entertaining that many major corporations are now doing is coordinated or overseen by the executive who is host. After all, having twenty of your most important customers visit your plant so you can introduce a new product line takes a lot of well-coordinated planning. In return, it offers more control, a chance to show off your offices or plant, and a more casual way of selling your products. One major manufacturer in New Jersey introduces a new line by busing in clients for a champagne and omelette breakfast.

"It simply works better," the sales manager of the company reported. "I know how much time will be spent eating and drinking. I can casually move the clients toward the product displays. Everything is much more soft-sell—the mood is festive. The salespeople simply circulate among the customers; there is no reason for them to push."

Acquiring an appreciation of the benefits of on-premises entertaining is easy enough, but many managers are unsure of how to go about setting up this entertainment. First, go over old entertaining budgets in company records to get some idea of what catering fees have been in the past. Call in one or two top caterers and discuss your plans with them. A caterer needs to know the time frame, the desired atmosphere, and exactly what you need to achieve. The days are long gone when caterers planned ladies' lunches and little else. Professional caterers are geared to business entertainment; all know how to help show off a product line, entertain your top four customers at a formal dinner, and, most important, control the time and money spent in doing so.

Above all, be open with the caterer about what you can spend. On-premises catering is generally cheaper than other kinds of entertaining anyway, so you may be able to plan a more elegant function than you realize. On-premises entertaining is less sterile and certainly less hard-sell than similar functions in hotels or rented halls.

If you have hired a caterer who comes highly recommended and you do not know much about food and food service, rely on his or her advice. A service representative, however, always enjoys working with someone who does have menu suggestions, so don't be afraid to offer ideas if you have them.

On the other hand, several caterers interviewed complained that people who have not had much experience in planning this kind of entertaining often become too involved. Remember that the caterer's business is providing food and service; just as you delegate other aspects of managing your business domain, be willing to do so with food service when you know you are dealing with professionals. And treat the caterer with courtesy; he or she will only work that much harder for you if made to feel good about doing so.

## ENTERTAINING AT PRIVATE CLUBS

If you are a member of a private club, it is often an ideal place to entertain business associates. Among other advantages, cash is almost never used, so there is never any question about who picks up the tab.

When you are invited to be a guest at a private club, you behave exactly as you would in any public restaurant. If you arrive before your host, you will probably be shown to a waiting room or lounge; wait there until your host arrives. If you want a brief tour of the place, ask your host when he or she arrives; don't roam around by yourself.

It is assumed that you are a nonpaying guest at a private club, so do not offer to pay for anything. Even offering to pay for a round of drinks may prove difficult since money is rarely used in private clubs.

### *Sports at Private Clubs*

If you are invited to play golf or tennis at a private club to which you do not belong, you are not expected to pay. You are expected to dress appropriately and, in many cases, conservatively, for the sport. Tennis whites and conservative golf clothes are still de rigueur at many clubs, and appropriate footwear is a necessity.

Especially if it is a posh private club, these clothes are still the best way to dress, if only because you won't want to stand out as the person who doesn't belong. Basically, this means no halter tops, inappropriate shorts, or T-shirts.

You are also expected to bring your own equipment. This shouldn't pose a problem unless you have misrepresented yourself as playing a sport when you don't—and doing so would be a mistake. A business invitation for golf or tennis assumes that you already play the sport, and beginners and learners are not particularly welcome. There's nothing personal here: It's just the way the games are played.

If you don't play a sport, then simply say so when you are invited to play. (Another issue is whether you should take up whatever popular sport your colleagues and clients play at the moment, and the answer to that question is probably yes.) But to repeat, it is never appropriate to show up for a sport you do not play or are just beginning to play.

If someone asks you to play one-on-one, the same rules apply. In fact, it gets slightly trickier, and the real issue is to figure out whether you play at the same level. Most players of any sport want to play with others who play on their level. This is easily determined by a few quick questions, and a gentle demurral when you find out you aren't a good match. You will never endear yourself to either a client or a superior by pretending to play a sport better than you do simply so you can have contact with someone. And besides, why would you want to go out on a tennis court or golf course and make a fool of yourself in front of a client or your supervisor?

## Entertaining on a Boat or Ship

Regardless of the size of the craft (any boat longer than 100 feet is technically a yacht), owners of sailing vessels refer to their crafts as boats and to themselves as sailors. So the first rule of thumb regarding yachts, whether you are a guest or an owner, is to avoid calling them yachts.

Being a guest on a boat requires some preparation on your part. First, take appropriate clothes—denims or cottons, rubber-soled shoes, sweaters and jackets even if the weather is warm, and some rain gear, if you will be aboard very long.

Second, plan to stow (put away) your gear as soon as you are assigned sleeping quarters. Because of the limited space on a boat, you must be a neat guest. Keep your personal gear out of sight when you are not wearing it, and ask where you are to dispose of paper or other garbage.

If a boat does not have a crew, be prepared to lend a hand, but only if you are asked. If you do not know how to do something you are asked to do, admit this right away, since trying to perform a task you do not understand could jeopardize the lives of everyone aboard.

If the boat has a crew, this is a sign to you that things are more formal. You may wear a suit, or, more likely, a blazer if you are a man, to lunch or dinner (always wear a suit if you are invited to dine aboard any large vessel), and women may be expected to wear long dresses to dinner. Check with your host if you have any questions as to the dress that will be expected.

## OTHER BUSINESS ENTERTAINMENT

Caterers and hotel food service managers report that less business entertaining is done at home than in previous years. The major reason, they all feel, is the change in women's roles. When both spouses hold executive positions, the time they spend together is precious and often limited, and they may not be willing to give up an evening at home to entertaining business associates, aside from the traditional bash they throw for the office staff or their colleagues.

As a result, there has been a rise in business entertaining in public places. There is still traditional entertaining at sports events, where companies give tickets to a football game to prized customers or even entertain them at the game, but there also has been an increase in entertainment in conjunction with the arts. A large Chicago bank buys a block of tickets at Ravinia, an outdoor concert park. The bank buses its guests out to the park, and the evening begins with an open bar, followed by an elaborate picnic under a tent. Following the concert the guests wind up the evening with drinks and sundaes.

There is little difference between planning an on-premises function and an arts- or sports-oriented function, such as the one just described. Begin by hiring the best and most professional caterer you can find; sit down and work out the budget, entertaining objective, and actual services and food required—then relax and let the caterer handle everything. The executives do function as hosts during the evening, but if anything goes wrong they can talk it over with the service representative who will be on hand to direct the party food and service.

## HOSTING A CATERED FUNCTION

There are just a few guidelines to follow if you are an executive or a salesperson representing your company at any official function. One, this is a business function; you may partake of the food and drink, but your interest in it should be downplayed. An executive host with any finesse will never be seen going through the buffet line with everyone else. When everyone is served, he or she may lightly fill a plate with a few tidbits and then circulate among the guests. Salespeople should be forewarned that the same is expected of them. While the atmosphere is soft-sell, there is a purpose to the function, and a salesperson should not see this as a festive occasion in which to eat and drink as much as possible.

As a guest, you should be aware of the gracious way to handle business functions at which food and drinks are served. Always eat lightly—look as if you are paid enough by your own company to eat regularly. Drink lightly, too, so that you are responsive to the business purpose of the function. Never walk up to a bar at a business function and request a double—it is an insult to the host, who has presumably made arrangements for you to be served an adequate-size drink, to say nothing of being a giveaway to sloppy drinking habits.

Unless a business entertainment is quite obviously intended to be purely social—you've been invited to a baseball game or a concert, for example, where your host couldn't and shouldn't expect to talk business with you—assume that some business will be discussed. This is especially true of any entertaining done on company premises. When attending events sponsored by a company, you should anticipate that you will be shown a new product line or introduced to a new service, and even over a quiet dinner, you may assume that business conversation is inevitable.

Finally, invitations to such parties usually state a beginning and ending time. Plan to leave before the party dwindles, and definitely leave before the time stated on the invitation. Again, if the image you want to portray is that of a busy, important person, you should look as if you have someplace else to go. Hangers-on, overeaters, and overdrinkers too often gain an undesirable reputation for being as sloppy in business as they are in their socializing.

## SEATING ARRANGEMENTS

One of the more complicated aspects of business etiquette, whether you are entertaining at home or in public, is arranging the seating for those present at a lunch, dinner, or other public meeting. Undoubtedly at times seating arrangements will require the use of protocol, a special etiquette used by heads of state, diplomats, and members of the military.

Seating arrangements are made by the host. It is never correct for guests to shift name cards or take a seat at a table other than one to which they have been assigned. It is a company's prerogative to decide how to seat its guests—and it usually has its reasons for the decisions it makes.

### Who Sits Where at Lunch and Dinner

When entertaining business associates at home, the head seats, at either end of the table, are taken by the host and hostess. At a round or square table, the head seat is wherever the host wants to sit. At a rectangular table, the head seats are at the ends of the table. Male guests, ranked according to their importance, are seated respectively to the right and left of the hostess. Female guests, according to their rank, are seated to the right and left of the host. The most important guests occupy the right-hand seats, with the second most important guests, if there are any, occupying the left-hand seats.

Unless protocol is being observed, other guests should not be seated according to their importance, especially since doing so would leave those farthest from the host and hostess feeling unimportant. (If protocol is being observed, then everyone present understands the seating arrangements.)

Seating should as much as possible be man-woman, man-woman. Mix young and old as much as conviviality and tact allow. For ex-

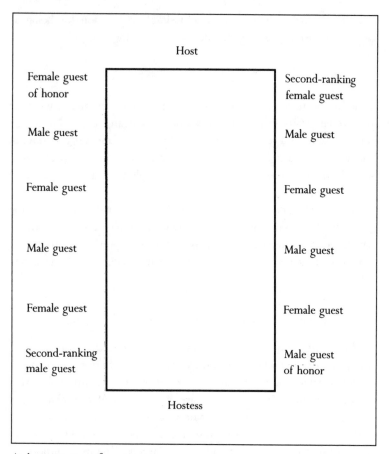

*At-home seating of executive guests*

ample, you wouldn't necessarily seat a CEO next to a junior staffer, but you might well seat an executive emeritus who is visiting for the day next to a young hotshot executive. Both should be flattered. Beyond these few guidelines, guests should be arranged in the way that the host feels will be most congenial for conversation. Husbands and wives are not usually seated together.

At a business lunch or dinner where spouses are not present, guests are more likely to be seated in accordance with their importance. The guest of honor is seated to the right of the host, with a second guest of honor seated to the left. Less important guests are arranged, often according to rank, around the table as the following drawing indicates.

## Ranking Your Guests

And how, you may wonder, do you go about ranking your guests? It's not so difficult as it sounds. Here are guests who would be honored:

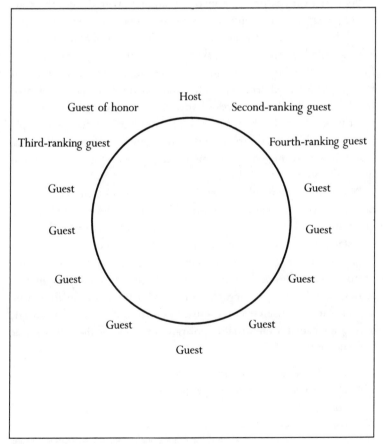

*Seating arrangement for business lunch or dinner*

- Visiting foreign dignitary or customer
- Guest with military or government rank
- Elderly guest
- Guest with distinguished career or other important achievement
- Guest who is celebrating an occasion such as a promotion, transfer, or birthday

## When Protocol is Involved

As noted earlier, protocol involves (among other things) the seating of government or military officials. It can be very complex, and if it will be a concern of yours, you would do well to obtain a copy of a book called *Protocol* (New York: Prentice-Hall, 1977). Another useful guide is the *Congressional Directory* (Washington, D.C.: Government Printing Office). Alternately or to establish the finer points of protocol, you may call the offices of your invited guests. Sometimes you must make the call, when, for example, you have invited two people of equal rank. If there are no other distinguishing factors, they are seated based on the length of time of their service—and for that you will probably have to call their offices!

Nowhere is protocol as complex as in Washington, D.C., where nearly every dinner has the potential to entangle a host in such arcane questions as whether a state governor outranks a federal judge or a five-star general outranks the head of the largest electronics company in Japan. Fortunately, most executives will not have to deal with protocol on this level, since they will rarely entertain many dignitaries at one time. Proper seating also varies with the occasion in Washington—and in business entertaining, as well. But to get you started, here is a loose and unofficial list of rank for most of the officials you will encounter:

- The President of the United States*
- The Vice President of the United States
- The Speaker of the House

---

* Or another head of state. This same list can be applied loosely to visiting foreign officials, but the safest course of action is to check with the appropriate embassy.

- The Chief Justice of the United States (and note that the title is as written, not "Chief Justice of the Supreme Court")
- Former President of the United States
- Secretary of State
- Secretary General of the United Nations
- Ambassadors of foreign countries
- Justices of the Supreme Court
- Cabinet members
- Director, Office of Management and Budget
- U.S. representatives to the United Nations
- U.S. Trade Representative
- President pro tempore of the Senate
- Senators
- Governors
- Representatives
- Aides to the President
- Chargés d'Affaires of foreign governments
- Undersecretaries of Cabinet
- Chairman, Joint Chiefs of Staff
- Members of the military, based on rank or length of service

The ranks of state and local officials are equally logical and are unofficially as follows:

- Governor
- Member of Congress (senators take precedence over representatives)
- State senators
- State representatives
- Mayors (based on size of city and/or length of service)*

There is also an informal protocol for seating corporate officials:

- The president of a company or CEO sits in the host's position, or next to the host in the guest of honor's seat.

---

* The mayor of a large or very influential city may be deemed to outrank a congressperson in the state legislature.

- The guest speaker, or guest of honor (if the CEO is hosting the event) sits on the right of the CEO.
- The toastmaster or person introducing the speaker sits to the left of the CEO.
- Other corporate officials are seated according to their rank.

The ranks of corporate officials are usually as follows:

- Chairman of the board of directors
- CEO
- Members of the board of directors
- Other corporate officials*

## Announcing Seating Arrangements to Guests

When seats are assigned, you must convey this to your guests. At a large banquet or formal dinner with many guests, there are two ways of doing this. The easier method is to issue a small table card to arriving guests that lists their table number. Place cards at the table will identify their specific seat. The more awkward method is to draw up a large chart showing the seating arrangements, but since this often leads to a traffic jam as arriving guests cluster around the drawing, it isn't the smoothest way to handle this situation.

The White House uses calligraphers to write table and place cards, but businesses can use typed cards.

Place cards are rarely used for fewer than ten diners. At dinners for more than ten at home or in a public place, place cards may be used. They may be handwritten or typed. No place card is used for the host or hostess since they will be sitting at the head of the table.

---

* Seated in order of importance. For example, a treasurer usually outranks a vice president in charge of sales, and an executive vice president may outrank a treasurer. These are highly individual and vary from company to company, but you won't have to work for a company very long to understand exactly what everyone's rank is.

## Dais Seating

Often executives arrange meetings where is is necessary to work out seating arrangements for a dais, or raised platform that seats a host and honored guests, who are usually speakers.

Perhaps the first decision you as the executive planning a meeting needs to make is whether to use a dais. The advantage to using one is that the speakers are readily at hand, and no time is wasted while they wend their way through a crowded room. Another advantage is that the invited guests can see a speaker about whom they may be especially curious. But that's also a disadvantage, since few people enjoy being stared at while they eat. Also, guests may enjoy having the speakers and honored guests mingle with them (and the honored guests often enjoy this, as well). If you don't use a dais, then seat speakers at front tables. Be sure to arrange for a podium whether you are using a dais or not.

If you do use a dais, it's a nice touch to cover it with a long cloth that at least lessens clutter and affords your guests an extra measure of privacy.

The guidelines for dais seating are fairly straightforward:

- The host sits on the right next to the speaker's podium, facing out.
- The most honored guest sits on the host's right.
- The next honored guest sits directly to the left of the podium.
- The second host (and there should be a host for every honored guest) sits to the guest's left, and so on.

Occasionally you will encounter an unusual dais arrangement where the podiums are at one or both ends of the table. It still makes sense to seat the host and guest of honor (or the CEO and next highest ranking official) in the center of the dais, with guests arranged to the right and left in descending order of importance. There is one exception: If one person will be moderating an event (and thus will be hopping up and down repeatedly to go to the dais), then he or she should sit near if not next to it. Few CEOs will relish being relegated to this off-center focal point, though, so think twice before you place your company's president or other very high-ranking officials in this seat.

If there will be a projection screen behind the dais (the usual reason for moving the podiums away from center), be sure it is high enough so that those seated on the dais don't have to shuffle around to new positions to enable the audience to see the screen. It is acceptable if those on the dais have to turn their chairs to watch the screen.

The drawing on the opposite page shows the usual arrangement for dais seating.

## Keeping a Door List

For reasons of security among other things, many companies screen guests before admitting them to a large party or other event. This is best done through the use of a door list. Guests can be required to present invitations, but anyone could obtain an invitation or simply hand the person at the door an empty envelope and then fade into the crowd. A door list—that is, a master list of who is invited—is the safest and most efficient method of screening guests.

Depending on the size of the party or function, one or more people stand at the door or at a table near the door with a list of invited guests. Unless security is extremely high, each person should have a complete list so as not to slow down arriving guests. Upon arriving, guests pause at the door to state their names, and the doorkeepers check them off before permitting them to enter.

Since door lists are kept as much for the security of the guests as anything else, it is rude to hassle the person with the list or to expect him or her to pass you through without checking your identity.

## PURELY SOCIAL ENTERTAINING

Business entertaining becomes social when you see a client or customer whom you like outside work with no business motive whatsoever—or at least this is how most executives define these

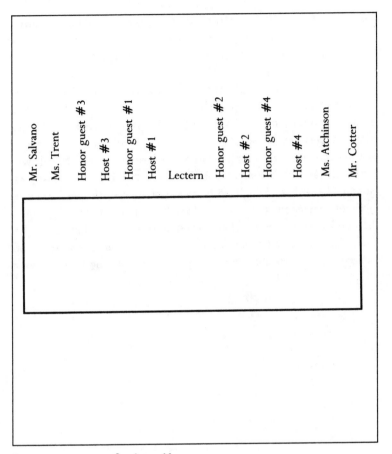

*Seating arrangement for dais table*

circumstances. Still, every executive interviewed qualified this definition by saying that he or she knew someone whose entire social life consisted of entertaining business friends—surely not a purely motiveless venture except in rare circumstances.

Generally, entertaining of a social nature—apart from big wingdings such as the Super Bowl or an occasional customer's night out at the opera, ballet, or theater—is not that common. You need not feel any pressure to ask a customer and spouse to dine with you—and indeed, it may be viewed as slightly aggressive if you push too far in this direction. Many times you simply will not be on the same social level as many of your customers, so there is no genuine reason for you to see each other socially except to advance your business relationship.

Occasionally two people or two couples will find that they do have something in common—golf, theater, a love of eating in fine restaurants. A genuine friendship develops. When this happens, the relationship becomes social; it's even smart not to discuss business on social occasions. You simply relate to each other as good friends who enjoy one another's company. A fine line between business and pleasure always exists, though, so be aware of your motivations in seeing a client or customer socially. It may hurt more in the long run to befriend a customer or client, even if you truly enjoy his or her company. The trend today toward separating business and social life is healthy and probably won't be reversed for a long time—if ever.

# 7

# Entertaining Moguls and Others at Home

ntertaining business associates in your home forges close work-ing ties that are likely to last long after the main event. In-ternational clients are especially eager to be invited to American homes. Americans are known throughout the world for their informality, and Europeans and South Americans are especially delighted when they are asked to an American patio party, buffet dinner, or a picnic.

Having company is an occasion to bring out your best manners, cleverest entertainment ideas, and most sparkling tableware. This does not mean, however, that you can entertain only with china, crystal, and silverware—if you have none of these things, you can still entertain using pottery, stainless, and a dose of ingenuity. While formal dinners are fun and elegant, the days when a boss must be entertained in that style are long gone. Today's entertaining is per-sonal and much more individual.

## Planning the Party

Having guests in your home is always a special event, and a certain degree of planning is necessary to make everything go smoothly, regardless of how informally you plan to entertain.

### Choosing the Kind of Entertainment

First decide on the type of entertainment that suits you best and that also suits the occasion. Although they are infrequent today, you could plan an elegant, formal sit-down dinner. Less formal entertainments include:

- A circulating buffet, where guests help themselves to food from a buffet table and sit throughout the living area of your house or apartment rather than at one table.
- A sit-down buffet, where guests serve themselves from a sideboard or table but then sit down at a table to eat.
- An informal, served, sit-down dinner.
- A party that, by definition, may be large or small and may or may not entail the serving of a complete meal. (A party menu can easily consist of only drinks and appetizers.)

Parties with themes are fun—you don't, for example, have to live in Kentucky to celebrate the Kentucky Derby with mint juleps and ham biscuits. You could also plan a Sunday afternoon Russian tea table; a Chinese banquet; a rijsttafel, which is a traditional Indonesian meal; or any other meal with an international theme. You can plan a costume party, a come-as-you-are party, or even a party of game playing, although if guests will be expected to participate in any way, it is only thoughtful to alert them to this fact when you extend the invitations.

### Planning the Guest List

Once you have decided on the type of party to give, write out the guest list—with care. The first thing to consider is the number of people you can comfortably fit into your house or apartment. If you are planning a large party with very simple food and drinks, a larger number can be accommodated. At a sit-down dinner, the number of people your table can accommodate becomes the important factor.

Within reason, invite people who will get along fairly well, particularly when you are mixing social and business friends. Don't use business parties to pay off old social obligations, especially to people whom you do not find particularly entertaining. If you think someone is a drag, the chances are your business associates won't like him or her either. You should strive for a guest list of people who will find each other interesting—for business or social reasons. You can, if you like, combine a husband's and a wife's colleagues and business associates at the same party.

## ISSUING INVITATIONS

Until recently, invitations were always extended by the wife of a married couple to other wives. Today, the etiquette surrounding invitations has become much less formal, in part because of the large number of single people in business and also because so many wives have active careers of their own that they simply don't have the time or inclination to maintain the family social calendar. These days invitations may be extended by whomever feels more comfortable doing so—a man often invites his colleagues and a woman may invite her colleagues.

Business associates are frequently asked to weddings and even anniversaries if the party or reception is large, but invitations to small, personal parties—birthdays, for example—are best extended only to those business associates with whom you have a close personal relationship.

Most invitations are issued by phone. This is more casual, and it usually produces an immediate response. If you telephone someone to invite him or her to your home, be sure to mention the time and place, the appropriate dress, and the occasion—if there is a special one—for the party or dinner.

For a large party, it is easier to send written invitations. Again, be sure to include all the facts, such as time, place, date, and occasion.

Some clever printed invitations are available, as are some very nice plain ones, but rather than buying something that is merely cute, write your own invitations on plain white or pastel stationery.

Occasionally it is a nice gesture to extend a written invitation even to an informal dinner. Use plain personal stationery and write something like the following:

Dear Jane,

Kenneth and I are having a few friends over for a cookout on Saturday, July 10. The dress is casual. I hope you will be able to join us.

Cordially,


Suzanne


For a formal dinner, handwritten invitations are a must. Use plain white cards that are already engraved on plain white paper on which you can hand-letter the invitation.

A formal invitation reads as follows:

*Mr. and Mrs. Henry Holt*
*request the pleasure of*
*Mr. and Mrs. Jones' company*
*at dinner in honor of*
*Emily and Robert Longsworth*
*on Friday, the fifteenth of April*
*at eight-thirty*

*RSVP*
*664 N. Lake Short Avenue*                    *Black tie*
*Chicago, Illinois 67676*

Notice that the guests' full names are not written out. Invitations to single or married women may be prefaced by "Miss," "Mrs.," or "Ms."

When inviting a married couple who don't have the same surname, use his name *and her* name. Many women choose to keep their own names when they marry, and it is rude not to use the name they prefer. A married woman who uses her own name is Ms., not Mrs. Address invitations to couples who live together in the same way, that is:

Mr. Jones and Ms. Parkhurst

An acceptance to a formal dinner is always written on plain white stationery in the following way:

> *Mr. and Mrs. Michael Jones*
> *accept with pleasure*
> *the kind invitation of*
> *Mr. and Mrs. Holt*
> *to dinner on Friday, the fifteenth of April*
> *at eight-thirty*

A formal regret is written in this way:

> *Ms. Jennifer Henborn*
> *greatly regrets that a previous engagement*
> *prevents her accepting*
> *Mr. and Mrs. Holt's*
> *kind invitation for dinner*
> *on Friday, the fifteenth of April*

## Handling Problems with Invitations

Once in a while someone will fail to respond to an invitation. When this happens, you have no choice but to call the person. You have a right to know who is and who is not coming so you can make plans. About one-third to one-half of the people invited to a large party will be unable to attend, so it is especially important, in order to judge the amount of food and drink to be purchased, to have a fairly accurate estimate of the number of acceptances.

When one of a couple is unable to attend a dinner at the last minute, a problem may arise. If you are the guest and this happens, call the host and explain the situation, saying that you and your spouse or escort will both decline if the absence of one will throw off seating arrangements. A gracious host will encourage the person to attend alone unless the dinner is very formal and the seating arrangements truly would be upset. Otherwise the host should make every possible attempt to accommodate a single guest.

More awkward is the situation in which you have a houseguest and have been invited to attend a party at someone else's home. Call the host and explain that you must decline the invitation because of your guest. If it is convenient, the host can encourage you to come with the guest, but if it is at all inconvenient, the host has every right to let you bow out gracefully. Alternately, you can explain the situation to the guest, help him or her find something else to do, and go to the party anyway.

Few people think anything of asking a single man or a single woman to come to a party with or without a date. The invitation to bring a date should always be optional, and no single person should feel pressured to do so. Single people in turn should realize they now have a responsibility to reciprocate. For many years, single men in particular were so popular at dinner parties that their only responsibilities seemed to be to show up. But today being single is no excuse for not entertaining. Single men and women should return dinner invitations and give the occasional large party.

Once in a while you will get an invitation when you are still in that touchy twilight zone of not having quite owned up to being part of a pair. If your supervisor doesn't know about your partner, he or she can hardly include him or her. It is up to you to make it known that you are part of a pair before the Christmas office party invitation or whatever comes along. If you do receive an invitation that is issued (out of ignorance) to you alone, the best you can do is to mention your partner and hope the host picks up on this and asks you to bring that person with you. Otherwise, your only option is to go to the party alone. And remember, there is no law that says companies must entertain partners or, for that matter, spouses. While social invitations must always be extended to both spouses or partners, business entertainment can be exclusive. Sometimes when the invitation comes to you alone, there is no mistake: It is meant for you alone.

## HOSTING THE LARGE PARTY

Big parties, if handled properly, require time and money. They are best planned far in advance, and they are ideally planned with the aid of a caterer or, at a minimum, a bartender. You can always ask a friend to play bartender to as many as ten people for a couple of rounds of drinks, but it is an imposition to ask someone to prepare drinks all night for thirty or forty. As a general rule, one professional bartender is required for every twenty-five guests. If you are also hiring servers or maids, there should be one for every twenty-five people. Often a caterer will supply people to work at the party in addition to providing the food. (See "Hiring a Caterer for Home Entertaining," p. 157.)

The menu for a large party often consists of drinks and appetizers. At a more elaborate party, a simple supper may be served at some point during the evening, but usually the larger the party, the simpler the food.

Once a very general menu has been worked out and the budget planned, contact a caterer or service agency to arrange for help. A skilled cook can prepare food for any number of people if he or she really has a mind to do so, but a party of more than thirty people is easier to handle if a caterer arranges for at least some of the food and service. This frees you to be a gracious host—an especially important factor in business entertaining.

Decide also whether you will need to rent any supplies, such as flatware, glassware, dishes, tables, chairs, or linens. For example, for fifty people, you will need approximately eighty glasses. This may sound like a lot, but they will all be used throughout the evening. If you plan to do a lot of large-scale entertaining, it may be worthwhile to invest in some inexpensive glasses, but such items are also easily rented. While checking supplies, don't overlook serving dishes and utensils, which can also be rented or borrowed.

## Bar Supplies

Here is a list of bar accessories necessary for a large party:

tablecloth
cocktail shakers and martini pitchers
water pitchers
bottle openers
ice bucket or other container for ice
jigger measures
corkscrew
bar strainer
teaspoon
long spoon for mixing and stirring
cocktail-size paper napkins
dish towels

For a party of fifty you will need the following kinds of liquor and condiments:

3 fifths Scotch
3 fifths vodka and/or gin
3 fifths each bourbon and rum
8–9 bottles wine
24–30 beers
2 bottles vermouth
8 large bottles each soda water, ginger ale, and tonic water
24 bottles Perrier or other good bottled water
24 small bottles soft drinks
ingredients for special drinks: lemon peel, orange and lemon slices,
    cherries, olives, cocktail onions, bitters, limes, sugar

People's drinking habits change over time. At the moment, wine is in favor, and the consumption of hard liquor has dropped in the United States over the past few years. Beer, once rarely seen at a cocktail party, is now a popular drink, and many people forgo alcohol entirely in favor of soft drinks or bottled water. Drinking habits also vary from one region of the country to another, with people's ages, and with the seasons. Wine is more popular at cocktail hour on the two coasts than in the heartland. Young people drink more wine and beer, while people predominantly in their fifties and sixties will consume more mixed drinks. In winter, people drink more Scotch and whiskey, while gin and vodka are favored summer liquors.

Buy ice at the same time you buy the liquor. When buying liquor in quantity, ask the liquor dealer for a discount and make arrangements to return any unopened bottles. If a dealer won't permit this, shop for a new merchant.

## Planning the Menu

Do yourself the favor of serving foods that can be prepared in advance and served with ease. Chips, nuts, and crudités with a good dip can obviously be prepared in advance. Stuffed eggs or mushrooms can be partially prepared, although they should be stuffed the day of the party. Cocktail sandwiches, small quiches, and tiny cream puffs can all be made in advance and kept refrigerated (covered with a damp towel) until serving time. Anything spread on toast or crackers is liable to get soggy and so should be prepared at the last minute.

## Preparing the House

Clean house well in advance—and it should be sparkling. That is a compliment to your guests. Glasses that are not used frequently may need to be washed, and silver may need polishing. The evening before the party is a good time to rearrange any furniture to accommodate the large number of guests. Several days before the party make a check to be sure there are enough candles, fresh soap, bathroom tissue, paper coasters, and guest towels.

If you are planning to have a centerpiece made up by a florist, it should be ordered in advance and scheduled for delivery early on the day of the party.

On the day of the party, you will only have to set up the bar, set the table where food will be served, and make last-minute preparations of food. Try to have everything done by late afternoon so you can take a few hours to relax and get ready. Immediately before the guests arrive, set out the food and the ice.

## Greeting Your Guests

You are now ready to greet your guests. Meet new arrivals at the door, take their coats or tell them where they may put them, and then usher the group into the room of the party and make at least one introduction so newcomers will have someone to talk with immediately.

## Hosting the Buffet Dinner

There are two kinds of buffet dinners. In each the food is put out on a table or sideboard and the guests help themselves. In one kind of buffet, the guests seat themselves as they would at any informal sit-down dinner; at the other the guests mingle or sit on chairs, sofas, or in any convenient place (including the floor). At the latter kind of dinner, the food must be of a kind that can be eaten with only a fork. With either kind of buffet, the food can be fairly simple: one or two hearty main dishes, salad, cheeses, and dessert. The only pieces of special serving equipment needed for a buffet dinner are warming trays that will keep the food hot.

If you are not planning a sit-down buffet, be sure there are enough chairs (and small tables, if you can manage it), so that everyone can sit down somewhere while eating. At this kind of buffet, the dining-room table is often the best place to serve the meal.

In setting a buffet table, the main thing to remember is that everything should be organized for the convenience of the guests. You want to promote a natural traffic flow. People will naturally need to pick up their plates and flatware first. Serving platters should be arranged in such a way as to help the flow of traffic rather than impede it.

## Serving the Dinner

When the guests arrive, offer mixed drinks or wine and give everyone a little time to settle in. It's a good idea to have bowls of nuts, olives, or other tidbits around for guests to nibble on early in the evening.

When all the hot food has been placed on the table, announce that dinner is served. If the meal is being catered and there are waiters, they will help serve the guests. If you are without help, be prepared to cut pieces of cheese for guests or offer them dessert—anything to facilitate their progress.

The main dishes should be ones that each guest can serve himself or herself. After everyone has been served, replace covers on dishes and return them to the oven if necessary. To offer seconds, bring the dishes back to the table or, if convenient, ask guests whether you can take their plates and refill them. When each person finishes eating, remove his or her dishes. Dessert can be served right away, or you may prefer to wait a while. The interlude between the main part of the meal and dessert is a good time to clean ashtrays and set out coffee and dessert dishes.

At a seated buffet, tables and chairs are provided for each guest. Don't forget that it is possible to borrow or rent card tables, thus allowing you to use your dining table for serving food. Chairs need not match, and unity can be created with tablecloths of the same fabric, centerpieces and candles that carry out a color theme, and dishes that match or coordinate. At a seated buffet, put the first course on the table before the guests are seated. If there are waiters, they can remove these plates while the guests help themselves to food at the buffet table. Waiters can also pass rolls and sauces and offer second helpings to the guests. The dishes will need to be cleared after the main course. Dessert can be served from the buffet table or brought to the seated guests, as can coffee.

A buffet table, as well as a dinner table, is often enhanced with a centerpiece. Although flowers are traditional, there is no reason to be limited to them. An absolutely lovely centerpiece can be made from vegetables in a basket; a bowl filled with lemons is stunning. There is really no end to the inventive ideas that can be put to work in a centerpiece. If flowers are ordered, be sure to purchase a low arrangement, especially at a sit-down dinner, so the guests do not have to dodge the centerpiece to talk with one another. Candles are always a nice touch at a company meal, and they go beautifully with flowers. If the table is already crowded with food, however, skip the centerpiece; it is not a necessity.

## Checklists for a Buffet Dinner

Here are checklists for the equipment needed for a buffet supper.

### Drinks

glasses
wine, liquor, soft drinks, bottled water
cocktail shakers and pitchers
ice
bottle openers and corkscrew
olives, lemons, limes, onions, and so on
napkins and coasters

### Dinner

enough plates, and flatware to serve everyone with every course
wineglasses
tablecloths, place mats, and napkins
food-warming equipment
salts and peppers, other condiments
ashtrays
sugar bowl and creamer

coffee cups and after-dinner drink glasses
extra tables and chairs if it is a sit-down meal

***Miscellaneous***

extra ashtrays
centerpiece
candles

## HOSTING THE INFORMAL DINNER

An informal dinner is not much harder to manage than a buffet. The number of people invited depends on the number that can be seated at your table; or again, you might rent small tables. If small tables are used, make sure they all seat the same number of people. Nothing is guaranteed to make a guest feel slighted faster than being seated at a table that makes one guest look less honored than another, as happens, for example, when six people are seated at one table and eight are divided between two small tables.

At an informal dinner, either a tablecloth or individual place mats can be used. The following drawing shows how to set a table for a sit-down dinner.

Perfectionists, take note: There is even an etiquette to putting flatware on the table. It goes as follows:

- All flatware should be lined up at its bottom edge.
- The blade of the knife should turn inward.
- The tines of the fork go up.
- All flatware should be placed about an inch from the table edge.
- The flatware that will be used first is placed farthest from the plate.
- The salad fork should go inside the dinner fork if you are planning to serve salad after the entrée; otherwise, put it on the outside.

If you are having a seated dinner for more than eight people, it is nice to have separate condiments, butters, and salt and pepper shakers

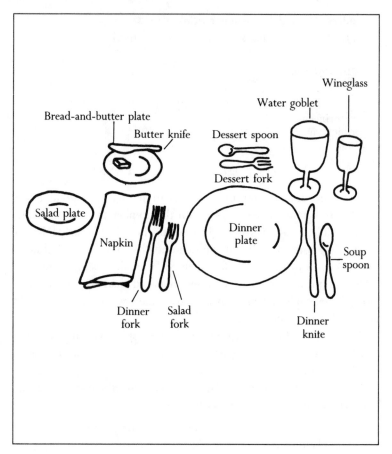

*Informal sit-down dinner*

for each end of the table. The one exception is a peppermill. Since so many people today have cultivated a taste for fresh-ground pepper, and since food tastes so much better with it, by all means pass the peppermill if you have one and dispense with individual pepper shakers.

## Checklist for an Informal Dinner

Here is a basic checklist for an informal dinner:

place mats, tablecloth or runners, and napkins
plates for all courses
flatware for all courses
wine- and water glasses
coffee cups, dessert plates, and after-dinner drink glasses
candles
centerpiece
salt and pepper shakers, butter dishes, condiments
serving dishes
serving flatware
coasters for wine bottles or carafe
trivets for hot dishes

## Serving an Informal Dinner

Food can be served from the kitchen or from a sideboard, whichever is more convenient. Since serving this kind of meal requires a great deal of effort, if you will be serving it without help, try to prepare simple dishes that need only minimal last-minute finishing.

You will probably want to serve drinks and possibly an appetizer as the guests arrive. Generally an informal meal is served anywhere from thirty to sixty minutes after the time on the invitation.

Being late at a dinner party is fairly inexcusable, since there is every chance that food cannot be held over past a certain length of time. If someone doesn't arrive by the time the food is ready, eat without him or her. This may sound discourteous to the latecomers, but it is, in fact, very courteous to those who arrived at the appointed time and who have a right to eat food when it is at its peak. Guests who show up when a meal is in progress should make quick apologies to the host, seat themselves without fuss, and take up at whatever course everyone else is eating.

In some parts of the country, it is fashionable to arrive late. On the

East Coast, for example, no one would arrive for a 9 o'clock party invitation much before 10 o'clock. But a dinner party is different since a host needs to time a menu. Even in fashionable late Manhattan, dinner party guests are expected to arrive within fifteen to thirty minutes of the appointed time—and fifteen minutes is preferred.

Put soup or any other first course on the table just before dinner is announced. Clear the first course and then bring out the main course. Wine is poured with each course. Be sure to bring out the rolls when the main course is served.

The manner of serving at an informal dinner varies depending on the part of the country lived in and how formal the social group is. In small communities dishes are often put on the table and then passed family-style. Meat is often carved in the kitchen. Sometimes the plates are filled there and brought to the table.

In New York, Los Angeles, and Chicago, meat is more likely to be ceremoniously carved at the table, and the host may fill each plate and then pass it to the guests. In either case, a sideboard may be set up to serve from rather than making numerous trips back and forth to the kitchen. An informal dinner can be juggled by one person, but is considerably easier for a couple to handle. One person can serve while the other clears. One person can offer seconds while the other readies the coffee and dessert.

If the dinner is very large and is being catered, waiters will, of course, do the serving. Even for a smaller dinner party of six to ten people, it is sometimes helpful to hire someone to help with the serving. Discuss with servers in detail what you will expect from them and write up a list to post in the kitchen. Work out what each of you will do—you will serve the soup, while the helper passes the crackers; the helper will clear the drinks glasses from the living room while everyone eats the main course; the helper will offer seconds to guests while they are seated. It's important to work out as much as possible in advance so the meal will go smoothly. Ten people is probably the most that one person or a couple who are hosting a dinner can serve without having the meal take on the aura of a three-ring circus. A single hired server should not be expected to handle more than twelve people.

A word of warning, though: When in a company town, do as the company people do. You may have just been transplanted from a sophisticated Boston or Dallas or New York milieu where no one thinks anything of being served by a maid even at a small informal dinner. In your new community, a maid serving dinner to so few may be considered putting on airs. In some towns and small cities, serving meals in courses rather than passing the food family-style is considered pompous. While everyone should be open to new dining experiences whenever possible, for business entertainment, the risk may be too great. Your closest friends may be delighted to be asked to a formal dinner party the likes of which they have never seen before, but your colleagues may feel they are being subjected to an ostentatious show of power. So before you undertake any entertaining, take the pulse of your guests and community.

## HOSTING THE FORMAL DINNER

Black-tie dinners are rarely held these days except for official entertaining in Washington, D.C., or other large cities or at the United Nations, but a special occasion calling for one may arise: an important European guest is visiting your company, an important business merger is being celebrated, or someone important within the company is celebrating something.

Formal dinners call for formal written invitations, as noted in the section on invitations. They are invariably black tie.

A formal dinner is usually served in courses. Although the number may vary, four is the usual number served today. Several wines are served: white wines first with the fish course and a red wine or different white wine with the entrée. Usually two wines are served, although three may be required depending on the food.

While you can do your own cooking at a formal dinner, you cannot do your own serving. Since you will hire a caterer or service agency to help you, be sure to check references before hiring to assure yourself that the caterer is trained to handle a formal dinner. This is not the time to skimp on the caterer or service personnel. Hire the very best you can afford. One waiter or waitress is required for every six to eight guests.

## Setting the Table

A formal dinner calls for good china, silverware, white table linens, candles, and a centerpiece, usually of flowers. Place cards are always used to indicate where guests sit. They go in the center above the plate and are handwritten in this form: "Mr. Brown," "Ms. Stettler," or "Mrs. Linden." If there are two Browns, write "Mr. James Brown" and "Mr. Everett Brown."

## Greeting the Guests

Guests are expected to arrive promptly for a formal dinner because there is usually a guest of honor, and he or she is not supposed to walk into an empty room. A guest of honor who knows his or her etiquette will also take care to leave first, although other guests who have a special reason to do so may of course leave whenever they have to. The rules have softened considerably on this in recent years. Dinner is usually served within thirty minutes of the arrival of the guest of honor.

## Entering the Dining Room

There is a ritual for entering the dining room at a formal dinner. The host offers his arm to the female guest of honor and the hostess is escorted in by the male guest of honor. Other guests can escort each other in as they see fit, but at truly formal dinners, one is likely either to encounter a seating chart or (in the case of male guests) to be handed a small envelope at the door telling each the name of the woman he is expected to escort in. The female guest of honor sits to the right of the host and the male guest of honor to the right of the hostess.

## Proposing Toasts

Toasts are de rigueur at a formal dinner, although they are appropriate at any time that good friends have gathered. At a formal dinner, the host offers the first toast to the guest of honor. It should be short and flattering. Everyone except the person being toasted drinks, even nondrinkers, who may raise an empty wineglass. The person being toasted is expected to respond. The shortest and perhaps most appreciated response is to stand, raise your glass to those who toasted you, and say "Thank you." More can be said, but remember that a toast is not a speech. Once the initial toast has been made by the host or hostess, anyone is free to offer additional ones.

## Serving Drinks

Whenever people gather socially, drinks are inevitably a part of the evening, although in recent years there has been a trend away from serving mixed drinks toward serving aperitif wines. Most hosts will want to be prepared for any requests.

Before serving anything, though, you will need an adequate selection of glasses. Only you can decide what kind of investment you want to make in these, in terms of both cost and quality you think you will need. Inexpensive dimestore glasses work very well, especially for those extra sets of glasses that are brought out only a couple of times a year for a large party. Although there are specially shaped glasses for white and red wine, many people choose to use an all-purpose wineglass. Other useful glasses to own are sherry, champagne (purists favor the tall tapered ones), small dessert wineglasses, and brandy snifters.

A well-stocked bar might include Scotch, bourbon, rye or blended whiskey, gin, and vodka. Today it also usually includes a dry sherry, a couple of aperitif wines, and vermouth. For mixes and those who do not drink alcohol, a bar should have a selection of soft drinks, soda water, a good bottled water, and tonic water.

The following chart shows the number of predinner drinks you can expect to serve. It is only a guide, and the amounts suggested are on the ample side.

| Number of People | Number of Predinner Drinks | Liquor |
|---|---|---|
| 4 | 8 to 16 | 1 fifth |
| 6 | 12 to 24 | 2 fifths |
| 8 | 16 to 32 | 2 fifths |
| 12 | 24 to 48 | 3 fifths |
| 20 | 40 to 80 | 4 fifths |

The number of drinks served at any social gathering is fairly easy to control. Simply cut off the predinner drinking—and do the guests' taste buds a favor—by announcing that dinner is served. At the end of the evening when it is time to wrap everything up, stop offering drinks.

The varieties of mixed drinks that can be served are too vast to list here and can be obtained from any good book on the subject, but there are a few things to know about mixing drinks in general. Always measure ingredients exactly. Bar measures are as follows:

| | |
|---|---|
| Jigger | 1½ ounces |
| Pony | ¾ ounce |
| Bar spoon | ½ teaspoon |
| Dash | 8–10 drops |

Drinks that contain eggs, fruit juice, and other ingredients of a texture that is different from the liquor should be shaken vigorously to ensure thorough mixing. Drinks with carbonated beverages should never be shaken but should be stirred.

Start mixing any drink by putting ice in the glass, and always put fresh ice in every drink when you offer another round.

Use granulated sugar to sweeten drinks, but when you are serving a lot of people, it is easier to premix a syrup of ½ pound of sugar in ¾ cup of boiling water.

## Serving Wines

Wines are easier to serve than are mixed drinks, since they only need uncorking and pouring. Selecting the right wine to go with a food, however, is an art. The best way to learn about wines is to befriend a knowledgeable wine merchant, take his or her advice about what to buy, and drink, drink, drink until you have developed a palate that tells you what wines are fine and what foods they complement.

In general, red wines go with red meat and other foods that are hearty except seafood and fish. White wines go with fish and seafood, some veal dishes (others are enhanced by reds), and light dishes that simply would be overpowered by a red. Sweet wines are served only with sweet foods, and they are meant to be served after dry wines. White wines are served before red wines.

There is a great deal of mostly misinformed debate about the best temperature for serving wines. Generally it is said that white wines should be served chilled and red wines should be served at room temperature. The catch is that the room temperature that is best for a red is wine cellar temperature—55 to 68 degrees Fahrenheit. So when serving a red wine, chill it slightly.

One apartment dweller we know puts red wines on a windowsill for a while before serving. Others chill the wine in the refrigerator for about thirty minutes before uncorking it.

Red wines should be uncorked an hour or so before serving to allow them to breathe. After opening a bottle of wine, always smell the cork for any sign of sourness; this means the wine has begun to turn to vinegar and should not be drunk. Save it for salad dressing!

Wineglasses are placed to the right of the water glass. The wineglass closest to the water glass is the first one used. If more than one wine is served during a meal, the empty wineglass is removed with each course. Pour wines at the beginning of each course, and do not lift the glass from the table to pour the wine. Fill the glass about half full, so, the wine can expand in the glass and the drinker can inhale the full aroma before sipping.

Many countries produce their own wines, and more and more of these are being imported into the United States. It is fun to experiment with these wines at tasting parties, but when you are serving a dinner that has taken effort and time to prepare, try to buy a wine that complements the food. Here is a general guideline:

*Appetizers, cheeses, canapés:* Sherry, vermouth, champagne, or any of the white aperitif wines.

*Poultry:* Rhine wine, dry sauterne, white burgundy, or white bordeaux.

*Seafood:* Chablis, Rhine wine, moselle, white burgundy, or dry sauterne.

*Beef or hearty or red-sauced dishes:* Red burgundy, red bordeaux.

*Veal and ham:* Red or white bordeaux or a white burgundy.

*Eggs:* Light red or dry white wine such as you might serve with fish.

*Desserts:* Port, sweet sherry, muscatel, or sweet sauterne.

*After dinner or with coffee:* Brandy, any of the various sweet after-dinner liqueurs, such as Benedictine or crème de menthe.

## SMOKING IN SOMEONE'S HOME

When First Lady Hillary Rodham Clinton declared the White House a smoke-free zone, it became easier for many people to enforce no-smoking rules in their homes. Only five or ten years ago, it would have been unheard of for a host to deny guests cigarettes. The gracious host in fact was more likely to have matches and cigarettes sitting around for anyone who wanted to use them. But as we have all become wiser about the dangers of even secondhand smoke, fewer and fewer of us are willing to tolerate smoke in restaurants, the workplace, or our homes.

Polite smokers should not assume that they can light up virtually anywhere. If there are no ashtrays around, that is a very strong hint that they cannot smoke. Some hosts make allowances for smokers by handing them ashtrays and showing them to the back hall (in an apartment) or back door (in a house). Some guests (good ones) show themselves to the door when they want a cigarette.

It is in especially poor taste to use clout to smoke. One advertising executive was entertaining a client with whom she had just concluded a big deal at a dinner in her home. He had been asked not to smoke on numerous other occasions in her house. After the deal, however, he brazenly walked in, asked for an ashtray, and challenged: "You have to let me smoke now. Look at how much money I just made for you." And if she had been a lesser woman (or man), she might easily have acquiesced.

## HIRING A CATERER FOR HOME ENTERTAINING

Although many people are familiar with what is termed semicatering—having trays of food brought in by a caterer for a large party—fewer people are aware of the full range of services a fine caterer can offer for at-home business entertaining. Caterers can serve an elegant formal dinner for eighteen members of the board of directors or for eighty of your top executives.

In full catering, and this is probably what you will need and want for business entertaining, the caterer can furnish everything—the dishes, chairs, tables, waiters, bartenders, chef, and of course, the food—or the caterer may use your dishes and silver according to your preference.

The best way to find a caterer is through referral. If others have been happy with a caterer's services, the chances are you will be, too.

The quality of caterers varies greatly, and while hiring a mom-and-pop group for a small party may work, probably only a full-service caterer can guarantee you the smooth-running operation you will want for a business party. A professional caterer also provides a complete package—and best of all, will clean up afterward, something many smaller caterers won't do. By all means, check a caterer's references. Ask for names of current and former clients and then call them.

Once you have found one or two caterers who are possibilities (even in large cities, there are usually only two or three truly professional organizations), make appointments to talk with their service representatives.

The most important thing to establish is your budget. It is a waste of your time and the caterer's if you decide to listen to the most elaborate entertaining package that can be offered and then announce two hours into the meeting that you can afford to spend only $12 per person. A qualified, professional caterer is willing to work within your budget, but he or she cannot do so until you have made clear what that budget is.

Explain the purpose of the party or dinner. Are you entertaining three of your most important clients and their wives and husbands? Are you entertaining international visitors? Is this your annual back-yard bash for your employees? Ask the caterer to come to your home to see the facilities. Together draw up a list of the equipment to be rented. Have the size of the guest list in mind before the first meeting, so you can talk in specific terms.

Caterers provide a cook, if that is what is called for, as well as bartenders and any other servers that are necessary.

As is true with most things in life, you get what you pay for, and the better the caterer you hire, the better the service personnel will be, as a rule. In addition, if you have any specific requests—you don't want the bartender to joke with the guests, for example—make this clear to the caterer when you plan the party.

In fact, it's better to leave nothing to chance. All your personal preferences regarding how you want to entertain your guests should be explained to the caterer in advance. If you want to use china and crystal, tell the caterer. Perhaps you want the wine to flow, or maybe you want it cut off at a certain point. You want white ta-blecloths with yellow napkins. You want the waiters dressed in white shirts and ties—all this should be mentioned when you plan the party.

Find out whether a staff person will be on premises to supervise. This person provides a nice buffer between you and any problems that arise. You tell the supervisor and he or she irons out any problems with food, service, use of facilities, or clean-up detail.

The caterer should be expected to clean up after a party, but ask in advance and make sure this is included in the written contract. And by all means get a written contract from the caterer, and ask before you sign whether it is all-inclusive, that is, whether there will be any extra charges.

Few caterers supply liquor or wine, so you will have to negotiate your own deal for this with the liquor or wine merchant. A caterer may be able to suggest someone reliable who will also give you good service. There is a case discount of 10 percent, and most liquor dealers will let you return unopened bottles. If your dealer refuses, shop around a little more.

A sales manager at Gaper's, the largest and best-known caterer in Chicago, said that anyone hiring a caterer should have a long list of questions to ask before finalizing the deal:

Will food be prepared on the premises?
What grade of meat will be served?
Will the vegetables be fresh?
Where will food be prepared?
How will food be prepared?
How many servers and personnel will be involved?
How many carving stations will be used?
Will there be long lines at the buffet?
Will there be long lines at the dinner?
Will they pour both red and white wines in case people want both?
What type and size wineglass will they use?
Will meat and fish be cooked to order?
Will they be able to serve coffee before dessert if someone requests it?

A good caterer should be able to answer these and any other questions that any good host would ask of himself or herself while planning a party.

As for a menu itself, when working out a meal with a caterer, you should have a few suggestions or ideas about the kind of food you prefer to serve to guests. A caterer's consultant will also have many suggestions, and a professional caterer can prepare almost anything (the limitations are usually your kitchen, not the caterer's cooking skill), but it helps if you know what you want.

## The Role of the Host

A host (male or female) has only one true responsibility: the guests. The entire event is planned for their enjoyment, and everything possible must be done to make them feel welcome and to ensure that they have a pleasant evening.

Begin by being ready and waiting for company. Few things hit a more sour note than greeting guests (especially the first ones, who find arriving first a bit awkward in itself) with the message that you are not quite ready for them and then letting them sit in the living room alone while you complete last-minute personal or cooking preparations.

Even if you saw your guests just a few hours ago at work, greet them at the door when they arrive, shake hands, and tell them how happy you are to see them.

Whether you kiss your guests in greeting probably depends on where you live. On both coasts, people often kiss in greeting, even if they know each other slightly or have just spent the day working together. In the rest of the country, a handshake is the usual form of greeting. Speaking of greetings, it is a true kindness not to indulge in a round of close contact when you are ill. Politer by far is to announce this fact and keep your distance.

Take guests' coats or show them where they can hang them. Notice the word "hang." If at all possible, plan a way to hang up coats. Clear out the front hall closet temporarily or rent or buy a portable coat hanger.

### Making Introductions

Escort new arrivals into the living room. If the party is small, introductions should be made all around. At a large party, introduce your guests to one or two couples or a group standing nearby and then excuse yourself to greet other guests. Since first names are used so commonly today, most introductions, with a few exceptions, are made with first and last names.

If you are introducing someone very much older to someone young, it is still courteous to use "Mr.," "Mrs.," or "Ms." Be careful about this, however, when guests are business associates. You never want to accord the status of wise elder to someone who will be offended by it, such as a very powerful man or woman who may indeed be older than his or her subordinates but has no desire to acknowledge this.

Ministers, rabbis, priests, and higher-ranking Catholic clergy, senators, and others above that rank, including judges, are often introduced using their titles, especially if the individual is the guest of honor. Medical doctors, dentists, and people with doctorates do not use their titles socially.

You will quite naturally want to identify a relative, but there's no need to qualify any other introduction except where necessary to start a conversation. Don't say, for example: "This is Jack Johnson, my very good friend." It is assumed that any guest in your home is a very good friend. It is helpful to say "This is Jack Johnson. He was my college roommate and is in town from Cincinnati for a few days." If you know two people are going to have difficulty starting a conversation, help them out by saying "Myra just got promoted to account executive at O'Grady Advertising," or "Jeff and Cindy just returned from a food tour of France."

Introducing two people who are living together to other guests often produces a moment of awkwardness; it need not. Simply introduce the people by their names and omit any reference to their relationship. Do the same thing when a married couple use two surnames; again, simply introduce them by their names and let later conversation turn up how they are related to one another.

When several guests have arrived and are seated, don't vanish to the kitchen if you can possibly avoid doing so, for your departure almost guarantees an awkward lull in the conversation except among very old friends. Stay for a while and keep the conversation rolling.

On the other hand, a host should always be subtle in manipulating a conversation. No guest wants to feel that he or she is being given the third degree, and some people are shy about discussing their work. Others may be overly gregarious, and your task may be to keep them from monopolizing the conversation—or the entire evening, for that matter.

Give guests room to open up in their own ways. No one appreciates a host who says "Jack is going to tell us about his trip to Greece now." If someone needs to be brought out, do it subtly, possibly in a two- or three-way conversation. A shy person won't be eager to be the center of attention anyway. If someone needs to be slowed down, do take advantage of even the smallest lull to turn to someone else and say "Not to change the subject, but what did you enjoy most about your visit to Costa Rica, Sally?"

The host is responsible for seating arrangements at a dinner. At a formal dinner, this is all planned in advance (see the section on formal dinners), but at informal dinners the host may use place cards or may simply indicate where each of the guests is to sit.

A guest of honor, however unofficial—an out-of-town visitor, an old college friend, a long-lost cousin—may be accorded the place of honor if there are no official guests of honor. When business associates are present, the highest-ranking one (such as your manager!) is given the place of honor. Seating is frequently more interesting when men and women alternate, although this is not a hard-and-fast rule. Try to separate people who see each other often and mix those who have just met.

A very good ploy with dull or shy people is to put them together. A shy person is often bowled over by an outgoing, aggressive person and will become even quieter, while two shy people often bring each other out beautifully.

If you are serving the meal yourself, excuse yourself quietly when you must leave the table. Do not let others pop up to help you, no matter how persistently they offer. Remember that you are expected to take the first bite of any course, so don't serve the soup and then vanish into the kitchen to pull the roast out of the oven. It's never appropriate to suggest that your guests start without you—somehow a gracious guest is just too aware of the trouble taken in preparing a special meal and wants the cook to take the traditional first bite.

Years ago, a host was expected to "turn the table" midway during the dinner. This was often done quite abruptly, by turning from one's partner on one side and saying to the person seated on the other side "Now I'm going to talk to you." Every person at the table followed suit in pretty short order. Fortunately that custom has given way to a more gracious one in which everyone present at a dinner table talks at some point to the person on either side whenever it is comfortable during the meal.

A meal is officially over when the last person has finished eating dessert. Coffee can be served at the table, but it is more often served in the living room, and guests are usually ready to move around after eating anyway. Shortly after the last person has finished eating dessert or during a lull in the conversation, the host should stand, a signal to the guests that everyone is going to move away from the table.

## Departing Guests

How guests depart depends to a large extent on the kind of party. If a party invitation specifies a beginning and an ending hour, as those for cocktail parties and open houses often do, then guests should arrive at least thirty minutes before the party is supposed to end and leave within thirty minutes or so after the time noted on the invitation. Guests at a dinner party are expected to linger no longer than an hour or an hour and a half. At a large party where a meal or buffet is served and only an arrival time is noted on the invitation, guests may stay until late into the night but once the party begins to break up, all guests should take the hint and leave.

Guests at a large party, a cocktail party, or an open house may go on to another social event if they choose to. Guests at a dinner party are not expected to have any other plans.

When you are the guest of honor, the rules are a little different. Generally, a guest of honor is expected to leave a party ahead of other guests because other guests cannot leave before the guest of honor has departed—or so the strict rules of etiquette read. While this rule is still observed in some places, especially where protocol is used, for most of us, this is a rule that is often broken—for practical things like train schedules and baby-sitters' deadlines. If you have to leave a party and diplomatic protocol is not being observed, simply do so, taking care to say good night to your host and the guest of honor. One word of warning, however: As a business strategy, you should always consider whether you want to leave before a CEO, valued client, or other honored guest if you can make advance arrangements to stay later.

When you decide it is time to leave, do so with little fuss. If the party is small, say good-bye to everyone. If it is large, say good-bye only to your immediate circle, taking care to tell any new acquaintances again that you were pleased to meet them. You should never leave any kind of party, though, without saying good-bye to your host and thanking him or her for the evening. Remember that the best compliments are specific. Better to say thanks for the "unforgettable soufflé" or the "stunning table" than for a "a great evening."

When you make a move to leave, it is gracious for the host to say "Oh, must you really leave now? We've enjoyed seeing you so much," but this is a mere formality. Departing guests still are expected to depart. The guests thank the host again at the door and the host thanks them again for coming. The host escorts guests to the door or to an elevator. Elderly people may even be escorted to their cars, particularly if the hour is late. Most guests who are going to call a taxi will ask where the telephone is and do it themselves, but if they are not familiar with the community, it is helpful for the host to call one for them. Hosts should try to keep good-byes with the first guests brief so other guests don't think they are being signaled to leave, too.

Single women frequently come and go unescorted today, particularly in large cities, but most hosts will show some concern for how a woman alone is getting home late at night. If possible, the thoughtful host will ask another guest to drive her or call a cab for her if the hour is very late.

Those who have drunk too much may require a little help getting home. This can be especially tricky when dealing with business associates. No one wants to be in the position of telling an important client or executive that he or she cannot safely drive home, but the situation may arise. As the host, try to avoid long-winded arguments over the issue.

If possible, just assume that the person will not be driving his or her own car home. Call a taxi and then tell the person what you have done. Better yet, ask someone else to take the overimbiber home, and tell him or her discreetly that you will bring the car over the next day or wait for it to be picked up. Assume that the person knows he or she will not be driving home under the circumstances.

Some guests, unfortunately, do not know when to leave, and a wise host or hostess needs a few signals for such occasions. First, you should stop serving drinks. Second, let a lull in the conversation hang. If you constantly jump in with new topics to keep the evening alive, your guests may never want to go home. As a last resort, start to clear glasses and ashtrays while still talking to your guests.

If all else fails, you will have to say something. Make it sound as if you would like the party to go on for days were it not for the fact that you have to meet a plane at 6 A.M. the next day or get up at 5 A.M. to finish a report. You need not even say this directly to a guest; just comment offhandedly that you wish you didn't have "that darned report" to finish tomorrow.

## CHILDREN AT A PARTY

Generally when you are involved in business entertaining, your children should not be present, even for dinner. They may, if you wish, come into the party or dinner when it is just beginning to meet the guests.

If you have very small children, you may want to hire a baby-sitter to take care of them so you do not constantly have to break away to handle their requests.

## The Price of Entertaining

Ticklish moments often occur when a guest spills a drink or otherwise damages something or breaks a valuable or cherished object. Think of this as the ultimate test of your poise as a host. Even if you want to put your hands around the person's neck and squeeze, act as if the incident were nothing. The wineglasses are cheap. The white sofa needed to be cleaned anyway.

As for the guest's responsibility, profuse apologies are, of course, in order, but there is more to be done. If the object is not of great value or is not too rare to be replaced, another should be obtained. A guest who breaks a wineglass or china plate should send a replacement to the host as soon as possible, along with a brief note apologizing again for the accident.

If you have broken something truly precious that you obviously cannot replace, you should still send a gift by way of apology. If your budget is modest, flowers, a book, or candy will do, again accompanied by a note of profuse apology. If you can afford a nicer present—not a replacement, but something lovely to compensate—send it along.

If you have damaged something, try to make arrangements for its repair. Most hosts will refuse to let you do this if you state your intentions, so discretion is called for. First check with your insurance agent the morning after a party to see whether your insurance will pay for damages. If so, ask an adjustor to call on the host and discuss the repairs needed. If you have burned a hole in a table or spilled something on a piece of furniture, call an expert and make arrangements for him or her to see the host to discuss repairs. Make it clear to the supplier that you expect to pay the bill and that it is not even to be discussed with the host. Since most people do start to seethe quietly (or otherwise) the morning after the party when they get another look at the burn in the coffee table or the liquor stain on the sofa, they are usually delighted to see someone who plans to repair their property, regardless of how much they may protest to you that the courtesy is unnecessary.

## UNEXPECTED GUESTS

Uninvited and unannounced guests are rare, but they sometimes appear. At an open house, an extra body is of no consequence, but at a dinner party, it can be deadly. If someone is actually rude enough simply to arrive with an uninvited guest, a gracious host should first of all try to make room for him or her. If there is no place to seat the person or if there truly will not be enough food, tell the person who has brought the guest that while you would love to have the extra person stay, it simply isn't possible. Explain why this is impossible (no extra chair, not enough food), so your refusal will not appear to be a mere ploy you are using because you are annoyed.

If someone has called in advance and you have both agreed that the extra guest is welcome, it is thoughtful to write or telephone the extra guest to extend a personal invitation.

## APPROPRIATE DRESS

Invitations usually note only when dress is formal, either black tie or, less rarely these days, white tie. Other than that, you're on your own except for any guidance you can muster from your host or colleagues who may have attended similar events. It is, however, especially important for business entertaining that you dress for the occasion.

One more caveat: Dress down when it's a business occasion. A black-tie dinner with VIP clients isn't the time to test a plaid dinner jacket or the latest in men's formalwear—unless you happen to work for a very fashion-forward company.

The same applies to women. Even when the occasion is formal, it's still about business. Save the extreme—low-cut, ultra-frilly, and extravagant—dresses for purely social occasions.

If conservatism is called for in your daily dress, then it most definitely is required for business-related entertaining as well.

\* \* \*

A final word about business entertaining: Relax and enjoy yourself. This is a time to get to know your colleagues or clients better, to cement your relationships, and above all else, to enjoy an evening of camaraderie in good company.

# 8

# The ABCs of Eating and Drinking

Table manners? Surely they don't belong in a book about getting ahead? after all, don't education, skills, contacts, personality—anything else, for that matter—count more? It is true that these other things are vitally important, but make no mistake about it, how you handle the task of putting food in your mouth is a very big part of your image—professional and social.

Business executives who have already made it to the top frequently lament the lack of social polish in their protégés—and one of the first places where rough edges show up is at the table.

Really polished table manners can take you to another level of sophistication. Obviously, everyone will notice (in a negative way) if you eat with your mouth open or use your flatware ineptly, but you can also really impress top executives if you also know the fine points of dining—how to eat an artichoke, for example, or snails. With these finer skills in hand, you become even more valuable as a representative of your company and even more sought after as a dinner guest.

Fortunately, while some other aspects of good manners are linked to personal qualities such as tact and the ability to get along with others, table manners can belong to anyone. No one is born with them, and once you have acquired a usable set, using them becomes second nature. Another bonus of acquiring good table manners is that learning about them necessities picking up knowledge about food and wine, and that has become a fascinating avocation for many people.

Once you have mastered the essentials of eating properly, it is fine to be casual about them. Many of the strict and unnecessary rules of even a decade ago have vanished. For example, it is not particularly important to follow the old rule about opening a dinner-size napkin halfway and a luncheon napkin all the way. Remembering to put the napkin in your lap is the important thing.

## Setting the Table

In these days of lightening up our diets, formal seven-course meals have given way to simpler four-course ones. At most meals, you will usually encounter an appetizer or first course, possibly soup; an entrée, or main course; salad, sometimes served with cheese; and dessert and coffee, which are often but not always combined. Salad also may be served between the first course and the entrée, American-style, despite a growing trend toward serving it after the entrée, as Europeans do.

At a very formal dinner, you may be served more courses. For example: an appetizer and a soup, followed by a fish or pasta course, an entrée, salad, cheese (seen more often in France and Italy than in the United States), dessert, and coffee.

The drawing that follows on the next page shows the typical plates, flatware, and glasses that you will encounter at an average, fairly formal meal at home or in a restaurant.

Two easy rules will help you confront the flatware. The first is that, as a rule, a place setting contains no more than three of any one kind of utensil. The second is that you typically work from the outside in when using flatware.

The place setting shows the pieces of flatware you are likely to encounter, but you probably would not see this much all at once. For example, if a place setting did include three forks beside the plate, as this one does, then the dessert fork would probably be brought in when dessert was served. And it would be unusual to serve a seafood cocktail and a fish course, as this place setting shows. In this place

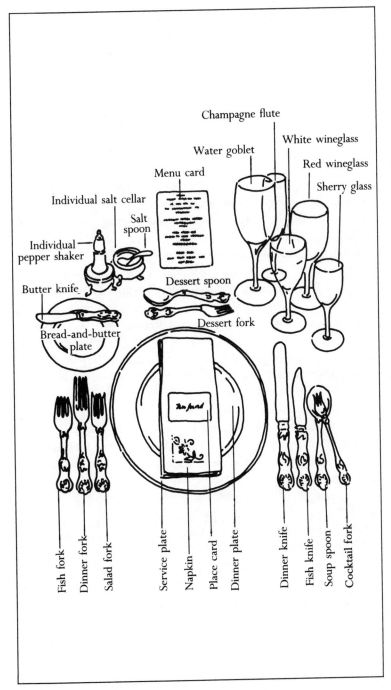

*Formal place setting*

setting, a quick glance would tell you that there will be an appetizer or first course, followed by an entrée, with the salad served afterward. The fork and spoon above the plate are always used for dessert. On the right, you encounter a seafood fork (the only fork to go on this side of the plate), a soup spoon, a fish knife, and a dinner knife.

## Glassware

The use of glassware is especially easy to understand because someone will fill up the glass from which you are supposed to drink. Your water goblet usually rests at the point of your knife, plus it is usually the largest glass. (In Europe, you may not be served water with meals, although you can always request it.) Other glasses are for wine, sherry, or champagne, and are arranged around the water glass. Rarely, though, will you encounter all these beverages at one meal these days.

If there are two wineglasses, you are having both a white and a red wine. A small sherry glass signals that this beverage will be served with the soup. At a formal dinner, champagne may be served with dessert. Each beverage will be served with its own separate course. And another general rule is that white wines are served before red ones, and light wines are served before heavy ones.

Wineglasses can and do vary in shape and size, according to the kind of wine that is being served. There is a special glass to hold burgundy, for example, and another for bordeaux. But it's usual today for a generic wineglass to be used for any and all wines. Each different wine should be served in a clean glass.

## Flatware

Here is what you will encounter on the left side of your plate:

- *Seafood fork.* This small fork is used only for shrimp, clams, oysters, snails, and other similar seafood usually served as a first course. It is either the first fork on the left (beside the other forks) or the first utensil on the right, beside the knives and soup spoon. Sometimes the seafood fork is brought in with the seafood course.

- *Fish fork.* The fish fork and salad fork are often interchangeable these days, although a true fish fork has one specially shaped tine, which is used to carefully pull apart the fish.
- *Place fork.* This fork is used to eat the entrée. Occasionally, if the entrée is fish, it may be used for fish.
- *Salad fork.* If the salad is served first, this fork will be to the left of the dinner fork. If the salad is served after the entrée, it will be to the right. You'll see what the fork is used for when your food arrives.

Here is the flatware you will encounter on the right side of your plate:

- *Seafood fork.* Remember, this could show up here as well.
- *Soup spoon/Fruit spoon.* If soup is being served, it will be the first spoon you encounter. If fruit is being served as a first course, the first spoon will be used for this.
- *Fish knife.* If fish is served as a first course, there may also be a small, pointed knife with which to eat it.
- *Dinner knife.* Used for the entrée.

And finally, here is what you will encounter above your plate:

- *Dessert/coffee spoon.* This goes immediately above the plate or occasionally to the right of the plate.
- *Dessert fork.* This goes below the spoon above the plate or to the left of the plate.

You may also encounter:

- *Butter knife.* This goes across the top of the bread plate.
- *Salt spoon.* This tiny spoon will be in a salt cellar. If there is no spoon in the salt cellar, use the tip of your clean knife.

Used flatware is removed after you have finished a course, although some inexpensive restaurants today insist that diners keep their flatware to use with the next course—a practice we deplore for its lack of elegance. Assume that your flatware will be removed unless the waiter tells you otherwise.

## Plates

The bread plate, accompanied by the small butter knife, is placed slightly to the left and above the dinner plate.

The salad plate (or bowl, as is often seen today) goes to the left of the dinner plate, or on the service plate, if salad is served as a separate course.

The small extra plate on the dinner plate that is so often seen in restaurants is meant to hold the seafood or appetizer course or the soup. It is a superfluous plate whose only function is to protect the dinner plate until it is used. You don't have to worry about it; the waiter will remove it if it isn't needed, as will a host at a home dinner party.

## Finger Bowls and Hot Towels

At a very formal dinner you may encounter a finger bowl, which is placed above and to the left of the dinner plate. The finger bowl is not used until you have finished dessert, even though it may be brought to the table with the dessert plate and flatware.

Finger bowls may also appear before the meal at a Chinese or Japanese dinner, in which case they are to be used before the meal. Whether they appear before or after a meal, the technique is the same. Dip your fingers into the water and move them to slightly below table level to dry your hands on your napkin.

In some restaurants (most notably, Japanese) and on certain international flights, before a meal is served, you will be presented with a hot towel. It is a courtesy to you. To use, liberate it from its plastic bag if it is in one, and open it fully. Use it to lightly wipe off your hands. Do not use it on your face. When you are finished with it, place it neatly on your tray or table. Don't refold or roll it.

If you receive a hot towel on a plane, using it is entirely up to you. If you receive one in a restaurant or in someone's home, though, it is best to use it —even if you just washed your hands.

## EATING EACH COURSE

Aside from the myriad questions that arise about eating in general, here are a few tips to help you handle each course.

## *Seafood*

Use the small fork and eat on the plate that is put in front of you. Sometimes seafoods come in small casserole platters that the waiter places beside your dinner plate. Use a large spoon to transfer the food from the casserole to the small plate on top of your entrée plate. If necessary, request a large serving spoon to facilitate this process.

## *Soup*

The important rule here is *Don't slurp.* Actually, any book for adults should not have to make this point, but, in fact, it is amazing to see the number of people who slurp their food or talk while they eat. So be forewarned but not nervous: An occasional sound may be unavoidable and easily handled with a small, murmured apology, but constant slurping—or talking with food in your mouth—is the sign of a boor.

It is fine to drink from a soup cup with two handles or no handles, but if you feel uncomfortable doing so, it is equally acceptable to use your soup spoon. Formal etiquette books state that the diner should move the spoon away from the body. This is the kind of rule that, fortunately, one no longer need worry about. Just eat the soup quietly, without slurping or spilling it. (Of course, it never hurts to eat exactly correctly; in this case, by moving the spoon away.)

Rest the soup spoon in the soup bowl if it is large and flat, or on the plate or saucer under it. If you want to drink the last tasty drop (and who doesn't) but it eludes you, tilt the bowl slightly away from you and spoon it out. Small oyster crackers can be put directly into a bowl of soup, but it is not acceptable to break larger crackers into the soup.

## *Entrée*

Historically speaking, in French menu parlance, entrées were small dishes that accompanied or followed the appetizer and prepared the palate for the pièce de résistance that was served later. Today the word "entrée" refers to the main dish, although some French cookbooks still make the distinction. An entrée or main dish, which generally consists of meat, fish, or poultry and accompanying vegetable dishes, is eaten with the large fork and knife.

## Salad

Generally try to use a salad fork to cut lettuce or other greens. If you meet resistance, using a knife and fork is perfectly correct. The salad plate should be to the left, unless the waiter or host has placed it in the center of the dinner plate, in which case it should be left where it is. When finished, leave the utensils on the salad plate.

## Fruit

The fruit course increasingly appears with or following salad these days. It sometimes substitutes for dessert, a tribute to the calorie-conscious era in which we live. At formal American dinners, fruit is peeled, quartered, cut up, and eaten with a fork. It is eaten this way at any type of European dinner. If you are at anything less than a black-tie, five-course formal dinner, however, you can usually simply pick up a nice red juicy apple and bite into it. Of course, there are those occasions when one feels more elegant peeling and cutting up a piece of fruit, and there is not reason not to do so—just do whatever is most comfortable for you.

## Dessert

Dessert may come with a fork or spoon, so merely eat away, leaving the utensils on your dessert plate when you have finished.

## AMERICAN VERSUS CONTINENTAL EATING STYLE

You can eat using the American or the Continental method or a combination of both methods. Most Americans, unless they have spent a great deal of time in Europe, are more comfortable with the American method, which is widespread in the United States.

In fact, if you are not comfortable using the Continental method, it will only look awkward, so while you may be tempted to try it, do so only in the privacy of your own home until you are sure you have mastered it. The drawing on the next page shows how to hold the utensils to cut food regardless of whether you will use the American or Continental method to transfer the food to your mouth.

The American method entails holding the fork in your left hand and the knife in your right hand and cutting the meat, then switching the food on the fork to your right hand before raising it to your mouth. (See the drawing on page 179.) Obviously, this method necessitates replacing the knife on the plate before transferring the food to the right hand.

In the Continental style of eating, the food is transferred to the mouth on the fork in the left hand. (See the drawing on page 179.)

Left-handed persons may reverse these procedures.

Many people prefer to use the Continental style of eating for everything but the meat, when they switch to the American method. Whatever method you choose to use, try to use it regularly so that you will feel comfortable with it. Some unacceptable ways of holding utensils are shown on page 180.

When you are finished eating, place your knife and fork together on your plate, as shown in the drawing on page 181.

## SITTING DOWN

Always move to the right of the chair when you are being seated. This is especially important for women who are being seated by a waiter, for this is what the server will expect women to do.

Without being stiff, make an effort to sit erectly at table. Good posture goes hand in hand with self-confidence, and slouching at the table is not a look you will want to present. The old elbows-off-the-table rule has pretty much been boiled down to elbows-off-the-table-

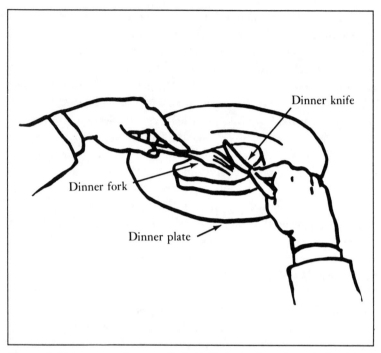

*How to hold your utensils to cut food: Hold the knife in the right hand with your index finger on the handle slightly overlapping the blade. Hold the fork, prongs down, in your left hand and extending down from your index finger. Elbows should be kept just slightly above the table level.*

while-you-are-eating. It is permissible to put *an elbow* on the table between courses or when you are talking after dinner—or even over coffee, for that matter. Just be careful not to rely on your elbows for total bodily support.

*The American method: Lay your knife on the plate, transfer the fork, with the prongs up, to your right hand, and then carry the food to your mouth.*

*The Continental method: With your left hand, bring the fork, with the prongs down, to your mouth.*

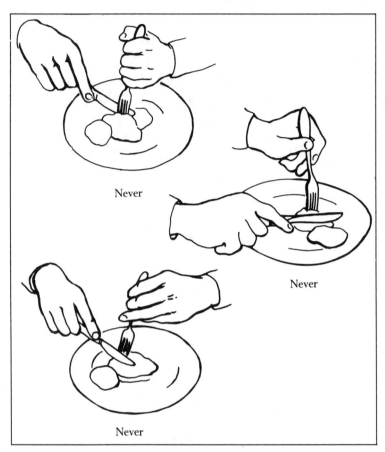

*Incorrect ways of holding a knife and fork*

## Excusing Yourself

If for any reason you have to leave the table during a meal, excuse yourself to those present. Don't just get up and leave. Reasons for leaving the table include the need to blow your nose, a sudden feeling of illness, and the need to make a trip to the rest room or take a phone call. Leave quietly to avoid making any kind of fuss. When you return, reseat yourself quietly and join in the conversation whenever appropriate.

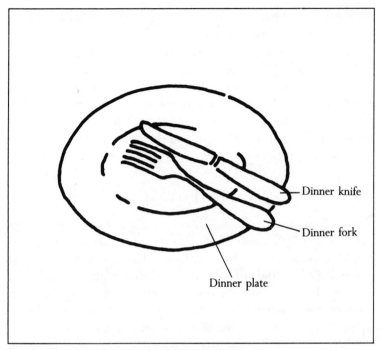

Dinner knife

Dinner fork

Dinner plate

*The finish position, Continental and American methods*

The one time you absolutely do not excuse yourself from the table is when you feel yourself choking on a piece of food. This is a life-threatening situation, and you must alert your fellow diners so they can perform the Heimlich maneuver on you. If you are choking on food, you will not be able to speak, so the universal symbol to indicate this is a hand on your throat—invariably accompanied by your own genuine look of panic.

## USING YOUR NAPKIN

As a general rule, wait for the host to put a napkin in his or her lap and then follow suit, or so the etiquette books of old say. What is important is to put the napkin in your lap shortly after you sit down. The rules for unfolding a napkin have also become more casual: Just open it to a comfortable size and put it in place. When you have finished eating, place the napkin casually to your left. Do not refold it.

Use the napkin to remove food crumbs from your lips before you drink a beverage. This avoids leaving a messy wineglass. Lipstick stains on a glass are also unattractive, but it is difficult to tell a woman who looks good in dark-red lipstick to wipe it off before she eats. (One trick is to blot lipstick carefully with tissue when applying it.) Just remember that lipstick on a glass repels some people—and one of those people might be your supervisor or a prospective client.

## Dinner Table Talk

No one likes a loudmouth, but this distracting feature of a personality can be especially alarming when eating in public. Try always to speak in low, intimate tones at the table. Some subjects, even these days, are not acceptable at the table. Details of illness, surgery, funerals, and anything that could make someone squeamish are topics to avoid. Remember that it is considerate to avoid not merely topics that make *you* squeamish, but also whatever might make anyone else uncomfortable.

Although well-mannered people talk freely of money, politics, and religion these days, the table is still not the best place to do so. For one thing, everyone is there to eat, and it is upsetting when one person presses an argument that makes anyone else uncomfortable.

## Talking to Servers

The days of servants are mostly gone, so you don't have the problem of deciding whether to converse with an old family retainer, but some people do eat regularly in their favorite restaurants and get to know those who help them. People who wait on you always deserve a fair measure of respect (especially if you hope for good service), and someone to whom you are friendly when you eat alone should be accorded the same respect when you are with friends. Generally it is polite to thank a waiter occasionally during a meal. You need not thank him or her for every little service. Certainly you do thank someone who performs an extra service.

## REACHING

Reaching across the table used to be strictly taboo. Today we're a little more realistic and generally take whatever is within reach of us, provided we do not have to stretch in front of another person to do so. If something is equidistant from everyone at the table, don't ask someone else to hand it to you but pick it up yourself.

## ASKING FOR WHAT YOU NEED

Too many people are timid, particularly in a restaurant, about asking for something they need or want, or about requesting a change in their food if it is not properly prepared. Since a good executive needs to be aggressive, it only makes sense to apply the same aggressiveness to such a seemingly minor situation as ordering and eating a meal. This is not to say that you should ever be the cause of a scene (a mistake too many would-be stars make), but rather that you should firmly and politely insist on getting what you want or ordered.

## PESTS IN FOOD

Ocassionally a water glass or salad will arrive with a small beast in it. The correct way to handle this is not to bring it to the attention of the others present at the table but to quietly request that the waiter remove the offending dish or glass and bring you a fresh one. Use the same technique for unclean flatware or dishes.

## REMOVING FOOD FROM YOUR MOUTH

Seeds, pits, and small bones obviously cannot be swallowed, so remove them discreetly, placing them on the side of your plate. Use your fingers, cupping them to hide the food, and also bring your napkin to your mouth.

## FOOD THAT IS TOO HOT

If you take a bite of food that is too hot to swallow comfortably, squelch it with water—again, as discreetly as can be arranged. Never spit it out.

## Catsup and Other Sauces

Americans, perhaps because they have for a long time lacked the elegant sauces of French cuisine, drench foods in catsup, steak sauce, and anything else that appears on the table in a glass jar. They have even taken to putting catsup on foods such as scrambled eggs. Most etiquette books point out that this is an insult to the chef. Most Americans don't seem to care. If, however, you are dining or lunching with someone you want to impress, it is safer not to drench a good piece of beef or (heaven forbid) your scrambled eggs with anything that was not personally prepared by the chef to go over the food. Particularly in light of the reviving interest in gourmet cooking, an increasing number of people look disdainfully upon such actions.

If you simply cannot eat a food without catsup or another bottled sauce, at least learn to use it correctly. Catsup, mustard, or any other condiment is put directly on an open-faced or closed sandwich. If you want to eat catsup with your French fries, do not drench them in it. Rather, pour a small amount of catsup on the side of the plate and dip the French fries in it as you eat them.

## Jams, Jellies, and Butter

Jams and jellies are transferred to your butter (or dinner) plate with the serving spoon that comes with them. You then use your butter knife or dinner knife to spread the jam on your food. The butter knife is also used to butter breads. But when you add butter to vegetables or any other food already on your dinner plate, use a fork.

## Stirring and Mashing Food

Even in these days of casual manners, stirring and mashing food have not become acceptable and are, furthermore, highly offensive to others.

## Using Bread to Clean the Plate

It is acceptable to use a piece of bread to get a difficult bit of food; it is less acceptable to use the bread to wipe your plate absolutely clean.

## Drinking

There is an art to drinking beverages when eating food. First, wipe your mouth with your napkin; then sip the beverage. This may sound time-consuming, but it prevents the unattractive situation that results when food particles have traveled far from your mouth across your face, as well as when food particles land on a drinking glass. If you have ever tried to carry on a conversation with someone who has a particle of food located somewhere on his or her face, then you will appreciate the beauty of the required sweep of the lip area with the napkin.

## Dropped Flatware or Food

When a piece of food or flatware is dropped, the general rule is to leave it where it lands, especially in a restaurant. If necessary, quietly ask the waiter or your host to bring another piece of flatware. Common sense should prevail, however, if you drop a really messy piece of food or spill a beverage in a private home. An immediate cleanup may be called for, but even so, no host wants his or her dinner party interrupted with a scene. So if the host tells you to let it go after you have quietly commented that you spilled red wine on a white carpet, then say no more. And if the host does decide to clean up, let him do so quietly.

## Removing Dishes

Do not push your plate away from you or stack your dishes to indicate that you are done eating. In so doing, you are likely to move the dishes closer to someone you are eating with, and if the dishes are unsightly enough for you to want them out of sight, imagine how they will appear to the other person.

A general rule of thumb in the United States is to serve from the left and remove dishes from the right, and in a fine restaurant, this is how food will be brought to you and taken away. In casual situations, a host or hostess may elect to take the food away from either side. It is never polite to reach across a guest to remove a dish, so as a host you should plan to do whatever is most convenient for the person seated.

## FOOD SPILLED ON THE TABLE

If you break bread or rolls over your bread plate, there will be few crumbs on the tablecloth. If you do drop crumbs on the table, just leave them alone. Small particles of food can be discreetly removed with a napkin when the dishes are cleared or slightly before.

## USED FLATWARE

Nothing is more glaringly offensive than putting a piece of flatware you have used on a white tablecloth—or anywhere on the table. Once you have used a piece of flatware, place it on a plate, either the dinner plate or the bread plate. A knife or fork should not rest half on a plate and half on the table. Also remember not to use your own flatware to dish up portions of food. Ask for serving pieces if they are not brought in with the food. (Your host will be grateful if you remind him or her of something like this that has been forgotten.)

A nastier situation occurs when you're in a not-quite-topnotch restaurant that tries to stint on flatware. Instead of giving you clean flatware with each course the way a really good restaurant does, many servers now nudge your used flatware onto the table when they clear your plate. The best you can do in this bad situation is to rest the utensils against your serving spoon or some other piece of flatware that has not been used. Alternately, you could place them on your bread plate until the next course arrives.

## SHARING FOOD

In these days of restrained eating, two or more diners may elect to share a dish. In some restaurants, if you indicate this to the server, he or she will divide the dish for you and bring it on two plates.

To divide it yourselves, one of you passes over a plate so the other one can divide the portion and transfer it to the plate. Unacceptable ways to share food involve simply reaching over with your fork to spear something and carry it off to your plate or eating food from someone else's plate. The only time food is truly shared is when two very closely related persons share a dessert. This doesn't usually apply to business associates.

It is wise to remain a bit reticent about sharing at a business lunch, particularly if you are interviewing for a position or otherwise trying to impress someone. Food is not shared as casually under these circumstances as it is among friends.

## SMOKING AT THE TABLE

Smoking at meals is a touchy subject. It is only civilized to refrain from smoking while anyone at the table is still eating, when anyone at the table indicates that he or she has an allergy or is ill, or even when you notice that someone appears to be annoyed by smoke. It is never polite or considerate to smoke during a formal meal, and if you notice that there are no ashtrays on a table in someone's home, take that as a hint that you are expected to refrain at least until after leaving the table.

A trickier situation presents itself in these days when restaurants are divided into smoking and nonsmoking sections. Where does a party containing smokers and nonsmokers sit?

No real etiquette has been established to solve this problem, but we have observed that the nonsmokers usually hold sway. Everyone sits in a nonsmoking section, and the smoker(s) excuse themselves to go smoke elsewhere.

The exception seems to be a business lunch where the smoker is a VIP or a potential (or current) client. Then nonsmokers often yield to smokers—with the accompanying risk to their health, of course.

## Tricky Foods

If you are confronted with something that you are not sure how to eat, never be afraid to speak up and say "I've never eaten this before. How do I go about it?" This should never be cause for embarrassment.

Invariably someone at the table will give you instructions and not think another thing about the incident. The paragraphs that follow contain useful descriptions of how to handle certain unusual foods. The only problem is that reading about eating them and eating them are not the same thing. The solution is to cook some of the foods that appeal to you at home and *practice*.

## Seafood

### Shrimp Cocktail

Use the seafood fork to eat a seafood cocktail. Use your fingers to eat each shrimp in one bite if the shrimp is small. If it is large, eat it in two bites. Place the tails on the seafood plate. Place the fork on the plate under the seafood dish when you are finished.

### Oysters and Clams

In open shells, oysters and clams are usually served on a plate of cracked ice. Use a seafood fork. Hold the shell in place with one hand, and with the fork, lift the whole oyster or clam out of the shell and eat it in one bite. Do not pick up the shell. Seafood sauce is usually served in a small bowl right in the middle of the ice; dip each piece in it before eating.

### Steamed Clams

Use your fingers to lift out each clam by its neck, then pull the body from it and discard the neck part. Dip the clam in melted butter or broth (often served separately) and eat it in one bite. Special note: If a clam shell hasn't opened during the cooking, don't eat it. The closed shell means it shouldn't be eaten.

## Snails

Snails are served in shells on a special plate that holds each shell in place. First, pick up and hold a shell with your napkin (snails are always hot) or with the special metal clamps usually served with snails. With the other hand dig out the snail with a seafood fork and eat it in one bite. If you like, you may sip the liquid from the shell, or you may dip small pieces of bread in it with your fork to soak up the butter-and-garlic sauce.

## Lobster

If lobsters are not cracked in the kitchen (and you may request this), they are always served with a tool that looks like a nutcracker. Use it to crack the two big claws and then break them wider apart with your hands. Next, pick up one claw and, with the seafood fork, dig out the meat in one or more chunks and put it on your plate. Cut it into bite-size pieces as you eat it. A butter sauce is served for dipping. Break the small claws with your fingers and either suck out the meat or dig it out with your fork. The coral-colored roe of the lobster and the soft green liver—both considered delicacies—are eaten with a fork.

### Meat

## Chicken

Eat chicken with a knife and fork unless you are at a picnic. Steady the piece of chicken on your plate with your fork in one hand. With the other hand cut away the meat a bite at a time.

## Frogs' Legs

Frogs' legs can be eaten partly with a knife and fork and partly with the fingers. First, though, sever the leg at the joint, then eat as much meat as possible from the larger part, using your knife and fork. Put the bones back on the side of your plate.

### Sauces

Horseradish, applesauce, mint jelly, béarnaise, and cranberry sauce are placed on your dinner plate, either to the side or over the meat. Dip small pieces of food into the sauce one at a time as you eat. Sauces such as lemon-and-butter sauce or tartar sauce are never poured over the whole fish. Instead cut off a small piece of fish and dip in into the sauce.

## Vegetables

### Artichokes

To begin eating an artichoke, pull off one leaf at a time and dip it into melted butter or sauce. Then pull it through your teeth, scraping off the soft part at the end of the leaf. Set the rest aside. When all the outer leaves are finished and arranged neatly on the side plate, remove the fuzzy part in the middle of the artichoke by cutting under it and lifting it off. Then cut the artichoke heart into pieces and dip each piece into sauce with your fork before eating it.

### Asparagus

Eat the soft tips of asparagus with your fork only and then cut the tender part of the stem with a knife and fork, if necessary.

### Baked Potatoes

Do not scoop baked potatoes onto your plate and mash them; instead, eat them out of the potato skin. Use the dinner fork or spoon to put any topping on the potato. You may cut up the skin with a dinner knife and fork and eat it.

### French Fried Potatoes

Eat fried potatoes with a fork after cutting them into shorter lengths, if necessary. Never spear a piece and bite away at it from your fork. At a drive-in or on a picnic, French fries become finger food.

*Fruits*

### Bananas

When served whole at a table, bananas should be peeled halfway or all the way and the skin put aside on your plate. Then the banana is eaten by breaking off pieces with your fingers or by cutting them off with a knife and fork. Do not chomp away at a half-peeled banana with the skin draped down over your hand.

### Grapes

Cut or break grapes from the main bunch in small clusters, put them on your dessert plate, and eat them from there one by one. Do not pick one grape at a time from the main dish. Remove seeds from your mouth with your fingers and put them on your plate.

### Kiwi

These lime-green fruits have become popular enough to show up in baked desserts and on fruit platters, where they are invariably cut into slices but aren't always peeled. The fuzzy outer coating doesn't taste good, so simply cut it away when you encounter it. Should you encounter a whole, unpeeled kiwi, peel it with a fruit knife, cut it into quarters, and eat it in bite-size pieces with a fork.

### Lemon

A slice of lemon served on meat or fish is not picked up; it is strictly for show. A wedge of lemon is picked up and squeezed or pressed against the prongs of a fork to let the juice trickle out. Shelter it with your hand to avoid spraying anyone.

### Oranges

Peel oranges spirally if you can do it gracefully. Then eat them segment by segment with your fingers. Remove seeds from your mouth with your fingers and place the seeds on your plate.

## Strawberries

Strawberries can be picked up by the hulls and dipped in whatever is served with them—sugar, whipped cream, or sour cream—and eaten with the fingers. Fruit in juice is always eaten with a spoon.

## Tangerines

Peel tangerines; then eat one segment at a time, preferably in two bites. Use the fingers. Remove seeds from your mouth with your fingers and place the seeds on your plate.

## *Miscellaneous*

### Food Served *en Papillote*

Food served *en papillote* is enjoyed renewed popularity, no doubt because of our diet-conscious ways. *En papillote* is a French method of cooking food sealed in a parchment (or, more likely these days, aluminum foil) package. It is up to the individual diner to open the package. This should be done carefully, as the escaping steam can burn you. Break a small hole in the package with your fork or knife on the far side away from you, and lean away while the first burst of steam emerges. You can then open the package even more, until it is nearly flat, and begin eating. The food is not removed from the package before eating.

### Candy or Pastry in Paper Frills

Pick up pastry or candy, paper and all, when you are served. When you are ready to eat, peel off the paper carefully, and leave it on your plate.

### Olive Oil

Authentic Italian restaurants often serve a bottle of olive oil with bread. Pour a small amount on your bread plate, and then dip small pieces of bread into it immediately before eating them. If the olive oil is brought in on a small plate, bread is communally dipped. Keep in mind that it is not polite to redip a piece of bread once you have bitten into it.

## Olives

Olives belong on the butter or salad plate, but if neither is provided, put them on a dinner plate. If an olive is large and has a pit, eat it with two or three bites, holding it with your fingers. Place the pit on the butter or salad plate. Small olives without pits can be eaten whole.

## Pasta

There are two ways to eat long pasta. You may either wrap it around your fork, holding the fork against the plate or bowl, until you have achieved a manageable amount, or you may hold the fork against a spoon until you have shaped the pasta into a manageable ball.

Smaller, more manageable pastas can be eaten in the usual way with a fork.

## Tea

When you are served a teabag and an individual teapot, you may make yourself tea in either the pot or your cup. If you want more than one cup of tea, it's more practical to brew the tea in the pot. Be sure to let the tea brew for a few minutes so you can savor its full taste. If the tea is brought to you already in the pot, you may want to ask the server how long it has been brewing. When you remove the teabag, place it on the small serving plate if one is under the teapot; otherwise, place it on your saucer. Occasionally, there will be neither serving plate nor saucer, and you will have to look for something else—a bread plate—or ask the waiter for a saucer. Don't put a teabag on a tablecloth or napkin because it will stain permanently.

A good trick is to wrap the teabag around your teaspoon when you remove it so it doesn't drip all over your saucer—and you—when you drink the tea.

Occasionally a pot of looseleaf tea is served with a strainer. After the tea has brewed, place the strainer over your cup and pour the tea into it slowly. A few tea leaves will fall into the strainer. You'll also need a small plate to hold the strainer; ask for one if you need to.

## Toothpicks

Never use toothpicks in public.

# 9

# *The Art of Executive Gift Giving*

The days when an executive could order calendars with a company logo on them and distribute them—with little or no ceremony—to two hundred of his regular customers at Christmas have vanished. Such minimal gestures fall short in today's business climate, where executive gift giving has been elevated to a high art.

This shift to more and better gift giving has come about in part because of increased international trade. In many countries, the exchange of business gifts is a normal and expected part of business. But gift giving has also proliferated in the United States and not many executives dare to ignore their secretaries at Christmas—or even, for that matter, on Secretaries' Day. Real estate agents now routinely give a gift to customers who buy from them, and growing numbers of physicians send flowers to patients after surgery, to cite just two gift-giving occasions that did not exist a few years ago.

Business gifts serve several important purposes. They strengthen ties to clients and colleagues. They tell people that you like them and value their business or, if they are colleagues, their assistance in the workplace. They reward people for a job well done. Gifts are especially useful in establishing goodwill. And they should never be ignored as a means of apologizing for a social gaffe—such as the time you completely forgot a cocktail party a client invited you to, or the other infamous occasion when you accidentally spilled wine on a client's suit.

## When It Is Appropriate—and Inappropriate—to Give a Gift

As important as knowing when to give a gift is knowing when *not* to give one. For example, any time that a gift could be misconstrued as a bribe, it probably should not be given. Gifts are typically not proper when a major project or contract is under consideration or in negotiation, nor should they be given when you are trying to get someone's business for the first time. Give a lovely gift after the deal is consummated or the merger goes through, not before.

In some businesses and parts of the world, there is *no* appropriate time to give a gift. Some corporations frown on their employees accepting any kind of gift for a job they are paid to do, while others routinely accept—and give—gifts. U.S. federal employees and the employees of several other countries, for example, cannot accept gifts in exchange for favors. But in some parts of the world it is literally impossible to conduct business without passing around a few gifts, gratuities that to the average American may look more like a bribe. And finally, there are the places, such as China, where gift giving may be officially illegal but is nevertheless a common practice.

In the face of all these confusing practices, the only recourse executives have is to educate themselves about any regulations, customs, and traditions—local or otherwise—related to gift giving before offering anything. It is perfectly acceptable to ask the potential recipient or, in the case of international business, to check with the State Department or the embassy of the country you plan to visit.

Here are some typical gift-giving events and occasions for clients and colleagues around the world:

- When a project is finished or concluded
- At holiday time

- When someone receives a promotion
- To celebrate a personal event, such as a wedding, the birth of a child, a move, or a retirement
- To celebrate a business milestone, such as a merger, the sale of a company, a restructuring, or a new job
- When you have offended someone or forgotten something important
- When you have caused someone to go to great trouble on your behalf

Sometimes it is appropriate to give a gift for no reason at all, or for no reason other than to express your appreciation for the continuing relationship. An executive we know recently received a lovely little book designed to record people's birthdays. It came with a note from the giver explaining that since she had appreciated receiving several birthday cards from the executive over the years, she hoped the executive would find the little book useful. It was the perfect gift, all the better because it was totally unexpected.

## CHOOSING THE RIGHT GIFT

In today's sophisticated business climate, business gifts should be creative, interesting, and obviously chosen with a specific recipient in mind. Business gifts, however, must walk a line between the personal and the impersonal. This is true whether you are giving a present to a client or a colleague.

If you choose the wrong kind of gift, a client may be bemused or even amused, especially if he or she is from another culture where the rules about what is personal may be different. A colleague, though, is more likely to be embarrassed or even to feel sexually harassed by an inappropriate present. Sometimes the error is accidental, but if you have done your homework, you should be able to minimize these awkward moments.

Most of us know when we are giving someone a gift for purely business reasons and when we are attempting to turn a business relationship into something more personal. Some impersonal items of clothing—a scarf or tie, for example—are acceptable gifts, but others—jewelry, lingerie, or an outfit—are not. Sometimes what is acceptable varies with the business. Unless you are in the fur business, for example, a fur coat or other similar expensive, luxury gift would always be seen as accompanied by an ulterior motive.

If you discuss a book over lunch, and a client indicated he would like to read it, it's a good choice of gift, provided the subject matter is general. If you discuss a book that's filled with torrid sex, that's probably not a good gift to give to anyone—unless, that is, you are perfectly aware of what you are suggesting. A box of candy would be fine, for example, but a piece of chocolate shaped like a woman's leg (or a man's) would be tacky.

Appropriateness is important, too. It may well be correct to send a jar of expensive caviar to a colleague who has just given you a great deal of business, but it would not be right to give the same gift to a client who gives you very little business. The client would rightfully be confused about your motives.

As noted earlier, the best business gifts are chosen with a specific recipient in mind—as opposed to being mass-ordered for all clients with no one and everyone in mind. Even when your company mass-orders a gift, there are times when you will want to send an additional something extra along to a favored client.

There are several approaches to choosing gifts that are creative and interesting. Most of the executives we talked to had special tricks to help them choose great gifts. First, they avoid the expected and the bland. One woman we know shops for business (and personal) gifts when she travels. She's bought unusual leather address books in Italy, sterling letter openers in Mexico, small papier-mâché boxes in Poland, and sherry glasses in France. Usually she has someone in mind when she buys something, but at other times, she simply buys an item that catches her eye and figures out later who's deserving enough to receive it.

Another approach is to look for the best or most unusual of a rather ordinary item. A sales representative we know sends her clients a box of chocolate cookies at holiday time. But these aren't just any ordinary chocolate cookies. They are from the kitchen of one of San Francisco's most renowned chocolatiers. Their remarkable quality shows in everything from the box they come in to how they taste. They are made with excellent ingredients (chocolate comes in several levels of quality, and you should learn the difference), and the tops of the cookies are worked with an unusual freehand design that is the signature of the baker. Each cookie is a small work of art. The same search for excellence is useful when choosing wine or liquor. Look for examples that are top of the line, vintage, or rare. In other words, don't just give champagne—give vintage champagne.

Try always to keep the recipient's taste in mind when choosing a gift. Don't give liquor to someone who doesn't drink or food to someone who is dieting—or worse, sugar products to a diabetic. Even if you know people's interests, take care to buy something they can actually use. Golfers don't like gadgets, for example, but cooks often do—provided they are of high quality and truly useful.

## Food

Food is always an appropriate gift, but it's important to choose something unusual or geared to a client's tastes. Fortunately, the proliferation of gourmet foods and food stores makes these gifts easier than ever to choose. You can give a ham or turkey, of you like, but give the best one you can find—a corn-cob smoked ham or turkey from a special butcher.

In choosing food gifts, one smart idea is to select regional, American-made foods if you can. These are especially good as gifts to international customers. Italians won't be nearly so enamored of a bottle of balsamic vinegar as they will be of a good sharp American cheddar or Texas grain-fed steaks.

## Flowers—the Universal Gift

Flowers, like food, are a traditional and universally accepted business gift. They are appropriate in most situations and even expected in some others. They are also a good cross-cultural gift, although you do have to be careful not to give certain kinds in some cultures. (See chapter 11.)

Around the world, red roses are a flower for lovers and are thus not appropriate as a business gift. The best and safest choice of flowers is often a mixed bouquet.

## Tickets to Performances or Other Entertainments

Tickets are a tried-and-true business gift whose value can never be underestimated. Many companies buy season tickets to the opera or theater as well as box seats to sports events with the express purpose of using the tickets to entertain clients. These are invariably welcome. You have only to inquire about someone's interests to find the perfect set of tickets to offer.

Tickets are also a popular way of rewarding employees. Everyone from custodial workers to account executives appreciates an evening that's on the company.

## WHO CHOOSES BUSINESS GIFTS?

Many companies select gifts for employees to give clients at holiday time. Throughout the rest of the year, executives are usually on their own. If your company does not order gifts, it may be up to you to choose gifts yourself, or you may want to select a more personal gift in addition to the company's standard gift—at your expense, as a rule.

## WHO PAYS FOR BUSINESS GIFTS?

Many companies have a fund that executives can draw on when they want to give a gift to a client, but even so, most executives above a certain level sooner or later find themselves using their own funds to buy a special gift. Note: If your company does not have a fund, gift giving may be against company policy. You should check this and then follow the rules.

## HOW MUCH TO SPEND

Business gifts need not be lavish. Most will cost between $25 and $50, with $100 being the outer limit. The exceptions are certain high-end businesses where lavish gift giving is the custom and certain metropolitan areas, where the standard of living is high. A decorator we know thinks nothing of giving a $200 pillow or some other small decorator item to a good customer. A real estate agent who sells only $1-million-plus houses will give clients a larger and more substantial gift than one who sells $200,000 houses. But as a general rule, a small but appropriate gift is better (and often more gratefully received) than a large, expensive, and sometimes burdensomely inappropriate gift.

Ceremonial gifts—to celebrate a merger or the completion of a very big deal—are the exception to the spending rule. In such situations, the gift is often substantial. One executive we know chose a lovely sterling bowl, which he had engraved, to celebrate the merger of his law firm with another firm. Another American who had recently concluded a deal with a Japanese company to manufacture products out of a plant to be located in the American Northwest presented his new business partners with an Inuit sculpture he had commissioned for the event.

## TIPPING IS GIFT GIVING, TOO

It's important to remember that tipping is a form of gift giving, one that is much appreciated by the people who provide us with services all year long.

If your company takes care of tipping the elevator person, the cleaning crew, the super, and the doorman, then you need not worry about this except when the person has performed some additional services for you during the year. If so, then a gift, usually in the form of a tip, is called for. This is one time when money is the expected and appreciated gift.

## HOLIDAY CARDS

Greeting cards are an easy, inexpensive way to wish clients and other business friends well during the holiday season. The best business greeting cards are nonreligious. Messages such as "Season's Greetings" or "Happy Holidays" and ecumenical symbols such as bells or wreaths convey the warmth of the season. Such cards aren't hard to find; several direct-mail companies specialize in holiday greeting cards for business.

The only exception to nonreligious cards is if your business is religious-based. Then it is acceptable and perhaps even expected that you will send cards with a religious theme. It is not acceptable, though, to send Christmas cards to Jewish customers or Chanukah cards to Christian customers. This is why most businesses avoid the entire issue by sending nonreligious cards.

Some companies choose one card for everyone to send and distribute them among their executives at holiday time. If your company does not do this, then you may buy your own cards and send them to business associates. In either case, try to sign the cards personally, if possible.

## Office Collections

While gift giving to clients has mushroomed, gift giving among colleagues has not enjoyed nearly so smooth a ride, largely because so many offices continue to use collections to buy gifts for colleagues. Being forced to contribute to a joint fund for someone you know well and for whom you would prefer to choose a personal gift (or, worse, for someone you barely know) simply isn't most people's idea of generosity.

For this reason, many but not all offices have given up on collections. If a collection system is burdensome, then it may be time to disband it. But if the majority likes using collections as a way to pay for presents, then workers should feel free to continue to use them. If your office still takes collections, and you personally dislike them, there's not much you can do but contribute. Refusing to do so makes you look like the ultimate Scrooge.

How much you are expected to give depends on where you live and your position in the company. In places like New York City, executives ante up as much as $10 to $15 every time an office collection is taken. In smaller cities and towns, $5 to $10 (and often even less) is the expected amount. And if you can afford to give only on the low end, then that's what you should give, with no apologies.

Collections are harder on some persons then others, so everyone should be especially tactful when soliciting money.

## OFFICE SHOWERS

It is tempting to think of bridal and baby showers as appropriate office events, but they aren't. They should not be held on office premises, nor should employees routinely be expected to contribute to or attend such events. It is perfectly acceptable, though, for a group of office friends to meet outside the office to celebrate an impending happy event for a friend.

Finally, if some people in an office—especially a small one—are excluded from an extracurricular party, it is only polite to be discreet about discussing the party so no one feels left out.

## GIFT GIVING AMONG COLLEAGUES

Apart from office collections, there are some times when gifts are appropriate among colleagues as well as some times when they are not.

• **Managers to employees.** Managers generally give gifts only to those with whom they work closely, which often means secretaries and personal assistants. A manager with a department of tens if not hundreds of people could hardly be expected to give each one gifts on special occasions.

Gift giving among coworkers should be modest and appropriate but generous in spirit. It's better to find the perfect, small gift than an elaborate, impersonal large one.

• **Employees to Managers.** Even though managers give employees gifts, employees do not necessarily give managers gifts in return. A secretary or personal assistant in a large company should have no difficulty accepting a gift from a superior without feeling obliged to return the favor. Similarly, a midlevel or junior executive who receives a gift from the company's president or CEO is not obliged—or expected—to give a gift in return. In the latter instance, the gifts have almost certainly been purchased with company funds and are really a gift from the company.

A personal secretary or assistant who is especially fond of a supervisor might want to give him or her something in return, but this can be small, even if the supervisor's gift was substantial. A bottle of wine, a small, attractively packaged item of gourmet food, or a book the supervisor has been dying to read is fine.

Managers, in fact, should not accept expensive gifts from those who work for them. Should someone not understand this and give the manager an expensive or inappropriate gift, the manager should firmly but kindly return the gift and say: "This briefcase is really lovely, but I can't accept so expensive a gift from you. I'm going to have to return it."

* **Colleagues to colleagues.** Colleagues can and often do accommodate gift giving during the holidays in one of several ways: by agreeing not to exchange gifts, with an office grab bag, or by drawing names. It's usual to put a limit on the amount that may be spent for such gifts, and the limit should easily accommodate the lowest-paid staff member. No one should feel obliged to buy more gifts than he or she can comfortably afford. The happiest offices are the ones where fuss over presents is kept to a minimum at holiday time.

On other occasions such as birthdays, weddings, and retirement, a colleague gives a gift or not depending on how close he or she is to the other person. If the two share a personal relationship and would ordinarily exchange gifts, they may do so—but then the gift giving should be viewed as personal rather than business.

Gifts exchanged among coworkers should be amusing above all else. In one department of a small advertising agency where the small staff shares a genuine camaraderie, the support staff joins together to buy their manager a modest but pertinent gift. One year when they had all worked very hard and put in a lot of overtime, the staff bought themselves and their manager team socks—matching argyles, to be exact.

A few years later, when they had come to know their manager well enough to realize that he had difficulty getting up in the morning, they presented him with the largest, loudest alarm clock they could find.

## BAD GIFTS

The smart executive realizes that company morale rests to a certain extent on the kind of gifts that senior management gives to the staff. During a bad business year or a recession, everyone can understand that gifts will be more modest, but they won't understand or readily forgive a mean-spirited gift.

Consider, for example, the executive who insisted on giving all his employees a book he had recently discovered on salesmanship in a year when he had also made it perfectly clear to them that they had not met their sales targets. Even worse, he inscribed the book with this message: "Hope for more business next year."

Another executive, who had long complained about his secretary's shrill voice, gave her elocution lessons for Christmas. The lessons might well have been appropriate to give her, but not as a holiday present. Less obvious but no less thrilling was the manager who insisted on giving each of his employees a fruit basket when the company refrigerator was always stocked with fruit for clients and employees.

Gifts like these reveal a spirit lacking in true generosity, and employees often feel surprisingly wounded about such gifts—sometimes even more wounded than they feel about small bonuses. And speaking of bonuses, companies that give them should not view them as a substitute for gifts. They are considered part of an employee's pay package.

## WEDDING PRESENTS

Whether to invite coworkers and your supervisor to your wedding is a dilemma for many, especially since a wedding invitation typically obligates the recipient to give a present. Fortunately, in a business environment, the etiquette is a little different. Under certain circumstances, a person who receives a wedding invitation from a coworker or an employee is not obligated to give a present.

If you are a manager and receive many invitations, you may need to make a policy. You will attend all weddings or no weddings; you will attend weddings only of those who work directly with you but no others. Then find out what the company policy is about wedding gifts. Some companies maintain a fund that executives can draw on to buy wedding gifts for their employees. If not, a gift is optional so long as you are consistent with all your employees. When an executive or other business associate declines a wedding invitation, he or she is not then obligated to give a gift—unless, of course, he or she wants to.

As for whether you should send your manager an invitation, there are no hard-and-fast rules. The answer depends on the corporate culture, the size of your workplace, and your relationship with your supervisor or the company CEO. Some corporate cultures encourage socializing; some don't. It's more common in small offices to invite everyone. If you have a close relationship, the answer is usually yes. But if your supervisor is a distant person who doesn't socialize with his or her employees, then you may do better to forgo the invitation. If you work for a large corporation that routinely gives wedding gifts to employees, then you should send the CEO an invitation.

Equally confusing is whether an invitation to the entire office obligates everyone to give a gift. In many offices, especially small ones, the custom is to post a wedding invitation on a bulletin board rather than to send individual ones. Anyone can then decide to attend the wedding, although generally only close friends of the couple will choose to do so. A couple who is serious about inviting the entire office should post a sign-up sheet next to the wedding invitation and should also ask people individually if they will be able to attend.

Blanket invitations do not obligate anyone to buy a gift. That is part of their purpose, in fact. But if you accept such an invitation and attend the wedding, then you should buy the couple a wedding present.

There is one exception to this rule, though: Technically, people who are invited to a wedding but not the reception need not buy a present. In small towns, it is customary for coworkers to attend a wedding but not a reception and to feel no obligation to buy a gift. Still more technically, though, if the couple is not having a reception, then an invitation to a wedding obligates a coworker to give a gift if he or she accepts the invitation. It's rare these days, though, for a wedding and a reception invitation list not to be identical.

Also, keep in mind that a wedding should not be used to pay back business obligations. Clients and customers should not be invited to a wedding unless they also happen to be friends. A client who receives an invitation from someone who is not a close friend may decline it and not send a gift.

## Gifts to the Ill

It is a kindness to remember any colleague who is derailed by illness. If you are close enough to visit, do so. If not, you can always send a card or a small gift. A low-maintenance plant is a good choice for anyone in a hospital. Bouquets are better sent to someone's home so hospital staff do not have to take care of them. Also appreciated are candy or other nonperishable food gifts, magazines, a current book, or a lighthearted joke gift.

## Birthday Gifts

In the United States, few managers or businesses feel obliged to give birthday gifts to employees. Often, though, a company may foot the bill for a small office celebration consisting of cake and coffee. If employees are taking a coworker out for lunch on his or her birthday, and a manager or executive joins them, he or she may choose to treat everyone to lunch.

Managers also need not send birthday gifts to clients unless they want to. Birthday cards are another matter. One very kind editor we know manages to remember all her writers' birthdays and always calls to wish them a happy birthday, as well. It's a lovely gesture.

## Retirement Gifts

Retirement gifts are a rarity these days, since few employees stay with one company long enough to earn one. When a retiring employee does have a long record of employment, though, it is appropriate for the company to reward the years of service with a retirement gift. Individual colleagues also may give retirement gifts.

The best gifts are geared to the retiree's interests. One large publisher is known for finding out what its employees hope to do in retirement and then offering a very nice gift of encouragement. One retiree who planned to return to her first love of music was given a piano. An amateur cameraman received a Hasselblad camera. Not all companies are rich enough to indulge in such generosity, but more modest gifts still can be found. Someone who's hoping to garden, for example, would enjoy some gardening tools, while a fisherman would appreciate some new equipment or a truly wonderful fishing rod or fly box.

## Acknowledging a Gift

Business gifts must be acknowledged (as should any other gift) with a written thank-you note. As the recipient, you should send the note as soon as possible, preferably within a few days. A phone call is fine, too, but it doesn't replace a note.

## Presenting a Gift

There is a special art to presenting a business gift. First, make sure the gift is timely. Don't give a wedding gift six months after the wedding or a gift congratulating someone on a promotion two months after it happened. Your best friends may understand that you spent two years looking for the perfect wedding gift, but your business acquaintances will merely be baffled.

Second, make sure the gift is beautifully wrapped. This, too, is a compliment to the recipient. Take some time with the gift card you enclose. Saying "We're so proud of you for how you handled the seminar last week" is far better than saying "Congratulations on the seminar." Use the message to get your point across as eloquently as possible.

Finally, learn to present a gift well, with a bit of flourish and ceremony. In some cultures, this is mandatory, and there are even customs about how a gift must be wrapped and when exactly in the course of a meeting it should be presented (see Chapter 11), but even in the United States it's important to present a gift with a bit of ceremony. To do this, call the person who is being gifted so he or she is standing next to you. Speak briefly about the purpose of the gift so everyone knows why it is being given. Then, as you actually hand the person the gift, observe how happy you are to be presenting it.

Keep your comments focused on the recipient. Don't brag about how hard you worked to find the gift or comment on it or the time, effort, or cost involved in obtaining it. This is immodest and puts the attention on the giver when it should be on the recipient.

## KEEPING TRACK OF GIFTS

Last, with all the gift giving that goes on in any executive's career, don't forget to keep a record of what you have given and to whom. If you have a personal computer, this is easily done. Just create a file called "Gifts" and then log every gift you give, plus your ideas for what to give in the future.

You can also keep records the old-fashioned way by writing them down in a small notebook or keeping them on notecards. Whatever you do, though, don't trust your memory. After all the work you've done to come up with creative and interesting gifts, it won't do to give the same gift twice to the same person.

# 10

# *Business Travel and Conventions*

Whether you are going to an annual convention or traveling abroad as a representative of your company for the first time, a special etiquette surrounds business travel, and it helps to know how to play the game before you get there. In addition, because there is often too little variation in the kinds of entertaining that occur at conventions, this chapter contains some innovative ideas for impressing important clients when entertaining them in places other than your own turf.

## AIRPLANE ETIQUETTE

Most business travel today is done by airplane. For years airlines have promoted the friendliness of their employees, and frankly, it is about time the rest of the world reciprocated. All the airlines we interviewed, however, did report that their smoothest, most courteous travelers were those who traveled regularly on business.

## Reservations

Have your secretary or assistant make airline reservations and any other travel arrangements as soon as you have set a firm date for the trip. Tickets—and sometimes even boarding passes—can be picked up or delivered far in advance to cut down on the amount of time you have to spend waiting in airports.

## When Things Go Wrong

Not only are things likely to go wrong occasionally when you are traveling, but also many people find themselves falling apart over what would be only minor issues at home. It helps to stay calm. It helps even more to be courteous. The airline cannot help it if you are snowbound in an airport or city where you do not want to be snowbound. Remember, too, that airline personnel also suffer when passengers cannot get to their planned destinations; they are deluged by miserable people. Therefore, it only makes sense that they will dispense courtesies such as alternative transportation, free food, and lodging more freely to those people who have made an impression on them, and courtesy makes a far better impression than outrage. The best strategy is to be persistent but polite. Make it clear that you want to get out on the first available airplane, but be courteous and even chatty when telling airline personnel of your needs.

## When a Complaint Is Called For

Sometimes service is too surly to ignore or you have truly been done an injustice. When you must make a complaint while traveling, firmness and courtesy will help you to do so faster, and speed is usually the essential element of business travel. One executive was rushing to catch a plane when a security person managed to turn her purse upside down, causing her keys, a good pen, and a business notebook to go flying in all directions. No one made the slightest effort to help her retrieve her things. As she raced to catch her plane, her anger grew. She knew that security was separate from the airline and therefore of no real consequence to the person she would be dealing with at the check-in counter, but lacking any other immediate source to complain to, she decided to explain what had made her angry in the hope that the airplane employee would pass on the complaint.

She managed to complain with grace and tact, saying "I know this isn't your fault, but I was just treated rudely at security in a way that could have caused me to miss this plane. I would like to complain to security directly, but I am sure the airline would also like to know that their passengers are being treated carelessly. Would you please pass this on to your supervisor or someone who can talk directly to the head of security?"

Since the person you complain to about poor service is rarely the one who mistreated you (always ask to talk to the manager, if possible), the words "I know this isn't your fault," can go a long way to ease the pain of a coming complaint.

## On the Plane

Airline personnel, including flight attendants, are highly trained professionals and deserve to be treated with respect and courtesy. While a variety of special services are available, such as blankets, hot tea or coffee, aspirin or other medication, and magazines, these are extra services, so phrase any requests for them as politely as possible, and be sure to thank the person who helps you.

Flight attendants may have time to sit down and chat with the passengers, but this is not, in fact, part of their jobs, so don't expect it.

## En Route

Many business people plan to work while en route, which poses no problem unless the person next to them wants to chat. If opening a briefcase and spreading papers out over the tray in front of the seat is not enough to discourage chatter, a more direct approach is called for. It is quite polite to say "I would like to talk to you, but I am afraid I have to get this work done." Even if you are reading a book for pleasure (half the world views this as being occupied and the other half seems to consider it doing nothing), you can say "I'm sorry I can't talk right now, but I'm very absorbed in this book."

If the flight is short and you do plan to work, probably the best place to do it is in a window seat. On long trips, however, most experienced travelers prefer aisle seats for the easy access they provide to all parts of the plane. When you must cross someone's seat to leave yours, say "Excuse me" when leaving and returning. Rather than inconveniencing others sharing the row of seats, request any special services you can from the flight attendants.

Requests for special diets required for health or religious reasons are gladly met by the airlines, but you need to mention your needs when buying your ticket so the food can be ordered and placed on the plane. Nonpork meals, kosher meals, and special dietary plates are not automatically available to those who do not request them in advance, but almost any special meal will be prepared at no extra cost for a passenger.

## *Deplaning*

Since the flight attendants are the people who have hosted your trip and made it as pleasant as they could, there is one often overlooked courtesy that attendants truly appreciate: the passenger who says "Thank you" when deplaning.

If a flight has been delayed en route and you are late for an important meeting, it is helpful to explain quietly your need to deplane immediately to an attendant who may then make sure you are one of the first people off the plane.

### EXPENSE ACCOUNT ETIQUETTE

This section is not about how to fudge on your expense account. If you decide to do that, you're on your own. In some companies, some areas of expense accounts are left very open, but this is a matter of company policy, and there is no etiquette involved other than to check discreetly with others to see what is and is not possible.

It is assumed that business entertaining is done on an expense account, particularly when one is out of town at a convention or traveling in a foreign country. Rarely will a customer or client even offer to pay the tab. These things are simply taken for granted by people who are used to them, so if a business colleague asks you to join him or her under these circumstances, accept your guest status graciously.

On the other hand, when you are using an expense account to entertain someone, it is best to be discreet about it. A potential or current customer or client with any business sophistication will not be impressed by your ability to spend the company's money freely and may well be offended.

Occasionally a client, if given the opportunity, will suggest an expensive restaurant that you feel is out of line for the occasion or your expense account. One way to avoid this is to be ready with your own suggestion when asking someone to lunch or dinner. If you have forgotten to do this, however, and a client has grabbed the chance for a splendid freebie, you still can steer things a little more in the direction you would like them to go. Simply say: "Oh, I was thinking of eating at Jake's Steak House—it's quieter there, and I thought we would have more of a chance to talk." If the client insists on the fanciest restaurant in town, you are, of course, stuck, but it is a rare person who will have the nerve to do so.

If you are trying to opt for less lavish entertaining, never blame it on your company—this makes you look disloyal and it makes the company look cheap, neither of which is good for your image.

## CONVENTIONS

Aside from the travel that may be a routine part of a job, conventions are the other occasion when you may be called upon to represent a company. There is no denying the freer atmosphere that generally prevails at conventions—many people view conventions as one big party—and you will indeed want to participate in some of the festivities, yet a smart executive never forgets that the real purpose of a convention is work, namely, representing the company. Whether you are doing direct selling, making new contracts, presenting a new product line, or entertaining major clients, the main purpose is business, not socializing.

If you are in charge of setting up corporate display or doing the entertaining for a convention, let the previous year's budget serve as a guideline of what to spend this year. If files are available, it is also a good idea to go over them to see what has been done in the past.

## Entertaining Important Clients

Most of the routine matters of convention work, such as setting up and operating a display booth, will be handled by support staff, but the entertaining of important clients is usually too important a task to leave to anyone else. Draw up lists of persons you want to entertain.

If you are planning a big bash, make arrangements well in advance, since every other company at the convention will have the same idea. Food and service arrangements for parties to be held at a hotel are always made by the hotel. Functions outside a hotel, however, can be handled by a caterer, and this is where some truly innovative entertaining ideas can be put to work.

Call the local tourist's bureau and ask it to recommend interesting local or historic sites that might be attractive places in which to entertain guests. Find out whom to contact and how to go about making arrangements. Many towns have lovely small museums where small private dinners can be held; historical homes or other sites can often be rented, particularly if a company is willing to throw in a donation. Is there an outdoor concert center where you might invite people for dinner and a concert? Is the city's local opera or symphony group an outstanding attraction? Is there an ex-president's home or the home of some other famous person that might be available for a function? In a city with a river or an attractive lakefront, a yacht or riverboat party quickly comes to mind.

The hardest-working people at conventions often spend the entire stay in the hotel headquarters or the convention center, so they frequently welcome the opportunity to relax away from the hotel and see something of the place they are visiting—and it is an added bonus if the event is combined with seeing business associates. Too many companies resort to the monotonous cocktail-party-in-the-suite routine, so if you really want to impress a few top clients, try to find something interesting and of local interest to entertain them. Go for an elegant dinner. The people you are entertaining may have been subsisting for several days on hotel food caught on the run.

Invitations to such functions need to be extended well in advance of the convention. Either call or write an important client or customer to confirm the date. Competition for people's time is never more fierce than at a convention, so put in your bid early.

## Throwing a Big Bash

If you decide to give one big bash—it may be a tradition and it certainly is a good way to entertain a large group—do your planning well in advance. Talk to a hotel party planner or a caterer's representative. Find out exactly what services and what food can be offered, what kind of bar can be set up, how the food will be served, and what the quality and grade of the food will be, as well as what security arrangements can be made, if necessary.

Party crashers are a real problem at conventions, but when you are spending your company's money to entertain clients, you have a right to control who attends even the largest party. Equally important is to be on the alert for someone obnoxious enough to ruin the spirit of the party. Conventioneers who are making the rounds of several parties don't get any mellower as the evening wears on, so either you or someone you have appointed or hired should be authorized to remove unauthorized guests. (An unauthorized guest is someone who does not know the name of your company or the nature of its business or who cannot name a single employee.) Such people should be politely but firmly asked to leave. Never permit anyone to make a scene over removing someone from the room. No matter how public the occasion or large the party, it is still a business function, and it is better to let a pest or uninvited person stay than to use bouncer's tactics to get rid of him or her, a quick damper to any party.

The same general rules of good taste that apply to entertaining clients at lunch or elsewhere in your own community apply at conventions. Representatives of the company do not eat as if they were being served their last meal. They should function as hosts, circulating among the guests and subtly (or not so subtly, depending on the occasion) conducting business.

## INTERNATIONAL TRAVEL

In these days of multinational corporations, executives are frequently asked to represent their companies abroad or even to live in another country for several years. International travel—particularly for large companies—has become commonplace, whereas it used to be a plum that went only to company presidents and top executives.

Even if you are planning a personal trip to another country, sometimes it is possible to work this into a work assignment—so it certainly is worthwhile to announce your travel plans at work. If you work for a small- to medium-size company that has one or more clients or suppliers in the place you plan to visit, mention this to your manager and say you would be willing to handle any business that might come up while you're there. If you work for a very large corporation, it probably owns affiliates, branches, or even companies where you are planning to visit. Ask whether you can make arrangements to visit these facilities. Even if your visit is not official company business, any contacts you develop will pay benefits in the long run.

If, on the other hand, the day arrives when your supervisor calls you into his or her office and asks whether you would be available to go to Germany or Belgium next month, say yes. If this will be your first trip outside the United States, there is no need to announce it openly, lest it give your supervisor second thoughts.

When you are asked to travel in another country for the company, it is safe to assume that the company will make the arrangements for transportation, accommodations, and any business. Should your secretary fall heir to this assignment, have him or her contact a travel agency with whom your company has done business or any reputable travel agency or the airline you will fly. Airlines will make hotel reservations and reserve a car for you, in addition to booking the flight.

As with all business travel, assume that you will fly whatever class you would normally fly for domestic travel for business purposes—increasingly today, that is tourist class. An international trip is definitely not the time to splurge on a first-class ticket, since it is considerably more expensive than domestic first-class.

You or whoever is making the travel arrangements should also contact the nearest embassy or consulate of the country you plan to visit. Personnel there will be able to answer any specific questions regarding the business you wish to conduct and can also supply you with background reading materials on business and economic conditions in their country.

## Travel Documents

Some things you will need to take care of personally. First, you must obtain a passport if you do not have one. Call or visit the nearest passport office. You will have to fill out several forms requesting information such as your parents' birth dates, your mother's maiden name, and so on, so go prepared with some degree of family history in mind or written down.

It normally takes two to four weeks during nonrush season (fall and winter) to obtain a passport. If your business is pressing, you can make special arrangements to obtain a passport sooner. If you know you are going to need this special service, make it easy on yourself and be very polite to the person who helps you from the first second that you step up to the counter. In a real pinch, you can get a passport in twenty-four hours.

To apply for a passport, you will need proof of citizenship (a birth certificate or naturalization papers) and identification that includes your signature and a description or photograph of you. You are required to have passport photos when your application is made. You will need 2- by 2-inch square color photos—there are other restrictions, so try to find someone who specializes in taking passport photos. This is easy in a large city, for the offices of such photographers are always located near the passport agency and the photos can usually be made in one or two hours. In a small community you may have to wait longer.

Health certificates and smallpox vaccinations are no longer required by the United States, but some other countries still impose restrictions when there is an outbreak of a dangerous disease. As a precaution, as soon as you know you are leaving, call the local health department to check on any inoculations that might be required in the countries where you plan to travel.

It's always helpful to study the language of the country you plan to visit, and for any business trip you will need to brush up on customs. Chapter 11 contains additional information about conducting business internationally, and includes customs and traditions in most parts of the world.

It will also be flattering to your hosts if you have a working knowledge of the country's current news and economics—and, of course, the business you will discuss. No one expects or wants you to be an expert on a foreign country, but if a major election has just been held or if business has taken a downswing, your advance knowledge of such affairs shows your interest.

As when conducting any business travel, you will want to stay within the general budgetary practices of your company, but the guidelines are generally a little more lax in foreign countries. Many executives, for example, rent limousines for local travel. It saves them time and it impresses people with their corporate status.

If you want to do any entertaining, ask the advice of local people and then follow it. Do not expect to be invited to the homes of those you see during the day; this is done less frequently in other countries than in the United States.

If you want to see a business associate for dinner (either to work or to repay courtesy shown to you), ask him or her to be your guest at a restaurant and then suggest one that you have heard is good. It is courteous to ask if the spouse would like to join you, but do not be surprised if this invitation is declined. A sharper line is drawn between business and social relationships in other countries—and, of course, in some Middle Eastern and Asian countries, women are still not included in business of any kind.

## Security

Security has increasingly become a problem for high-level corporate executives traveling outside the United States. If your company has security officers, check with them about any special arrangements. It also helps to have a set routine and to stick to it, so that people who are depending on you to show up somewhere will become concerned if you do not. Common courtesy can also be put to work on this front. Befriend hotel and restaurant personnel and tell them, for example, whether you will be away for a few days or whether you are planning to return the same evening.

## TRAVEL PRECAUTIONS FOR WOMEN

Everyone has now become more aware of the special hazards encountered by women who travel alone. Hotels were once thought to be much safer than they have, in fact, proven to be. Yet obviously a female executive will want the same freedom to travel on business as her male associates. The solution is for you to be savvy about making your trip as safe as possible.

While it is imperative that you take certain precautions, the best way to do so is tactfully. You want to retain the support of the staff whom you may need to call upon for help, and you also want them to be aware of your presence so they will look out for you.

- When booking your room, ask your travel agent to inquire about safety measures for women, and choose a hotel that offers them. These include double locks on the door, windows that lock securely, rooms that are located in a safe part of the hotel, ample hotel staff to ensure your safety.
- If you will be conducting business meetings at your hotel, inquire about meeting rooms or consider a suite. Even apart from the safety factor (and the sexual harassment factor), it's not profes-

sional for anyone to hold a business session in his or her bed-room.

- Generally book yourself into a hotel rather than motel. You want to exit and enter through a lobby rather than going directly into your room. If possible, book yourself into a good hotel. According to a *Wall Street Journal* report, much of the crime against women in lodging occurs in bargain-rate motels.

- When you arrive, go to the front desk and make arrangements for your room quietly. Don't say anything so loudly that someone listening in the lobby can overhear. You don't need to whisper, but be discreet. In short, don't call attention to yourself as a single female traveler.

- You definitely don't want your room number called out in a public area of the hotel when the desk clerk summons a bellhop. Should this happen, you must assert yourself politely but firmly. Simply say: "Now would you please give me another room, and not call out the number when you summon the bellhop."

- Just outside your room, look around to be sure no one has followed you or that no one is lurking in the halls. This is a good procedure to follow anytime you enter the room.

- Once inside the room, before the bellhop leaves, check all spaces, including closets and the bathroom. Check the door if there is an adjoining room to make sure it is locked. Make sure the windows lock, and look outside them to be sure there are no ledges or balconies that would give easy access to your room.

- If the room proves to be unacceptable for security reasons (or for any reason), call the front desk and request another room. They will understand.

- If you ever come back to your room and sense that something is wrong, don't go in the room. Summon hotel security. There are legitimate reasons that something may be off about your room—a workman has been in it, the maid is cleaning it—but you don't need to take chances with this kind of thing.

- Be kind and friendly (but not overly friendly) to the hotel staff, so they will recognize you and look out for you.

- Don't be kind and friendly to strangers who approach you for whatever reason. Con artists and criminals who work big-city luxury hotels are slick, so they won't be obvious. They will often look and dress like the men you work with. The only solution, unfortunately, is to be guarded.

- Never open your door to anyone whom you are not expecting. You aren't even obliged to let the housekeeper in to turn down your bed, if the hotel provides this service. If you have requested room service, let the other person identify him- or herself. Don't say "Are you the room service that I ordered?" Be sure anyone at the door clearly states that he or she is from room service, and feel free to open the door with the chain on to double-check. Never admit a tradesperson without first checking with the front desk, and even then, think about asking him or her to do the work another time unless it is an emergency.

- Finally, it helps to realize that hotels have already done a lot to accommodate women who travel alone. While it's smart to take necessary precautions, it's unnecessary to become paranoid over your safety.

## A FINAL WORD

There are several places you can go to learn about foreign customs and ways of living. Begin with the consulate or embassy of the country you are planning to visit. Embassies are located in Washington, D.C., and can be reached in writing or by phone. Consulates, located in other large cities such as Chicago and New York, will also be happy to supply you with any information about local customs or business practices.

You can also check your library or bookstore for books on the country you plan to visit.

If you are planning an extended visit abroad or will be living in another country for any length of time, you may want to contact people who have lived there. Call your local university to ask if a faculty member has lived in the country of your interest or inquire about local clubs related to the country in which you are interested.

# 11

# *Etiquette in the Global Economy*

I t is intimidating to think about doing business in another language, let alone another culture. Few American men, for example,
know what to do when an Arab man wants to stroll down a street
of his country holding his guest's hand. (Let him. It's his country's
custom. But it's okay to remind him that we don't do it that way
when he's in yours.) What do you do when the main dish at dinner
in Mexico is sauteed gecko? (Start eating.) How do you know not to
enter a home in Chile until you have been invited? Or that in Malaysia
you must remove both your shoes *and* your sunglasses before entering
a home?

The answer is that you don't know the answer to these and
countless other questions unless you have taken the time and trouble to learn about other people's customs and traditions. In some
parts of the world, you must learn how to fit in before you can
hope to conduct business, while in other places, you can get along
without paying too much attention to the local customs. But everywhere, you will be infinitely more successful if you show an
appreciation of local culture and at least try to follow the local
etiquette.

## LESS ETHNOCENTRICITY, PLEASE

Seasoned travelers know they must recognize their own cultural quirks before they can hope to appreciate others' idiosyncrasies. While it's a real skill to be able to let go of your ethnocentric thinking and sink into another's culture, it's one that will contribute enormously to your business—and personal—success.

The United States is an unusually ethnocentric nation. Perhaps it is the fact that we are so geographically isolated that makes us this way, but one thing is certain: Americans dote on American methods, mores, and manners in a way that no Belgian or African, for example, does. We even believe the word "American" belongs to us exclusively, a fact that offends both our Canadian and our Latino neighbors who also consider themselves American.

The first rule of being well-mannered in the international arena, then, is to stop thinking that the United States is the center of the universe. (The rest of the world gave up this thought some time ago.) Refrain from making comparisons, especially unflattering ones, between how we do things and how the rest of the world does them.

## SKIP THE INSTANT FRIENDSHIP

The next step is to give up the instant friendship. Americans are very friendly. It is one of our best traits—and one of our worst, especially when we take it abroad. The rest of the world, almost without exception, is less casual than we are, less quick to use first names, more attentive to titles, and slower to allow friendship. We do better abroad when we're slightly—and sometimes considerably—more reticent. Hard as it may be to rein yourself in, it will help you infinitely in your attempts to conduct business in the international arena.

## GENDER RELATIONS AROUND THE WORLD

Recognize that gender relations vary with the culture. Where women have achieved prominence in business, they are more likely to be treated as equals. In terms of business manners, this means that men may not scramble to let a woman go through a door first, nor will they offer to carry her briefcase. They may not stand when a woman approaches their dinner table, let alone their conference table, to cite just a few social customs that have changed as women have entered the executive ranks. In places like France, where over 60 percent of all women work, and China, where women have steadily made progress toward equality, women expect and receive more egalitarian treatment.

But in places where women have not moved into the executive ranks, such as Germany or the Arab world, manners have remained more old-fashioned, not least because the women you encounter in these places will be executives' wives, not female executives. Men may stand, for example, each time a woman enters a room or approaches a dinner table, or hold a woman's chair for her.

It is also important to realize that in some parts of the world, how women are treated goes far deeper than mere manners and touches upon a complicated, often unwritten code of behavior. For a man (or a woman, for that matter) to touch a strange woman in a Muslim country, even to shake hands with her, is to risk giving grave cultural offense.

Your best strategy when dealing with women in business—and in social situations—around the world is a defensive one. Let your instinct guide you. Do use your own good manners as you would on any occasion, and, in addition, take a cue from others. It won't hurt to let a woman go through the door first anywhere in the world, and you can always be prepared to leap to your feet to greet a woman when others begin to do it.

Furthermore, be very conservative in your approach to members of the opposite sex, especially when you are in a religiously conservative country.

Female executives may also want to be aware of their behavior. In male-dominated cultures, such as Japan, women are rarely seen in positions of power, and there simply are no guidelines for treating female executives. Japanese businessmen have only reluctantly begun to do business with female representatives of corporations, and they still don't include them in the dinners that feature so prominently in their business dealings. Similarly, a woman might be sent to an Arab country as a representative of her country, but she would have to observe certain customs, such as never touching a male client—even to shake hands. She would also have to dress more conservatively than she might otherwise.

## THE POWER OF FACE

No one can conduct business in the international arena without understanding "face." This is what Americans refer to as "saving face," but the concept accounts for far more in other cultures, where it is often a dominant facet of everyday life. To Americans, saving face is more or less a psychological concept, nice to use to smooth the path but not necessary. In the rest of the world, face is built into the code of etiquette; it is obligatory; and woe to the person who does not understand its subtle nuances.

Face, which is most associated with Asian cultures, means in simplest terms that you do nothing to embarrass another person, especially one with whom you hope to have a business relationship. So motivated are the Chinese to save face that they will even give up a potentially lucrative relationship to do so. Put another way, this means if you embarrass them, they will prefer not to do business with you regardless of what they are giving up.

The primary reason that Americans fall short about "face" is that they do not bother to do the necessary research before they visit another country. They do not find out what will be embarrassing or awkward to others, but assume, with their American casualness, that the rest of the world will adapt to their freewheeling ways. Not true, and the savvy businessperson is well aware of this.

## LEARNING THE WAYS OF OTHERS

Although no book can teach you everything you need to know to behave correctly in another part of the world, there are a few things that can help you get started. It helps, for example, to know how to greet people, visit with them without giving offense, and give gifts at appropriate times and in an appropriate manner. Surprisingly, it may not help to know much more than this before you go because so much of the world is rapidly becoming more Westernized. As a result, manners that were perfectly acceptable even two years ago may be outdated today.

Even with advanced Westernization, it is important to do some homework about others' manners. In many parts of the world, it is still a mistake—a big one—to think you can enter into another culture and attempt to conduct business there without knowing something about the local etiquette. Western manners may be spreading, but the world remains a collection of ethnic enclaves, each with its own customs and traditions. These must be honored by the traveler passing through who hopes to penetrate another world, and they must especially be honored by anyone hoping to build a business relationship.

## GREETINGS AROUND THE WORLD

Handshaking is the most common form of greeting around the world, but you also are likely to be greeted with bows, applause, and prayerful hands. In some parts of the world, looking someone in the eye when you meet gives offense, while in others you will be perceived as shifty or dishonest if you do not meet someone's eyes directly. Using both hands to shake hands or patting a new acquaintance on the shoulder, gestures that Americans regard as friendly, are considered overreaching in some places. On the other hand, in some places, a handshake will be more physical than Americans are used to.

## VISITING CUSTOMS AROUND THE WORLD

Similarly, it helps to know how to behave when spending time with others. Will people invite you into their homes, or should you anticipate that all entertaining will be done in public places, such as restaurants? Is it more important for you to entertain someone in public or to invite the person to your home? And when you are out with someone socially, when is it acceptable to conduct business?

## The Not-So-Universal Art of Gifting

Around the world, it is generally accepted that you bring a gift when you are invited to someone's home. But what you bring and how it is presented can also be of enormous importance.

For that matter, the whole question of gifts is one of considerably more importance outside the United States than at home. The executive who works in the international arena must understand the gift-giving customs of others.

Even though the customs regarding gifts may differ, nowhere in the world does business-related gift giving not incur some form of obligation. It is important—and sometimes difficult—for Americans to understand this.

Giving the wrong kind of gift—one that is either too expensive or too cheap—can get a business relationship off to a bad start or kill it before it has a chance to flourish. Also alien to many Americans is the idea that a bribe, even a gift of money, is not only acceptable but required in many parts of the world. Gift-giving customs in some countries are even styled so as to make the giving of a bribe easier. There are also places where gifts are not given until negotiations have been completed, lest they look like bribes. Americans who want to be successful must learn to put aside their own code of ethics and accept others' ways of doing things.

The presentation of a gift often takes on great significance. Sometimes it is better to present a gift in front of others while at other times it is better to do so when you are alone with the recipient.

It's also difficult for Americans, who love spontaniety, to understand that in many parts of the world, a gift will not be opened in front of the giver. Even the thanks for a gift that is just right may be less effusive than most Americans expect. Never fear: If you have chosen well and presented well, the gift will still accomplish its intended purpose of cementing relations.

A small point that Americans are often unaware of: When giving a gift almost anywhere in the world, it is better to enclose an informal or handwritten note than a preprinted card. Cards have not yet won the widespread acceptance elsewhere that they have in the United States.

Finally, on the subject of gifts, here's a tip for female executives offered by one woman who travels the world: Women should think about giving a gift that is suitable for a man's wife or family as well as for him, especially in a part of the world where women don't participate in business as fully as they do in the United States. It helps to smooth the path with a wife who might otherwise be resentful or less than sympathetic to a female executive. (The exceptions to this are the Arab countries, of course, where it is in bad taste to even acknowledge that a man has a family.)

## The Power of U.S.-Made

It's a nice touch to give American-made gifts when appropriate. These need not be expensive, although what people favor will vary around the world. Here are some suggestions, both expensive and inexpensive, for "American-made" gifts:

- Anything made of local products—a paperweight or small vase made of indigenous marble, wood, or stone
- Pure maple syrup or maple candies
- Albums and compact disks
- U.S. collectors' stamps
- U.S. mint coins
- U.S. tools and gadgets
- U.S. small appliances—including things electronic (But make sure they are made here. Don't give the Japanese an electronic datebook that was manufactured in Japan but bears an American label.)
- Sports equipment
- Mugs
- Photographs of the United States by U.S. photographers
- Drawings or prints by U.S. artists
- Photography books about American life or art
- T-shirts or other mementos from U.S. colleges and universities

- Western jewelry
- Pottery
- Native American art or jewelry
- Cowboy art (runs the gamut from trinkets to Remington sculptures)
- Sterling from U.S. jewelers—letter opener, small bowl, cup
- Steuben glass (very expensive but America's own)

A word of warning: When planning gifts for those in other cultures, take care to do your research, especially with regard to animal motifs or colors. The Chinese would find anything with a fox, the symbol of fertility, or a badger, the symbol of cunning, highly amusing when coming from a potential business associate. Red is the color of good luck in China, and would thus be a good choice there, but it is the color that casts spells in Mexico and would thus be somewhat suspect for anyone anticipating business dealings.

### Flower Power

American executives also need to be well versed in the art of flower giving since flowers are a universally accepted gift around the world. They are almost always an excellent gift to take to someone's home. A few guidelines will help you choose flowers around the world:

- Favor an uneven number of flowers over an even number, but don't give someone thirteen flowers in a Christian country where the number is considered unlucky.
- Skip red roses. The flower of lovers, they are considered too intimate in most places.
- Some flowers—chrysanthemums in France and Germany, lilies in Italy—are funeral flowers and should be avoided as a gift.
- Some colors—yellow in Mexico and white in much of Western Europe—connote death and should be avoided.

And how do you avoid some esoteric posy with bad connotations that is not described here? Try putting yourself in the hands of a competent florist. Floral gifts are best sent rather than hand-carried, anyway. If using a florist is not possible, choose a mixed bouquet, on the theory that at least any offense you give will be limited to one or two flowers.

Whatever you do, don't let the rules intimidate. Flowers are a wonderful gift, especially when you do not know someone very well and wish to show your appreciation for almost anything. The expense of buying good flowers is always well worth it.

## DRINKING CUSTOMS

As Americans have begun to reduce their alcoholic intake, they have encountered new problems in their international business dealings. In some parts of the world, most notably Japan but also in other parts of Asia as well as Eastern Europe and France, being a teetotaler can put a real damper on business relations. The Japanese, as a rule, do not settle down to serious business until they have tested a guest's stamina with food and drink. Sharing a few shots is hospitality personified in many parts of the world, and of course, in France it is an insult not to indulge in the many excellent wines.

It is not surprising, therefore, that abstainers need some ploys to help them get through an evening of alcoholic merriment without giving offense. Here are a few guidelines that will help:

- If you can drink moderately, do so.
- If you cannot drink at all, then offer a medical excuse. It is the only excuse that is truly acceptable in a culture where alcohol is part of the social ritual.
- Consider feigning drunkenness. This is not so far-fetched as it sounds. Some Japanese executives we know have confessed to using this tactic.

And remember this: What drinkers seek is conviviality. If you can supply this without indulging or overindulging, you will have accomplished your mission.

## Aren't There Any Universals?

In this morass of confusing and detailed rules, can anyone hope to visit another country and not commit a faux pas of the kind that is likely to kill a business deal? The answer is an unequivocal yes. Consideration and common sense can get you through almost any business situation anywhere in the world. And good intentions help a lot. This means if you do make a mistake, own up to it and apologize. If you even sense that you have erred, say you're sorry. Here are a few hints on handling others' cultures anywhere:

- Talk less rather than more about the United States. Less ethnocentricity from Americans is always appreciated. For that matter, talk less rather than more whenever you are unsure what is expected of you. Reticence rarely gets anyone into trouble.
- Show respect—any way you can. Show respect to the elderly, to children, to the poor, to clients' families. If you are in a culture where it's expected that you trample old people to get past them, you can always learn to do this. But if you're in a culture where the utmost respect is shown to the elderly, and you haven't managed to show any, you can't undo the error.
- If families are mentioned or present, ask about them. If they aren't around or aren't mentioned, don't ask. Don't ask if they are healthy; don't ask if they exist. The reason for this is that lots of people have close family ties, but the ties don't always spell pleasure. As an example, in much of Latin and South America, close family ties are cherished, and your business friends will be pleased if you are considerate enough to inquire after the health of family members whom you may not even have met. But in the Arab world, family ties are more often a source of pressure, and wives and children, to say nothing of brothers and cousins, may be kept out of sight. It is rude to ask how they are, where they are, or why they aren't joining you for dinner.
- Don't tell anyone to do anything—open a gift, go through a door first, talk business, or remove an article of clothing—that he or she seems inclined not to do. Let others take the lead and you will be more in sync with their culture.

- Try to look at the big picture. Other cultures really do view the world from a different perspective. An Indian, for example, may not concern himself too much with the return of a personal favor since she assumes that what she has done has also helped her soul.
- Punctuality qualifies as another universal. In some places, such as Western and Eastern Europe and most of Asia, tardiness is tantamount to rudeness. The Chinese consider lateness a character flaw, the sign of an insincere or inconsiderate person. So it's important to be on time in these parts of the world. In other parts of the world, people are not especially prompt about appointments, but they know the Western habit of punctuality and will consider it something of an insult if *you* do not arrive on time. Only in Latin America are people relaxed about running a little late.
- Finally, make it your goal to fit in without making a fool of yourself, especially when courting business contacts. In Japan, for example, you will rarely be offered a Western-style chair. Instead, you will be expected to sit on the floor on folded legs. It's okay to ask for a cushion and to sit cross-legged if you can't sit on a folded leg for any length of time—and few Westerners can. If you simply cannot do something, better to own up to the fact than to make a fool of yourself trying.

    The one exception is eating. Always try to be adventurous with new food. Around the world it's one of the greatest compliments you can pay any host.

## ETIQUETTE AROUND THE WORLD: A BRIEF TOUR

### Western Europe

*Greetings*
The typical greeting in Western Europe is a handshake. But unlike in the United States, where people shake hands only the first time they meet or if they haven't seen each other for a long time, in Europe

the handshake is a more common greeting, often used each time two friends meet. The Western European handshake is more reserved than the United States greeting. Skip the shoulder thumping or two-handed grasp until you know someone really well.

### Visiting

Mild offenses at home can be major ones elsewhere in the world, so keep your hands out of your pockets when talking to someone, don't chew gum, sit up straight in chairs, and don't cross your legs so the soles of your shoes stare someone in the face. Use titles (even university professors and others who don't use "Dr." in the United States often use those titles socially in Europe), and be slow to use first names.

Learn to call people what they prefer to be called. In the British Isles, use "British" instead of "English." A person from Scotland is a "Scot." He or she is never "Scotch"; that is a beverage.

Much of the time, don't discuss politics in Ireland or Great Britain, for example, where politics is a problem. On the other hand, the French like a good political-philosophical discussion over dinner (or lunch) but, in general, the more conservative the culture, the farther away you should stay from touchy topics.

Dress is generally more conservative throughout Western Europe than in much of the United States. Suits and jackets are expected of men during the day and at night, and women do not usually wear pants to work or to evening social occasions.

### Gifts

Gift giving is less ritualized in Europe than in Asia. You need not exchange business gifts at all, but if you visit someone's home, you should bring a small gift of candy, flowers, or liquor. Don't give U.S. wines in the countries that pride themselves on their wines.

If someone does you a big favor (invites you to a weekend at his or her country home, for example), then a present is called for. Western Europeans like silver. A tray or small bowl is a good choice. Avoid giving gifts for the home or personal use that are too intimate.

Perfume, for example, is considered an intimate gift in most of Western Europe.

Don't embarrass someone by giving a gift that is too large, either. Remember this is not ritualized gift giving but is, rather, a purely personal option. It is better to save gifts for a second visit, so you don't seem overeager. Similarly, while you are under no obligation to give any business gifts, if you do, give one after a big deal has closed, not before, or the second Christmas you do business with someone rather than the first.

Gift wrapping is a nice touch, but avoid white wrapping paper, and white, black, or brown bows, which are not considered festive enough. An enclosure card is a good idea, but use your own informal with a handwritten message rather than a printed card.

### Eating

Throughout Western Europe, table manners are much like ours, and you will feel comfortable despite a few minor differences.

## Eastern Europe

### Greetings

Greetings are the same in Eastern Europe as in Western Europe, with the handshake being preferred.

### Visiting

Visiting is also the same as for Western Europe. Take flowers or candy when visiting someone's home.

### Gifts

Gifts are slightly different in Eastern Europe than in Western Europe. People welcome products from the West, even utilitarian ones such as small appliances, mechanical toys for children, coffee, or Western delicacies. When food is in short supply, it is usually a welcome gift, although try to bring something festive without being ostentatious. Good food gifts are chocolates, pastries, coffees and teas, also liquor. It is okay to give small articles of clothing that would be considered too intimate in Western Europe—gloves, nylons, perfume. It is also okay to notice what is in short supply and give that to someone.

## Japan

### Greetings

The Japanese have been bowing in greeting for hundreds of years, and Westerners have been shaking hands for hundreds of years. A problem arises, therefore, when East meets West, both want to please each other, and there is no protocol for what to do first. To complicate matters further, the Japanese exchange business cards before either bowing or shaking hands.

The Westerner often tries to cover this awkward moment by shaking hands and bowing at the same time, but, to the Japanese, the more natural order of events is to exchange business cards, bow, and then shake hands.

While in the United States, the Japanese often try to follow the U.S. custom of shaking hands, but in Japan, they are pleased when Westerners make an acceptable pass at their customs. Technically, three degrees of bows are used by the Japanese, but the very deepest, called a *sai-keirei* (sigh-kay-ray), is rarely used except by very elderly Japanese in the presence of their emperor. This leaves the medium (or formal) bow and the light bow.

The medium bow is about 45 degrees deep and is held for several seconds, perhaps three or four. Holding a bow is a sign of respect. Done right, the hands rest on the thighs.

The light bow, most often seen today, is about 20 degrees and is held only for a second or two. Your hands may be at your sides or on your thighs.

If your hands are full, make a downward gesture as a show of respect. Similarly, if you are seated at a banquette and cannot give the proper greetings, apologize. The Japanese look at the floor when meeting someone for the first time. A direct stare is considered immodest.

Another Japanese custom is the exchange of name cards or business cards. This card exchange delineates who you are and how much respect you should be accorded, an important fact in a hierarchical society like Japan.

Not surprisingly, there is an art to exchanging cards. First, move slowly and carefully, as this is a small ceremony. Pull out a pristine card (nothing less will do anywhere in the world, actually), and be sure to hold it so it can be read by the recipient.

Because the Japanese have difficulty pronouncing English names, just as we have trouble pronouncing Japanese names, it's helpful to get your card printed in both languages. Just be sure the Japanese is facing the right direction when you present the card.

Hold your card with both hands, and hand it to the other person, simultaneously accepting his or her card and announcing your name and saying, "Pleased to meet you."

As soon as you receive the other person's card, read it and then determine how much respect he or she should be accorded. If you have just accepted the card of a CEO or other important official, or if you simply want to make a good impression, give a medium bow and hold it for two or three seconds. If the Japanese visitor should bow more deeply to you because of your higher rank, let him and return the gesture with a light bow.

## Visiting

The Japanese entertain foreign male visitors at long dinners in restaurants or other public places. Women still are excluded from business entertaining. They don't feel you really know someone until you have eaten and drunk with him, and they may not settle down to discuss business until several of these social events are out of the way.

They are also loath to let anyone else pay the bill, so either let them do it or, if it should be your responsibility, make arrangements in advance to pay.

No one in Japan says "no" directly. The language has no word for no. So visitors have to learn to read the signals that mean no—drawing breath through teeth; saying "sah," a meaningless expression that nevertheless seems to mean "no"; or observing "That will be difficult to do." Remember, too, when talking with Japanese that laughter often signifies embarrassment.

When visiting a Japanese home, it is customary to remove your shoes at the entrance on a special floor called the *genkan*. Place your shoes neatly together pointing toward the outside. You will be given a pair of slippers that can be worn everywhere except in a room covered with tatami mats. Never step on this straw mat that covers the floors in some traditional Japanese homes when wearing shoes or slippers.

In one corner of the home will be the *toko-no-ma* (toe-ko-no-mah), the family's altar. You need to know two things about it. One is to treat it with respect. Never rest anything on it. Second is that the seat nearest it is the seat of honor. Never take this seat without being invited to do so.

The Japanese are a modest people who are often put off by Westerners' gregariousness. This is important to remember when talking to them, and also when visiting in Japanese homes. For example, don't compliment a Japanese host's home excessively, or he or she may feel obligated to give you something. When you are offered anything, from a cup of tea to a gift, defer at first. Similarly, when you are complimented, deny that you could be that good.

Fruit, whiskey, sake, or candy are welcome gifts when visiting someone. Even small gifts taken to someone's home are presented and received with both hands, somewhat ceremoniously.

## Gifts

The Japanese may well be the most gift-giving people in the world. This is a regular part of conducting business in Japan, and, yes, it is intended to obligate you—and vice versa. The Japanese even have a word—*giri*—for the type of business gifts that impose an obligation.

Since the Japanese do not open a gift in front of others and all gifts are wrapped, people can easily incur an obligation through the presentation of an expensive gift. In the Western ethos, this might be considered a bribe, but the Japanese do not view such gifts in this manner.

No occasion is needed to give a gift, but two business gift-giving occasions that must not be missed are Chugen, or midyear on July 15, and Toshidama, at year's end, or January 1. Other occasions that call for gifts are bereavements, birthdays, illness, graduation, and promotion. Most of the acceptable gifts for these occasions are the same as in the West. Personal accessories, desk accessories, wine, and liquor, and sports equipment are all suitable presents. When someone dies, take or send a wrapped gift consisting of money, incense, flowers, fruit, or food.

When the Japanese travel, they often take along *o-tsukai mono* (oh-tsee-key-moe-no) or small "things to be used." These gifts, which consist of fans, Japanese paper, scarves, inexpensive electronic gadgets, are given to anyone who does them a favor along the way. The Westerner would be wise to think in these terms when visiting Japan. For these kinds of gifts, small uniquely American products are good: herb tea, candies, state pins, statues of the Liberty Bell or Liberty, long-handled shoe horns.

Gifts should always be presented in a low-key way. You may have gone to considerable trouble to get the right gift, but this should not show. Do not expect the recipient to open a gift in front of you or even necessarily to be effusive in thanking you. This is not the Japanese way.

There is a definite art to wrapping gifts in Japan, and the task is best left to department stores, where it will be done correctly. Black and white papers, for example, are used only for bereavement gifts. Western bows and ribbons are unattractive to the Japanese, who consider rice paper and bows of twisted paper to be tasteful. And indeed, Japanese packages are quite elegant once your eye adjusts to the seeming austerity.

Finally, let the Japanese give the last and the biggest gift. It's their custom, after all.

## China

### Greetings

At a formal gathering in China, foreign guests may be welcomed with a round of applause. It is appropriate to applaud in return. Handshakes are often then exchanged.

Name cards (business cards) are as important in China as in Japan, and you should have yours printed in both languages. Get them printed in Asia or you run the risk of their being done in an old-style script that is no longer used in China.

### Visiting

So important is eating in China that the traditional greeting is "Have you eaten?" Thus it is not surprising that foreign guests are treated to a welcome banquet.

There are basically two types of meals in China: family style and banquet style. Chinese banquets start at six-thirty and end at eight-thirty.

At a banquet, the guest sits facing the door, and the host sits with his or her back to the door. Honored guests' seating starts to the left of the host.

No one lingers after a banquet. When the meal ends, the party is over. But the meal itself may last through ten or fifteen courses, so pace yourself.

At the end of a trip or the conclusion of an important negotiation, foreign visitors are expected to entertain their Chinese hosts at a banquet. Everyone who was invited to the welcome banquet should be invited to the farewell banquet. There are four classes of banquets, and the one you give should be the same rank as the one you were given. Restaurants that handle banquets can help you with this.

Don't jump to entertain at home in this country, because the Chinese consider this more lowly than outside festivities.

*Gifts*

Gift giving is as important in China as in Japan, but bribery is officially illegal, so the rules change a little. In terms of bribes, the size of a gift does not matter; it is the giving of it that gets someone in trouble. Despite this, gifts are often given and willingly accepted, even though occasionally someone gets in trouble for accepting one.

Good gifts to high-ranking officials are household appliances and electronic equipment. Lower-ranking officials enjoy desk accessories, books about travel, pens, calendars, and magazine subscriptions to American magazines such as *National Geographic, Arizona Highways,* and *Natural History.*

Some visitors to China report that personal gifts should be small enough so the recipient can take it home in a pocket without attracting attention.

It is expected that you will exchange small gifts when first meeting someone. Don't give surprise gifts, though, because this will cause the recipient to lose face.

Always have a reason for a gift. It makes accepting it easier. Be sure your gift is personal and explain why it is right for the person. One executive, for example, who presented a Chinese business friend with a striking set of calligraphy brushes, explained: "I've seen how beautifully you write, so I thought you might enjoy these."

Don't give money because U.S. currency, including commemorative coins, is illegal in China. Don't give clocks to anyone Chinese because our word for clock sounds like their word for funeral.

Personal or one-on-one gifts should be given when you are alone with someone. Keep the gift giving low key. It is not appropriate to brag about or even discuss the lengths to which you went to get a gift. Lavish gifts are neither expected nor acceptable.

Gifts are exchanged at a Chinese banquet, especially if an important deal has just been concluded. These are usually collective gifts in that they are presented to a company or to a group of people with whom you have worked. You should make this clear when you present the gift to the group's leader. Appropriate banquet gifts are photographs of the U.S., plaques, and small artworks. Jade is considered a prized and lucky material in China, so anything made of it will be especially treasured.

Two big Chinese gift-giving occasions are October 1, National Day, and Chinese New Year in February.

Finally, gifts may be wrapped, but there is no special etiquette to follow here as there is in Japan.

## Throughout Asia

Although the rest of Asia comprises many cultures, much of these countries' heritages have been handed down from China, and many of the same customs and traditions are followed.

### Greetings

Except in Japan, handshaking has become the norm throughout Asia. The exception is Thailand, where you may be greeted with the Buddhist *wai,* a gesture in which both hands are gently folded together in a prayerful position at chest level.

### Dining in Asia

Everywhere in Asia you will be expected to eat with chopsticks. Try to use them if you can, not least because forks may be difficult to come by. Asians consider it barbaric to spear food. A few guidelines will help you cope with chopsticks:

- Ask for help if you need it. Your hosts will be flattered and pleased to help.
- Use chopsticks as a scoop if you cannot manage more intricate movements. (Think about practicing at home for a week or two before you leave.)
- Use the small end of a chopstick as your eating utensil, and the large end to serve others.
- Rest chopsticks on your plate or a chopstick rest when not using them. Never rest them in or across a rice bowl.
- You may use your rice bowl as a safety net, holding it close to your mouth as you eat.

- Sometimes rice is the last course. If you need it to eat other courses, apologize and ask for it.

In Malaysia, pork, the staple of Chinese cooking, will not be served, and Buddhists and Hindus around the world do not eat beef. Don't ask for these foods when dining with people who avoid them.

## The Mideast

### Greetings

Arabs are a warm people who greet others of the same sex with kisses and hugs. Kisses are planted on both cheeks, and are the common greeting between men. Israeli men also sometimes kiss on greeting, although a handshake will be more common when greeting a westerner.

### Visiting

Men often walk hand in hand in Arab nations, and it would be rude not to go along. Similarly, the distances people stand for conversation are closer than in the West. It is best to take a cue from your host, but don't back away lest you seem rude.

Muslims pray five times a day. This means that business grinds to a stop. You will not be expected to pray, but you will be expected to respect the custom and show absolutely no annoyance with it. The Muslim week runs from Saturday to Thursday, and Friday is the Sabbath. In Israel, everything closes down for twenty-four hours on Friday night—the Jewish Sabbath.

You may be invited to an Arab man's home, but you will not set eyes on his wife or children, nor should you ask about them. Israelis, many of whom have family ties to Westerners, will welcome you into their homes—and will welcome your inquiries about their families.

Because you are in a religiously conservative part of the world, conservative dress is expected of you. In Arab countries, this means business suits for men and nothing tight-fitting, low-cut, or short-sleeved for women.

Arabs dress in their traditional garb, long flowing robes for men and women. Do not ask an Arab man to remove his headcovering or a woman to remove her veil.

Hardly anyone wears a suit for business in Israel, and casual dress seems to be a point of pride. It's not a bad idea for a westerner to wear a suit to a first meeting, though.

### Gifts

In Arab countries, gifts of course are given to men only. Welcome ones are fountain pens and mementoes from the West such as books, maps, small boxes, and other somewhat ceremonial objects. Gold is favored over silver in this part of the world.

Do not give a gift to an Arab businessman when the two of you are alone. It will be perceived as a bribe, plus receiving a gift in public makes the host looks good. Also, do not give gifts on the first meeting, because this, too, looks like a bribe.

Don't admire objects an Arab owns because he will feel obligated to give them to you. It is flattering to an Arab, though, to ask for an English-language edition of the Koran.

Present and accept gifts in a Muslim country with the right hand or with both hands, never with the left hand alone.

### Eating

Arabs are known for their hospitality and their meals, which often start considerably later than ours. You may be expected to take several helpings, so pace yourself.

Alcoholic beverages are becoming more common even in Muslim countries, but Muslims do not drink, so do not ask for alcoholic beverages. Even when drinking is permitted, drunkenness is considered gauche and definitely does not lead to camaraderie.

You may be expected to eat with your fingers—your right fingers only, please.

Israeli food is both mideastern and western. Eating customs are the same, though, as in the West.

When visiting an Israeli home, take the same kind of gift you would when visiting a Western home.

## Latin America and South America

Latin and South America encompass a lot of territory, but most of the countries share customs and traditions, and these are for the most part European in origin. The most important thing in Latin America is to fit in. Without doing this, you will never be able to conduct business successfully there. For example, most of this part of the world closes down for siesta every day. If you let the siesta get you down or try to get someone to conduct business during this period, you will meet with the most subversive kind of resistance. Nothing much will get done, as we noted, until you settle into the local customs. And all things considered, the pace of life is quite pleasant. Everything gets done in good time.

### Greetings

Latin Americans shake hands on greeting and, once they know you, may embrace you as well.

In this culture, people touch more than North Americans do. Actually, almost any culture touches more than the more patriarchal United States, but, in Latin America, it is necessary to accept the touching—man to man—if you want to do business. A businessman may touch your lapel or fondle your shoulder to press his point, for example, and you should accept it rather than moving away.

### Visiting

Latin Americans also stand closer than North Americans find comfortable, and they consider eye contact very important. When attempting to do business in Latin America, stand closer and look longer and more directly at your clients than you ever would in the United States.

Latin Americans do not consider punctuality important, and they do not usually expect it of others. Meetings routinely begin twenty to forty minutes later than scheduled, especially in Mexico City, where the traffic is always bad.

Latin Americans, like many Asians, do not say no directly, largely because they want to please you. Therefore, you must learn to read the gestures that add up to no. Expressions such as "That will be difficult" or "Possibly we could do that," for example, are really polite ways of saying no and should be interpreted that way by North Americans. Occasionally someone will even say yes when no is meant.

The daily clock is completely different in Latin and South America. Work begins gradually sometime between eight and ten. Between one and three or four o'clock, everything closes down for siesta, mainly to avoid the hottest part of the day. Stores and businesses reopen after siesta, and the business world goes round until about eight. Dinner is at nine or later.

Latin and South Americans may well entertain you in their homes, in which case you will meet your host's family, on whom he or she will dote. Welcome gifts are flowers, candy, liquor, or toys for the children if you know what is appropriate.

Even though the climate will be hot, businesspeople should wear business dress, especially in the big cities, where life is sophisticated in the manner of Western Europe.

## Africa

Africa is divided into three distinct parts, each with its own customs and culture. There are the Muslim countries of the North, whose customs echo those of the Mideast; the black African countries; and South Africa. Within these countries there will be diverse regional differences in customs and traditions.

### Greetings

Throughout much of black Africa, handshaking is the accepted greeting. There are exceptions, however, and a business traveler should be prepared for them.

### Visiting

Be prompt even though your host is not. Africans do not consider punctuality important, but they are aware of the Western emphasis on it and may be insulted if you arrive late.

Similarly, you should dress conservatively even if your hosts don't. But be warned: In the large old colonial capitals of Africa, a business suit is de rigueur. Women should wear skirts, if not suits, for business meetings.

Use last names and titles until you are invited to be more familiar.

Do not presume to ask an African what "tribe" he or she belongs to. Once you are acquainted, you may ask what "group" or "ethnic group" he belongs to.

In some parts of black Africa, only men are included in invitations, and you will not meet a man's family when you visit his home. In other parts, wives may be included. To be safe, take a gift to a man, not to his wife or family. Small presents that are appreciated include pens, calculators, state pins, statues of the Liberty Bell and Liberty, and ties.

Gifts are not usually part of the normal conduct of business, but in some African countries "dash," or tips, are very common and very widespread. They are expected before a service is performed. Dash may be expected for everything from watching your car to facilitating transportation—both personal and commercial.

The distances between two people of the same sex is closer than in the United States. Let the other person establish it.

Africans do not think of themselves as belonging to a backward region of the world and should not be treated to conversations that in any way condescend toward their culture or industrial development.

South Africans are more like Europeans than Americans. Expect more formality in everything from table manners to dress when visiting.

## India

India is very much a blend of East and West, and the customs vary depending on which part of the country you are visiting. Expect to encounter Hindus, Buddhists, Muslims, and Sikhs.

Eating customs and the type of food vary greatly from region to region, so you should do research before you go.

You are safest everywhere using your right hand to touch food and pass and receive gifts.

Relations between sexes are far more formal than in the West, and visitors should respect this.

Gift giving is expected only after you have become acquainted or when you are invited to someone's home. Flowers or candy are excellent gifts.

Punctuality is expected throughout India.

Dress is typical of that found in large Western cities even if your hosts are not wearing the same kind of clothes. Do not ask a Sikh man to remove his turban.

## Australia

Americans are very much at home doing business in Australia because it is so much like the United States and because Australians like Americans. Most customs will seem very familiar. First names, for example, will be used right away, and the casualness of life will be very familiar. It would be difficult to give offense in Australia so long as you maintain the same good manners that you use at home.

It is wise to remember that these basic hints are mostly a starting point on a very complicated topic. More detailed information can be obtained from the U.S. State Department as well as the embassy of the country to which you will be traveling. A number of books also can help you learn about other cultures. We recommend the following:

*The Travelers' Guide to Asian Customs & Manners,* by Elizabeth Devine and Nancy L. Braganti (New York: St. Martin's Press, 1986).

*The Travelers' Guide to Latin American Customs & Manners,* by Elizabeth Devine and Nancy L. Braganti (New York: St. Martin's Press, 1988).

*The Travelers' Guide to Middle Eastern and North African Customs & Manners,* by Elizabeth Devine and Nancy L. Braganti (New York: St. Martin's Press, 1991).

*The Travelers' Guide to European Customs & Manners,* by Elizabeth Devine and Nancy L. Braganti (Deephaven, MN: Meadowbrook Press, 1992).

*Japanese Etiquette & Ethics in Business,* by Boye Lafayette De Mente (Lincolnwood, IL: National Textbook Co., 1986).

*Korean Etiquette & Ethics in Business,* by Boye Lafayette De Mente (Lincolnwood, IL: National Textbook Co., 1988).

*Chinese Etiquette & Ethics in Business,* by Boye Lafayette De Mente (Lincolnwood, IL: National Textbook Co., 1989).

*Do's and Taboos Around the World,* by Roger Axtell (New York: John Wiley & Sons, 1990).

Traveling abroad on business offers a rare opportunity to look into others' lives. And manners, which are anything but universal, are one of the invaluable and fascinating keys to opening another culture.

# 12

# Dressing for Business:
## MEN

Ever since the day Adam felt he needed to clothe himself in a fig leaf, clothing has been an important status symbol. It denotes class and reveals much about one's position in the world. Dressing is the way eccentrics give vent to their need for individuality, and it is also the way that most of us show that we belong.

The problem, then, with putting on a suit every morning is that there are many subtleties that must be mastered to make that suit say what you want it to say about the kind of person you are: mobile, intelligent, right for your profession.

## THE UNWRITTEN DRESS CODES

Dressing, like so many other areas of good manners, is not something anyone will necessarily tell you about—if you aren't doing it right, that is. In fact, by the time you hear that your dress is inappropriate, permanent damage may well have been done to your career. For example, if a superior calls you in to tell you that full-face beards or any kind of facial hair is not welcomed by your company, he or she has probably been seething about it for several months, and unless you are prepared to shave off that beard immediately in a gesture of deference and then toe the line very carefully, it is safe to assume that your image has already been tarnished.

Of the executives in large corporations, banks, law firms, and mid-size businesses who were interviewed for this book, none admitted to having a written dress code for their executives. When we wondered about the fact that so many bright young executives had obviously figured out how to dress, largely because of the great similarity in their appearances, one executive laughed and commented: "Why should we have a dress code? The rules are all right there in unwritten form. Those who dress to fit in get ahead. Those who don't—well, they get lost along the way, unless they're too damned brilliant to let that happen to them."

But "fitting in" doesn't necessarily mean dressing in a white shirt and a conservative three-piece suit. The key to successful—and tasteful—dressing lies in observing the successful people in your profession (and your supervisor is most likely one of those people) and modeling your dress after theirs. You may not be able to afford the same quality of materials as they wear, but the styling should be similar.

For those who bristle at the notion that what they put on their backs is nearly as important as what is in their heads, cheer up. As one company president noted, "Society's much looser now, thank God. I have a mustache now, but when I sold computers for four and a half years, I never wore anything but a white shirt, conservative suit, and a very short haircut. And in four and a half years, I reached the senior executive management level by playing that game, which was more important to me than having a mustache simply because it was in vogue. How you dress depends on the value judgments you make for yourself. An individual must look the part he or she chooses to play. Then, too, in many businesses, things have eased considerably, although anyone who wants to get ahead should think long and hard about whether he fits the image of the company he works for— whether his appearance would irk the most conservative board member." The important thing to remember is to dress to suit those figures of authority who control your professional destiny—if you're planning to climb to the top, that is.

## Buying a Business Suit

Suits are the basis of a business wardrobe. The first consideration in buying one is quality. Buy the best you can afford. On the other hand, no one in business should overdress—a $20,000-a-year employee who strolls in wearing a different custom-made $1,000 suit every morning is immediately suspected of being frivolous at least and, at worst, having his hand in the till.

Business suits are either off the rack or custom. The difference, aside from price, is the amount of special alterations one receives. With an off-the-rack suit, the store will offer you a first fitting, and you will do well to insist on a second fitting when you return to make sure everything has been done according to your specifications. Good stores never charge for alterations on their suits, which range from $250 to several thousand dollars if you buy a designer suit.

A custom suit costs $500 and up. You can have any fabric and any tailoring detail or style you wish, and if you are buying a custom suit, your tailor or salesman should be telling you how to look well dressed.

### Fitting the Suit

Regardless of the kind of suit you buy, you need to know how it should fit. First, consider the jacket—something that not enough men do. It should fit the back securely. The collar should not stand out at all from the shirt collar, and it should not wrinkle, either vertically or horizontally, across the back when you are standing normally.

Move around in a jacket; it should feel comfortable and should not gap or wrinkle anywhere. Make sure the vents hang properly. Vents on a jacket ensure ease of movement. Generally, two vents are considered sportier and more high fashion, but they also allow greater freedom of movement. A single vent is more traditional, and many older conservative men have clung to it, despite changing styles. A ventless jacket is very stylish—and also looks best on a slim body in a meticulously fitted suit. Double-breasted suits are currently enjoying enormous popularity, so much so that even men who look like sausages in the style are stuffing their bodies into them. They are a high-style look that is considered too flashy for some businesses. If you buy one, take a long, hard look at yourself in the fitting room to see if the suit really looks good on you, and then be sure the jacket is fitted smoothly.

Take a good look at the sleeve of the suit before you buy it. Setting in sleeves is one of the hardest tasks of tailoring and is often poorly done on cheap suits. Look to see that they are smoothly sewn in. You should be able to move your arm freely without causing the jacket to hike up. The correct, best length of a jacket depends on your body proportions, but, for most men, it should be long enough to rest in your bent fingers when they are cupped around the bottom of the jacket when you are standing normally. The sleeve should come to about midway through the wristbone— enough to allow for a half-inch of shirt cuff to show when your arms are hanging at your sides.

A vest requires fitting, too. It should fit smoothly with no wrinkles or gaps, especially at the armholes. For the most successful fitting of a suit jacket and vest, wear the same style and weight of shirt that you plan to wear with the suit when you are shopping.

Pants should not be tight; they should fall straight when you are standing and should not bag anywhere. They should have loops for a belt if you are buying a traditional, fairly conservative business suit.

Cuffed pants come and go with the current fashion, although cuffs always continue to be around for casual wear. They should be about 2 inches deep and worn only on lightweight business suits to avoid the appearance of bulk.

If you have cuffs, have the pants length finished straight across. Their length is best when they break slightly (but only slightly) over the tops of your shoes. A major fault in fitting suits is to make the pants too short, so have them done ½ to ¼ inch longer than you think you need.

Uncuffed pants should also break over the tops of your shoes. In the back, they should drop to the tops of the heels of your shoes. Needless to say, you should be wearing the shoes you plan to wear with the suit when it is fitted.

## *Following Fashion or Fad*

Most business suits are strictly tailored. Avoid extra flaps, colored stitching, self-belts, patches or contrasting fabric anywhere, yokes, and anything that is part of the leisure suit look.

Designer suits, while beautifully cut and frequently better fitted than other suits, are still not acceptable in many businesses. They look effete to many older conservative businessmen, who have yet to accept the fact that men's styles do change, but if you work in a profession where high fashion is accepted or even expected, designer suits may well be the norm. They are worn more in large cities.

Watch styles carefully and avoid new ones until they start to show up in the more conservative stores. Single- or double-breasted suits can look dated if they are not the current look, as do lapels that are two wide or too narrow, uncuffed pants when cuffs are in fashion, and loosely fitted suits when slightly more fitted ones are in style.

## *Colors and Fabrics*

The best colors for business suits are gray, beige, blue, and shades of these color families. Also acceptable are pinstripes, chalk stripes, and muted plaids. Avoid bright colors (especially in the blue and brown family), pinstripes in garish colors such as rust and scarlet, and any plaid that is not muted.

Men's suits today come in a variety of fabrics. Natural fabrics are favored—wool, preferably, or cotton or linen for summer. Suits are also being made of new blends of cotton and linen, which provide the best attributes of both fabrics, and tropical wools, a wonderful lightweight fabric that can virtually be worn year-round.

Some very finely made polyesters look and feel just like wool. If you truly cannot tell them from the real thing, by all means go ahead and buy them. Their great advantage is that they are practically wrinkleproof.

## Taking Care of the Suit

The number of times a suit can be worn before it needs pressing varies with the individual and the fabric. It goes without saying, though, that a wrinkled suit looks messy and should be sent off for pressing if not for cleaning.

## Buying Shirts

The well-dressed man has learned the secret of buying shirts to go with suits rather than the other way around, or worse still, simply collecting shirts and ties. A general guideline is to have three or four shirts for each suit if you have three to five suits. If you have five to ten or more suits, you can make do with fewer shirts for each suit. Since a shirt is worn only once before laundering, the need for any one color may vary depending on how quickly your laundry can turn around your shirts.

Shirts to go with the basic conservative business suit should be, of course, fairly conservative. This generally means that white, pastels, and pinstripes are most acceptable. Avoid shirts darker than a suit and try to select a tie that is darker than the shirt, or you may find yourself looking like an underworld figure. Shirts should be of dull-finish, flat weaves. Cotton is best, although some men can wear magnificently tailored silk shirts. Shiny fabrics, prints, plaids, wide stripes, and bright colors are out, except for those who work in professions where high fashion is accepted. (See "Dressing for Your Profession" on p. 260.) If you opt for striped shirts, those made of white fabric with stripes in subtle colors are preferable. All shirts to be worn under suits should have long sleeves.

Custom-made shirts are expensive, but they are a smaller luxury than a custom-made suit—and they do have status. Custom-made shirts always fit better than ready-mades. Custom shirts often do not have pockets, presumably because people who can afford custom-made shirts need not carry such mundane items as pens and pencils. Very small and very large men may find it to their advantage to order custom-made shirts for a better fit. In large cities, some stores have semicustom-made shirts. A variety of fabrics and styles are offered and the shirts are made to your measurements. These shirts sometimes start as low as $35 but can go much higher. Sometimes a minimum quantity must be ordered.

## Buying Ties

When you buy shirts to go with a new suit, also plan to buy coordinating ties. The first thing to look for in a tie is fit: It should come to the tip of your belt. Most ties are 55 to 56 inches long. Choose a tie you already own that fits perfectly and use that as a guide when shopping. The more expensive a tie is, the longer it is likely to be, so very short men may find it necessary to order custom-made ties. A tie should have a tab on the back through which the smaller section passes.

Silk is the best tie material, but silk and polyester is a good combination. Again, the best rule of thumb is to buy nothing that looks synthetic, but to go ahead and buy any synthetic that looks and feels real. Wool challis is another good tie material, and cotton ties are often worn in warmer climates. Knit ties also enjoy periodic popularity. The material must be thin enough to hold a neat knot.

Ties have broken the conservative mold more than any other item of men's dress, and it is now acceptable in many professions (but not all!) to wear flowered prints, large abstract prints, and even ties that tell stories, reveal your politics, or support a favorite charity. This outburst of colorful and evocative ties came along about the same time suspenders made a comeback—and both can be traced to the movie *Wall Street,* in which Michael Douglas set a new standard for moguls' dress.

In conservative circles, the smaller the print, the more acceptable the tie. Polka dots and diagonals are perennial favorites. Club ties and ties that display heraldic emblems, golf balls, fishing gear, and other such tiny prints are acceptable in most corporations, law firms, banks, and businesses, but in sales they may not be, depending on who your customers are. The same is true for Ivy League ties. Some midwesterners and westerners see them as signs of the eastern establishment and just don't like them. The best basic all-round tie is a muted paisley.

For most business purposes, bow ties are considered too eccentric, although they are still popular among some scholars, lawyers, and others who have risen high enough to wear anything they please.

## BUYING OTHER ACCESSORIES

When executives were asked what they did to prepare for an important event, such as a meeting with a client or a presentation, they all replied that they got haircuts and had their shoes shined. And while any well-dressed man should know enough to keep his shoes shined and well heeled, many are at a loss as to the best kinds of shoes to wear for business.

### *Shoes*

Black and brown are the best shoe colors, and laced or wing-tip shoes are worn by most conservative businessmen, although a general loosening in shoe styles has become apparent over the last few years. Plain slip-on shoes are fine as long as they aren't decorated with flashy hardware.

### *Jewelry*

Flashy jewelry may be fine for disco dancing on Saturday night, but it does not fit in with the corporate image. A wedding band, a small gold ring, and a plain watch are the only acceptable jewelry as far as most corporate business, bank, and law firm executives are concerned. Small gold or silver cuff links are fine, too.

Avoid any symbols that give away your personal life: class rings, which have never had any status, Masonic rings or insignia, religious symbols, and school or regional ties. Anything reminiscent of your school days, as a matter of fact, lacks status and makes a man look immature.

Judging from the number of fancy watches seen today, one would think they are power symbols, yet where it counts—in the board-room and the CEO's office—they aren't. The only real status symbol is a very expensive, plain, thin gold watch. Since most young exec-utives cannot afford this kind of watch, you should buy a plain serviceable watch with a leather band—the kind that looks more expensive than it is. If you can lay out the cash for a good-name watch from a jeweler such as Tiffany or Cartier, by all means do so. What even the best class ring won't get you in status, a good label on a watch will.

## Handkerchiefs

White handkerchiefs tucked in the front pocket are still seen in many conservative business suits on older men. They look a bit stuffy on young men and a silk scarf in a conservative color or pattern has now become acceptable. The scarf should coordinate with the suit you are wearing.

## Leather Goods and Umbrellas

Successful dressers pay attention to accessories, too. For example, umbrellas of powerful, prosperous men are invariably black. A small good leather wallet or, better yet, a pocket secretary that slips in and out of the breast pocket is a sign of a successful man. Briefcases, particularly for men, should be of the best leather you can afford and brown or black. A small canvas bag is fine for carrying postwork sports equipment.

## Hats

There are no hard-and-fast rules about hats, probably because they have been out of style for so long that most young men can't re-member a time when a man had to wear a hat to be well dressed. Until the late 1950s, a hat was required to complete the outfit of any sophisticated man. Today they are perhaps the only item where a man can express his personality if he chooses to do so. Providing you have the nerve, you can wear anything from a ten-gallon number to a Greek fisherman's cap. Some executives even adopt unusual hats as their one departure from totally conservative dress.

## Gloves

Gloves are no longer required as a sign of good manners. They are, however, a necessity in much of the country during the winter. The glove that works best is leather and brown, black, or dark gray, whatever looks best with your overcoat.

## Coats

Although styles in men's clothing have loosened considerably in the past decade, the beige trench coat—preferably with a good label in it—is the totem of the successful executive. Dark trench coats, unless they are very high style, don't have as much status as khaki ones. More leeway is permitted in overcoats; cloth, suede, and leather are fine. Cashmere is the ultimate status symbol for conservative businessmen.

The emphasis on conservatism may rankle some—particularly those young executives who know they look good in some of the new cuts of men's clothes. This is understandable, but it is helpful to keep in mind that most executives are older and more conservative. Furthermore, while dress for men has become considerably more interesting in recent years in terms of variety in styles and fabrics, this revolution has mostly taken place in the large cities such as New York, Chicago, and San Francisco. In the rest of the country, the executive who must be impressed with your ability to dress to fit the corporate image is still conservative and a bit old-school.

## GROOMING

Needless to say, any well-dressed man falls far short of the mark if his personal grooming standards are not as impeccable as his taste in clothing. Deodorants and antiperspirants (most come in combined forms) are a necessity; colognes and scented aftershave, popular a few years ago, are now considered sophomoric unless they are very discreet.

## Facial Hair

Facial hair, a symbol of antiestablishment freedom, is still frowned upon in many places, especially corporations, law firms, and banks. This is a shame because a little well-placed facial hair has been known to hide a wide assortment of defects, such as a receeding chin, lips that are too thin, and youth.

Some young men continue to go against the mainstream on the subject of facial hair, which, as many executives interviewed for this book repeatedly noted, often solicits a comment from the supervisor. Unfortunately, by the time the supervisor comments, he or she is usually pretty steamed about the hair, and the damage to the rising young executive's image may be irreparable.

Goatees are definitely unacceptable, possibly because they look too satanic, and handlebar mustaches are thought to indicate a fairly large ego, to say nothing of looking just a little silly on a grown man. Even the executives interviewed who didn't know what handlebar mustaches were called knew that they did not like them on their young executives. Full-face beards—a stage that almost no one in a corporation ever gets to anyway—are mostly out of style these days.

## Dressing for Your Profession

Each profession has an unwritten dress code. A good way to observe the varying codes is to visit a large bank in a big city and ride the elevator with a group of executives, all of whom will be dressed surprisingly alike. Move on to a federal court building and observe the dress of successful lawyers. People in publishing and advertising, doctors, and salespeople all seem to have their sets of unwritten rules about dress. The most successful salesmen, several surveys have shown, are invariably those who are best dressed *and* those who dress most like their customers; so salespeople, take note.

Interviews with people in various professions indicated that there is a lot more room for individual tastes than one might expect. No one gets fired for owning one high-fashion suit or wearing bright ties or even a bow tie occasionally. Very powerful men even use their dress as a power symbol. One executive, who numbers among his acquaintances many chairpeople of the board and company presidents, told of a very successful businessman who always wore a ten-gallon hat while he worked. He wore the hat inside as well as outside his office—a gesture that was both eye-catching and a definite sign that he was the most powerful person in the room.

If you feel the need to be eccentric—and who doesn't occasionally?—go ahead. Just do it carefully. Don't use eccentricity as a power tool, the way the man in the ten-gallon hat did, or at least not until you own the company. Finally, be eccentric only because you truly want to. Otherwise, the gesture falls flat.

## Corporate and Financial

If your goal is to reach the top of the corporate or financial ladder, then be prepared to dress in only the most conservative clothes. Most corporate presidents, bank presidents, and stockbrokers wear the conservative, traditional business dress described throughout this chapter. Beards and mustaches are barely tolerated in corporate boardrooms, and any sign of flashiness is frowned upon and considered frivolous, if not effete, and cause for not promoting someone.

In a corporate setting, men who wear jackets to work often follow a prescribed etiquette about wearing them at work. It goes like this: A man may remove his jacket while working in his office or moving around his immediate office area. In some offices, he may even roll up his shirt sleeves. But whenever he moves outside his immediate work area (to visit a higher-up, attend a meeting, or go out for lunch, for example), on goes the jacket. This unwritten dictum holds even on the hottest summer day.

## Law

What a lawyer wears depends on the firm. Some old-line conservative firms are more traditional than any business corporation. One young lawyer who went to work in a very conservative Wall Street firm was appalled to learn that no one removed his jacket and rolled up his sleeves during the work day.

Lawyers who spend a lot of time in courtrooms soon learn to dress for judges and juries. One lawyer who earns over $400,000 a year said he always wore a slightly frayed white shirt for one particular old-fashioned judge, who disliked rich lawyers. Many lawyers in large cities have led the peacock movement in male dress, while others own closets full of traditional business suits. If you go to work for a law firm, take note—quickly—and dress the way everyone else does. Since lawyers deal with clients, senior partners keep an eagle eye on the dress habits of youngbloods. If you are shooting for a partnership, you simply cannot afford to dress differently from the older members.

## Medicine

Among the professionals, doctors veer farthest from the traditional, conservative look, but doctors also experience very little pressure to conform to any standard of dress, as they basically work for themselves. Their sign of authority is the white office coat, and they seem to feel little need to use their other clothing to show power, so doctors frequently wear sports coats and casual slacks at work. Many doctors also wear short-sleeved shirts, since a longer sleeve could interfere with their work.

## Sales

Sales is the most difficult category of all to describe because there are so many different areas. The best general guideline is to dress at least as well as your customers and to dress in the same style as they do.

## *Publishing, Advertising, and Art-related Fields*

Publishing, advertising, and art-related fields are the professions where a man can show a little individuality and even eccentricity in dress—and sometimes be rewarded for it. Wild ties, dark-colored shirts, striped or pastel shirts with white collar and cuffs are all generally acceptable in these professions. Again, though, be sure to check the atmosphere of the particular place in which you happen to work, which, like all other places of work, will have its own unwritten dress code. Dress is infinitely more individual in these professions.

## *Formal Attire for Executives*

As an executive, you may on occasion be expected to represent your company at a formal event. Business events are usually black tie. White tie is rarely seen these days, certainly not in business circles.

If you get invited to enough events, it may be worthwhile to invest in formal evening attire. Otherwise, rent what you need from a reliable company, and follow the salesperson's advice about what to wear. While in some fields it will be acceptable to wear the latest style, unless you work in the fashion industry, a formal event is neither the time nor the place to experiment with color or unusual styles. Elegance in men's formalwear invariably is reflected in a conservative cut and style.

# 13

# Dressing for Business:
# WOMEN

Since women entered the executive ranks in the early 1970s, the question of what constitutes appropriate—and effective—executive dress has been a topic of hot debate. Would dressing like men help? Some years it did, and women took to wearing pinstripe suits, often with ties. Other years, women were chastised for the menswear look. Following the advice of an ever-proliferating group of experts who dedicated their lives to telling executive women how to dress, they added lace handkerchiefs and, silliest of all, lace bodysuits under the pinstripes.

In the late 1970s, John T. Molloy systematized it all for women in his book *Dress for Success.* The trouble with Molloy's style of dressing, though, was that it was lacking in personality and individuality. Plus, by the time it had been adopted by every executive wannabe, it was no longer the right look for executive women.

Throughout much of the past twenty years, executive women have lived in fear of not looking powerful or successful enough. Then sometime in the mid-1980s, working women grew weary of following others' dictates and began to ignore the office-success merchants, the fashion designers (who had *no* idea what women should wear to work), and anyone else who tried to tell them what to wear. The result: Female executives today look more varied, fresher, more stylish, and, best of all, more interesting than at any time since women began worrying about how to dress for the executive suite.

While creating an individual look is possible, it still does not mean that you can ignore the unwritten—and occasionally written—dress code that exists in every office. Lawyers still do not dress like book editors, and advertising people do not dress like bankers. Even while asserting your own sense of individuality, you still must be attuned to the norms within your profession. And there are few professions that tolerate much eccentricity.

With the price of women's clothing at an all-time high, most executive women out of necessity settle on a classic look. This means a wardrobe built around separates, which can be mixed and matched to create the impression of more outfits than are actually owned. Of enormous help to women planning a wardrobe like this is the book *Color Me Beautiful* by Carole Jackson (New York: Ballantine, 1987). First published in 1980, this fashion classic has taught millions of women how to wear the colors that flatter them, but, more important, how to coordinate a wardrobe.

Depending on where you live and what profession you work in, suits are acceptable, as are blazers, shirts and blouses and skirts. Pantsuits are acceptable on some occasions and, in many offices, so are good-looking slacks, a shirt, and a sweater or jacket. Actually, pants wax and wane in acceptability, depending on current styles, where you' live, and the profession you are in. Those working in conservative professions such as law, banking, and financial services rarely wear pants to work, and, if they do, they tend to wear a matching jacket. In less conservative professions, such as advertising, publishing, and fashion, pants are worn when they are in style.

More important than what you choose to wear is the ability to dress tastefully—in short, to show that you know the right thing to wear on any given occasion.

## How to Look Like an Executive

Discreet signals that say you know you belong at the top can be conveyed through dress. Secretaries and clerks, in part because they are young, and the young wear different fashions these days, tend to dress in a campy, high style that is not appropriate to the executive woman. They also get away with wearing cheaper clothing.

As an executive woman, you need not wear designer clothes, but you should be buying good bridgewear (the name the fashion industry has designated for women's clothes that fall between mass-market ready-to-wear and designer garb). A few well-designed and -tailored suits are better than many sloppily sewn, badly tailored, cheap ones.

For women as for men, the key to dressing for any profession is to dress for the particular office in which you work and to use the small status symbols that show you belong to your profession.

## The Signs of Status

For more than a decade, clothes and accessories with a designer logo have enjoyed enormous popularity, but with the pared-down 1990s well under way, such obvious status symbols may be on the way out. In any event, what's important is not the logo, but quality. Those in the know will see that you are sporting a good leather briefcase or a well-made leather purse even when there is no flashy designer label on it. Logos may come and go, but quality always impresses and is worth the investment.

In conservative professions and in large cities, most women build a wardrobe around neutrals—beiges, taupes, and browns, blues and grays, burgundy and forest green. In summer months and in the South year-round, lighter colors are worn.

Also try to wear good wool or linen skirts or pants and wool or cashmere sweaters rather than polyester, pastel outfits. Where you buy your clothes does not matter one whit so long as they manage to convey the look you need to get ahead.

Good shoes are a smart investment, but they should be appropriate. In the same way that a man would not appear at work wearing hiking shoes with a suit if he knew how to dress, a woman headed for the top would not wear platform shoes in a bright color when an elegant pump in a dark color would convey her message more effectively.

## SELECTING AN OUTFIT

Some women dress poorly because they do not know how to buy a well-fitting garment that is also well made. First, let us consider the matter of quality.

Natural fibers connote quality. For years now the world of fashion (and most of us) have been crazed to wear only natural fibers. Cotton, linen, wool, and silk have been our status symbols, and, indeed, they are classic fabrics that are acceptable everywhere. But they pose problems, especially for women who work twelve-hour days. Linen wrinkles five minutes after it is put on, and while wearing the wrinkles may be fine for the art-gallery circuit, it doesn't work in most law firms. Cotton also looks worn after a few hours. For years, many secure, fashion-conscious women have ignored the injunction to buy only natural fabrics and have worn polyester blends, which do not wrinkle as much. Polyester is now even working its way back into favor, in a fiber called microfiber, which looks, feels, and supposedly even breathes like silk and resists wrinkling. New blends of old fibers are giving them new life as well and, more important, are turning materials like wool and cotton into year-round materials. Other good additions to a wardrobe are silk-wool, cotton-silk, linen-cotton blends, and new (or revived) all-season materials like gabardine, tropical wool, silk crepe, and wool crepe.

Try to buy clothing that is well made. Look for seams that are wide enough to withstand the tension of normal wear and that also can be let out if necessary. Facings, too, should be wide enough so they are not constantly flipping out at inopportune moments. The seams should be neatly and evenly sewn, particularly where stitching shows, such as at the cuffs and around the collar. The plainer a garment, however, the less likely that poor quality will be obvious, so if you want to buy an inexpensive blouse or shirt to go under your expensive new suit, look for a simple style.

Skirt length is another problem. Whether you want to stay with a conservative just-below-the-knee look or go with a high-fashion length is a matter of personal taste, as well as a matter of noting what is appropriate in your office or profession. Try to strike a happy medium without being afraid to show your individuality. If you like a new look but it is not being worn in your office, go ahead and try it and see what the reaction is.

## Clothes That Fit

Fit is just as important in women's clothes as it is in menswear, and smoothness is the key. A jacket, skirt, and especially pants should fit smoothly—not so tight that they wrinkle anywhere and not so loose that they bag. Pants especially need to fit well when they are part of an office outfit. Even if you have a beautiful body, tight pants are not the way to adorn it if you are serious about your work.

When having pants fitted, be sure to wear the shoes you plan to wear with them. Pants should break just slightly over the instep of the shoe and fall over the beginning of the heel in the back. Women's pants can be tailored in the same way as men's, that is, at a slight angle that is lower in back than in front, or they can be hemmed straight across. Just make sure they are long enough to look good with the shoes you plan to wear them with.

Sleeves should be smooth at the armhole, and free movement of the arms should not be hindered. Collars should neither ride up nor pull away from your neck.

## Buying Accessories

### Purses and Briefcases

A purse is the major accessory for most women. It may look extremely businesslike to carry only a briefcase—until you are in an important meeting with a client and your spare pair of panty hose pops out or a lipstick rolls across the floor. If, like many women, you find it awkward to carry a purse in addition to a briefcase or tote, one solution is to buy a flat, envelope purse that can be tucked into your briefcase.

Your purse and briefcase should show that you mean business. Brown or black leather for a briefcase and any good leather for a purse is acceptable. Leather may be expensive, but it is worth every penny for the note of taste it adds to your overall look. This is the place to splurge if you can afford to.

## Gloves

Gloves as a pure fashion accessory are no longer worn, but most of us still need them for protection for two or three seasons out of the year. Leather gloves are the best choice for an executive woman. Save the cute knitted styles and the heavy-duty mittens for weekends. For work in fall and spring, choose an unlined or silk-lined leather glove. In winter, cashmere- or wool-lined leather gloves look good and keep you warm. If you cannot afford leather gloves, plain wool knitted gloves will do, and, with some coats, they are even the glove of choice. Avoid white gloves—cotton or kid—as they look too prim. Since gloves are no longer coordinated to outfits, choose them to match your coats.

## Hats

In cold climates hats are a necessity; most women coordinate them with their winter coats. Felt hats are the most popular. Knit hats are somewhat less acceptable, except in really cold weather when people lower their standards a little for the sake of keeping warm.

In warm climates or during the summer, a smart-looking straw hat is a good idea. Head scarves are acceptable when they are in style.

## Shoes

If you have a limited budget, you can own as few as four pairs of shoes—two for summer and spring, and two for winter and fall—

provided you color-coordinate them with your clothes. The fastest way to ruin your budget is to splurge on a wonderful pair of shoes that don't go with anything you own.

In conservative professions, plain pumps and T-straps are still the best choice. You can ride trends sparingly, though. Specifically, this means that when the fashion mavens are walking around on 1½-inch platforms, your shoes could have a conservative ½-inch addition to their soles. In less conservative professions, you can obviously adopt the newest styles right away if you choose to.

However you decide to play your shoe wardrobe, buy the best shoes you can afford. Better to invest in fewer pairs of really good-looking leather, suede, or nubuck shoes than in more pairs of cheap ones.

Heel heights no longer matter much, although most executive women seem to have settled on a relatively comfortable 2½-inch heel. Low heels and flats are now acceptable at work, stiletto heels slightly less so, but if they work for you, go ahead. The only warning we can offer is not to wear shoes that slow you down. If there's one thing you want to do in the executive ranks, it's to move with the same ease and speed as your male counterparts.

Shoe manufacturers—some of them at least—have begun to cater to women's demands for comfortable shoes, but without continuing pressure from women themselves for shoes that really fit, they will probably retreat as soon as they feel it is safe to do so.

When and where to wear the more extreme styles is a matter of taste most of the time, the exception again being the conservative professions. When knee-high boots enjoyed a brief moment of popularity a few seasons ago, they weren't showing up in law firms. On the other hand, a conservative high boot can be worn with a suit in most offices these days. Cowboy boots belong only in offices where the offbeat is tolerated or, better yet, cherished.

Much as we sympathize with the impulse behind rain boots and running shoes, now that manufacturers have begun to make comfortable pumps, we don't think they belong on any woman's feet once she gets to work. Wear them to and from, if you must, but switch to more traditional shoes once you're there.

The days of coordinating shoes and purse are over. There is nothing wrong with doing it, but it is far better, if your budget is limited, to invest in one good leather purse that will go with everything. If your purse coordinates with anything, it should be with your winter coat; it need only blend with an outfit.

## Coats

A winter coat should be of the best quality you can possibly afford, stylish but not of such high style that it cannot be worn for four or five years. Black is a good color if you will also wear the coat for evening wear. Otherwise stick to any neutral color—brown, camel, burgundy, beige, dark green, navy, possibly red.

If you find an inexpensive coat that looks great, buy it and then buy an expensive set of buttons to put on it; it will instantly make the coat look much better than it is.

The life of a coat can be prolonged by relining, and any coat that has taken a hard winter of wear will surely need some lining repair. Never wear a coat with a torn lining or a missing button; it looks sloppy. Also regularly check a coat to make sure that the lining does not hang out in back; if it does, have this fixed before wearing the coat again.

Raincoats should look businesslike. This is one place where a direct imitation of your male colleagues does not hurt: Buy a beige raincoat and carry a black umbrella. Resist the urge to go to bright colors in either an umbrella or a coat; they simply look too frivolous. You might consider buying a folding umbrella if, like most women, you are already burdened with a briefcase and a purse; the umbrella can be slipped inside either.

Fur coats have fallen on hard times recently, due in part to the economic times and in part to protests by animal-rights activists. If you are in a profession where they are worn and are acceptable, go ahead. But these days, no one looks askance when the wardrobe of an otherwise well-dressed woman excludes fur.

## Jewelry

A professional woman should wear conservative—and, if at all possible, good—jewelry. Either gold or silver is fine, and yes, the two are mixed today in many interesting styles.

A watch is a necessity. The most sophisticated and desirable watches are simple in design, with a gold, silver, or leather band. Silver-banded watches are rather rare, but if you wear silver rather than gold, there is no reason not to buy one. Watches with diamond or crystal bezels, so popular now, are overkill, especially in the workplace. They look and are faddish.

In fact, with the exception of engagement and wedding rings, diamond jewelry should be saved for evening wear. It has become popular for daytime wear, but, ironically, daytime diamonds have become the style of secretaries rather than executives.

Avoid any jewelry that looks too much as if it should be worn only for evening, even if the piece is made of precious stones. If you want to wear fancy jewelry after work, take it to work and put it on just before you leave.

## Hairstyles

Executive women don't have much more leeway than executive men when it comes to hairstyles. Conservative is still best. Some of the hair taboos are hair that is too "big," too short, too long, too braided (even though the rest of the world has discovered the elegance of braided styles), or too obviously artificially colored—all subject to personal interpretation of course. Standards vary from one milieu to another.

## Nail Polish

Painted nails are now accepted almost everywhere, but the smart corporate executive still keeps her nails short and wears a light shade of polish. Even if you choose not to wear nail polish, make sure your nails are well manicured at all times. It exudes confidence.

## Scent

Wearing any kind of scent in an office can be tricky since scents usually send a sexual message. You'll want to rule out any heavy or very sexy perfume in favor of a light, unobtrusive cologne or toilet water. (Both are lighter versions of perfume.) If you encounter a lot of different people during the work day (especially clients) or work in an airtight office, it may be more considerate of others to skip wearing any kind of scent. It's certainly kind to those who have allergies.

## CONCLUSION

Dress for executive women has loosened up considerably since John Molloy dictated that women wear solemn suits and plain, plain pumps. Female executives now routinely wear nonmatching suits—a bright-red blazer with a dark-colored skirt, for example—or even silk dresses with jackets, outfits that would have been unsuitable for office wear only a few years ago. Accessories now march to the beat of fashion in all but the most conservative offices. Only in certain corporate settings and law firms has an unwritten dress code persisted in keeping women's styles nearly as conservative as men's. But even though female executives can now dress stylishly and individuality can assert itself, the truly savvy, upwardly mobile executive still takes a long look around at what everyone else is wearing before going shopping for work clothes. And then she buys what will make her fit in.

# 14

# *For Women Only*

Although we don't believe that women need to do anything differently from men to get along in this world, two brief reports that appeared on the same day on the front page of the *Wall Street Journal* gave us pause regarding the condition of female executives.

The first noted that women will need approximately one hundred years to crash through the glass ceiling at their current rate of progress. Their pay and power won't be equal to that of men until the twenty-first century, or until this generation's grandchildren are running corporations.

The second noted that sexual harassment complaints lodged with the Equal Opportunity Commission have climbed dramatically in three years. Complaints numbered 728 in the last quarter of 1990 compared to 1,244 in the last quarter of 1991 and 1,608 in the last quarter of 1992.

When these two situations are remedied, we will no longer consider it necessary to include a chapter exclusively for female executives in a book of executive etiquette.

Women who reach the executive ranks are painfully aware that they encounter—and must counter—a great deal of prejudice along the way. The only question for most is how to deal with these problems, that is, whether to rely on restrained tact or use a bludgeonlike approach. Although we can appreciate the urge to use a club, we believe that many situations can be resolved with manners—and a lively sense of humor.

## THE LITTLE COURTESIES THAT HURT

It's often the little things such as having a door held open or packages carried that are the most painful to a woman. Some women simply acquiesce in the name of getting ahead with the least amount of pain, while others feel they are sacrificing a principle if they permit men to offer them these small courtesies.

If you are among the latter, you can still tactfully tell a male colleague that you don't appreciate such attentions. A heavy hand is only alienating and rude. To make a point about holding doors, for example, you might deliberately hold a door open for one or more male colleagues. You can simply *refuse* to let anyone carry your papers or packages. A colleague who refuses to pick up on these not-so-subtle hints is employing his own power tactics.

## WHAT YOUR LANGUAGE SAYS ABOUT YOU

Most men today, unless they are very apolitical or very old, are aware of the connotations of terms such as "lady," "girl," and "woman." Most liberated women today have strong feelings about not being referred to by such patronizing terms. The problem is how to deal with the person who persists in using them.

First, consider the source of the problem and the cost of proving your point. If the chairperson of the board, who happens to be eighty years old, comments on what a fine young lady you are, do you really want to lecture him about your political views? And isn't there a possibility that you should consider deferring politely to his age, just as you would to that of any other aged person?

When your colleagues use derogatory terms, it is more important to make it clear that you don't appreciate them. Since most men today know what they are saying when they speak this way, they follow the slur with a challenge such as "I suppose you are one of those women's libbers who doesn't like to be called a lady," or "I know it's in to say woman, but I still think of you as a lady." When you have such an obvious parry to counter, simply say, with your biggest smile, "That's right; I don't appreciate such language" or "I really do think I'm old enough to be called a woman." What you say isn't nearly so important as how you say it: with a smile and a light tone.

If you aren't given an opening by a colleague who persists in using such expressions around a hardworking woman, you can still smile and say "I work awfully hard for a living, and I really would like to be referred to as a woman."

Numerous women reported that one or two honest but polite comments often are not enough to end the jibes, but there is nothing to stop you from always commenting that you do not appreciate being called a "girl"—over and over and over again.

## Woman as Servant and Secretary

Too often executive women report that any kind of food or beverage service still seems to be their domain. A woman has every right to resent this, but it still may be easier to make her point subtlty or humorously. For example, if someone is rude enough to ask you to get coffee or food, smile and say "Sure." Then call out of the meeting room for a secretary and pass on the food and drink order to her or him. You probably won't be asked to provide food service again, and your point will have been made without rudeness to your supervisor or coworkers.

In the same way that men often assume that women have some innate ability to bring on the food and drink, they also assume that taking notes is a natural talent of all women, so unless you own the company, it is better to be prepared to ward off such requests graciously than to assume they won't occur.

The solution is simple, although it takes a little nerve and may surprise the men present. But don't worry about that: Business involves a lot of gamesmanship—men know it and women know it—and if, once in a while, women have to create a few new ones until the battle of the sexes has equalized somewhat more, so be it.

If you are asked to take notes at a meeting, simply smile (again, it is more than a polite gesture; it deflects hostility) and say that you are not prepared to do so, not having brought a notepad of any kind with you. Generally your point will then be made; occasionally someone will be loutish enough to ask another man to give you his notepad. At this point, you must take a stand, albeit a politely phrased one. Look the person making the request straight in the eye and in your calmest, most disarming voice say "I really would feel uncomfortable being the one to take notes."

Another tactic is to say "I think it would be better to have someone else do that." Then sit through what will seem like endless silence. If all else fails, or if you have been asked to take notes one too many times, when you are asked again, call a secretary to sit in and take notes. Need we say that this should be done with extreme politeness?

If these tactics are employed in a disarming, casual way, you probably won't get caught in a direct confrontation or power struggle. Few men today are looking for confrontations with what, in too many cases, are still their token female executives.

On the other hand, until it becomes obvious that you *are* being harassed, assume that any man asking you to do things that are not in keeping with your status is not doing so maliciously, and give him the benefit of the doubt until you learn otherwise.

With all these techniques, persistence is of the utmost importance. You simply will have to correct a supervisor or coworkers not once but many times. Try always to do it graciously and in a way designed not to offend someone you will still have to work with or for.

If a coworker does appear to be malicious in his intentions, then treat his actions as you would those of any other competitor. Techniques for this are discussed in Chapter 1.

## Intimacies—Accepting and Rejecting Them

Most instances of men touching women at work have an erotic base. While a man may casually fling an arm around another man's shoulder or pat him on the back, these actions rarely have the same intentions when directed toward women.

The way any woman handles sexual overtures is a highly personal matter, but assuming that you want to maintain a degree of professional distance and reject the pass, then try to find a gracious—or humorous—way to do so. Often making a joke or saying "Does your wife know you're loose?" is enough to stop someone.

And some men don't realize they are doing something offensive. One man we know, who wouldn't dream of cheating on his wife, nonetheless had a habit of massaging the shoulders of colleagues—male and female. He worked in a casual business where the hours were long, and his hands were considered a national treasure by some—and offensive by others. His wife had tried unsuccessfully to convince him that some women didn't appreciate his gesture. It wasn't until he sat through the Anita Hill–Clarence Thomas hearings that he finally "got it." He no longer offers uninvited shoulder massage.

Often sexual overtures begin with flattery. There is a difference, as every man and woman knows, between a compliment about how attractive one looks generally and how sexy one looks specifically. Any woman's antennae should go up when she hears the latter. Some men, entirely lacking in subtlety, make a physical approach. If the come-on involves touching, you have a right to remove whatever part of his body is touching yours. Usually it is smart to follow this up with a statement that makes your position very clear, such as "I'm sorry, but I don't go for that sort of thing at work." Then leave quickly; don't hang around for conversation about where and when you *do* allow that sort of thing.

If a man persists in making sexual overtures, you may have to take a sterner tack and bluntly tell him to stop whatever he is doing. In such a situation, remain calm and poised. Try to talk to the offender out of earshot of others. Be very specific about telling him what he is doing that displeases you. This is no time to be ambivalent or abstract.

Keep your reason for not getting involved as impersonal as possible so you don't offend someone you have to continue to work with. For most of us, this is easy. Many executives, male and female, simply don't want to get involved with someone they work with.

On the assumption that the man will cooperate now that you have unequivocally expressed your lack of interest, be friendly to him the next time you see him. In other words, give him one more chance.

## When It's Sexual Harassment

Some men simply do not get the message and back off, and their advances are sexual harassment. While our legal system may not yet have a good definition of sexual harassment, it is much like pornography: We know it when we see it. If a gesture or conversation makes you feel uncomfortable, then it's inappropriate—and probably sexual harassment.

In the past few years businesses have become much more sensitive to issues of sexual harassment, and many women now find they can take such complaints to a superior—or, if need be, a supervisor's superior—and get support.

If support is not forthcoming from within the company, your only other course of action may be to file a sex-discrimination lawsuit. Unfortunately, companies do not look kindly on this, and while we wish we could tell you that life will continue in the same way after you file one, the fact is that you will find it very uncomfortable to continue working in an office after you file a lawsuit charging your employers with sexual harassment. Still, the only way that sexual harassment will be stopped is if enough women speak up about it.

Should you continue to work somewhere after filing a complaint, brace yourself. As for your actions, this is truly a time when good manners (and a steely will) will help to get your through a rough period. Treat everyone as kindly as possible—even if coworkers don't return the courtesy. Ultimately this can only work in your favor.

## Lunch with Colleagues

Perhaps the most challenging aspect of being a female executive is forging relationships with peers. Let's face it: Men tend to form bonds with each other, and rarely do they do this better than at work. It is usually up to a woman who wants—and for business reasons, needs—to break into these male-bonding groups to take the initiative in establishing the kind of working relationships she needs.

If your colleagues seem shy about asking you to join them at lunch, ask them to join you. And as in any other situation, set the tone for the way you would like to be treated during lunch. If you prefer to remove your coat without assistance, do so quickly, out of range of those who might help. If you don't want someone to pull out a chair for you when you sit down, seat yourself promptly upon reaching the table. (On the other hand, if a maître d'hôtel is planning to seat you, it is rude to ignore his attempts. After all, it is part of his job to provide this service, and while you may have a chance and a reason to reform your coworkers, it is not appropriate to do the same for the waiters of the world.)

Some men still feel awkward about letting a woman pay for a meal, although so many women now work in executive circles that most men have adapted and readily share the tab with a female colleague or let a female client pick up the tab. And many women feel even more awkward about not paying for themselves, especially when they are with their colleagues. Female executives report that there are two approaches to this problem. The first, and gentlest, one is to play a waiting game. Always offer to pay, but don't argue about it. Eventually, most men who lunch regularly with a female coworker will relent, if only to salvage their own budgets.

The second approach is equally polite, although slightly more aggressive. Simply insist that you want to pay your share. Take money out of your purse and give it to the person you are with or place it on the table in a way that indicates that you will indeed walk away leaving a $10 tip for a $20 lunch unless the money is used for your share of the bill.

As a last resort, if a man persists in trying to pick up the tab for lunch, gently explain how awkward you find this situation and that you will have to stop having lunch with him if he does not let you pay. He will probably relent and breath a secret sigh of relief.

The exception to paying your own way is when lunching with your superior, who may ask male and female colleagues to lunch and treat. It is only gracious to accept this gesture.

Unless this really matters to you, who pays for what is not really worth making an issue over the first couple of times you encounter the problem. Old manners do die hard, and even the most liberated man may feel he has to make the gesture of offering to pay when he does not know a female colleague well. Such men often willingly let a woman pay for herself, or even treat occasionally, after one or two lunches, so the situation is best handled by not making an issue of it until it is obvious that a man is making a chauvinistic gesture rather than exercising manners he has not quite been able to let go of.

## CLIENT RELATIONSHIPS

Most of the strategies you use to handle colleagues can readily be applied to relationships with clients or customers. Set the tone for the way you expect to be treated and make your feelings clear without hurting anyone else's. Often a male client or customer is slightly ill at ease about how to treat a high-powered executive who happens to be a woman, so he is eager to follow her lead.

About the only persistent hurdle that women encounter with male customers today occurs when the bill arrives. Many women solve this problem by using a credit card. For some reason, if men do not see money, they do not get as nervous about having a meal bought by a woman. A credit card is also a definite signal that the company is paying, and not the woman, and that suits most men just fine.

If the waiter places the check beside the man, simply reach over and pick it up. If you frequently go to the same place for lunch, the waiters should quickly learn that you are to be given the check. If they don't, then you should speak with the manager.

## How to Get Credit for Your Work

A common complaint with junior-level female executives, particularly those who have come up from the secretarial ranks, is that their superiors frequently take credit for work they have done. If you want to get ahead, however, your work must be noticed by top management. Therefore, it is important to get credit for the work you do.

You can ensure getting credit by putting your name on your work in a prominent place. A more tactful ploy with a manager who consistently fails to recognize your work is to draw up a list of responsibilities and take it to the manager, seemingly to ask his or her advice about how you are allotting your time and what your priorities are. Such a list will force the manager to take an objective look at what you actually do—and, one would hope, to see that credit has not been given to you for doing it. If the oversight is accidental, you will probably find yourself gaining due recognition in short order. If the oversight is due to the manager's own insecurity, however, it may continue, and you may have to find another way to combat it, or even find another job.

## Problems with Other Women

Not infrequently a female executive may find that some of her worst enemies at work are those members of her own sex who are jealous of the power she has attained. Anita Hill certainly found this to be true when several of her coworkers readily testified against her—for no seeming reason other than the fact that she had power they lacked.

Clerical workers can do considerable damage in sabotaging someone's work if they put their minds to it. An additional factor that may create tension is the college-educated woman who got stuck at the clerical or low-management level and resents someone with a similar education moving ahead more quickly, as frequently happens these days.

Handling this situation is not unlike walking a tightrope. You should be the one to take the initiative in setting the tone for these relationships, and it requires tact. Because you are also a woman, one would hope you would find considerable empathy to use as a base in establishing relationships with female clerks and secretaries. Anyone who has ever served time in the clerical ranks should not have too much of a problem recalling the things that were most degrading. It is then a relatively simple matter to refrain from doing those things: asking a secretary to get coffee all the time and never returning the favor; insisting on unrealistic deadlines that may infringe on a secretary's personal life; and even expecting a secretary to interrupt the work he or she is doing for you to make a telephone call you could just as easily make yourself.

On the other hand, you do have executive responsibilities, and it is important that you exercise them. This requires a sense of balance. Do not make your secretary's life so visibly easy, out of sympathy for his or her plight, that your actions are noted by your colleagues and superiors, thus gaining you a reputation for being unnecessarily soft.

Avoid socializing excessively with subordinates (unless it's the norm where you work), not because you do not respect them as people, but because people normally socialize with their peers at work. Rather than seeming rude to the secretaries, you will probably find that maintaining some distance makes everyone feel more at ease.

And speaking of easing a secretary's way, while you are showing respect for clerical work, make sure that you are truly respecting *that* work. Realize early on that some secretaries do not aspire to executive positions and take great pride, quite justifiably, in doing clerical work. It is arrogant to assume that every female clerk who comes through your office door wants to become your protégée and follow in your footsteps to the executive washroom.

Showing a normal amount of empathy and enlisting clerical workers as your allies, plus waiting through the inevitable period when they are taking your measure, has often won a tactful female executive better relationships with other women in the office than any man can ever hope to attain.

## YOUR ATTITUDE

The best way to get equal treatment from colleagues is to expect it. Don't let yourself resort to ploys, manipulations, or any other of the tactics by which men and women have frequently guided their personal relationships. Create an aura that makes it clear that you expect equal treatment from your colleagues.

Just as important as creating this attitude is the need to fit in with a company. It is not a coincidence that lawyers in one law firm all lean toward wearing their hair the same length and wearing gray pinstripe suits. For years men have sustained their power structures through the use of such visible signals to one another. It is easy, therefore, to imagine the threat presented by a female executive who can and does wear pastel colors, carries a purse in addition to a briefcase, and does not wear her hair at all like any of her male colleagues. Although many articles and books suggest that women try to look as much like the men they work with as possible, we do not advocate such an approach, on the grounds that it is ridiculous and can actually be a detriment to your image as a woman. Even if a woman buys a gray pinstripe suit, it is a pretty sure bet that she won't look quite like one of the men. And if she cuts her hair like theirs, she may even find herself out of a job. So what is the solution for a woman willing to fit in with the look of her company or business?

Compromise. Pick up on the mood of the company, just as any ambitious young male executive would do. If it is indeed a gray pinstripe kind of place, buy conservative clothes, jewelry, and accessories. Studies have shown that women tend to choose quieter, less colorful clothing and accessories as they gain more power, and one wonders if this is perhaps a subconscious way of appropriating the "company look." At any rate, do dress in keeping with the mood of the place where you work.

In addition, follow the company line in manners and operating methods as much as you can without sacrificing your sense of identity. This is, after all, how men climb the corporate ladder, and it behooves any woman who wants to make her way to the top to do the same.

# 15

# *Landing That Big Job:*
# THE ETIQUETTE OF
# THE JOB SEARCH

Job hunting is not unlike a ritual courtship dance. The chances of getting a highly desired job increase greatly when you know the correct pattern of steps. If you don't know the steps, or blindly break the pattern, your chances diminish. You will have ruined an opportunity to get the job you want. But, as in all instances where actions are guided by etiquette, once you know the rules you can use them—or not use them—to your advantage.

It is not the purpose of this book to provide you with every detail concerning a job change. There are many excellent books that deal in depth with how to handle an interview, a headhunter, salary negotiations, and other aspects of job hunting. This chapter will show you how to handle the etiquette of the job search. I will show you how to develop the poise and tact necessary to get the job you truly want.

## Tapping Your Network

Once you make the decision to look for another job, it's an accepted practice to call business acquaintances and ask for help. This is not a time to rely only on friends, and it is definitely not a time to rely on colleagues with whom you work, unless you are very sure they can be trusted. Call or write anyone else whom you think might be useful. If you are hesitant about calling someone you do not know well, remember that people like to help each other and that you can return a business favor at a later date. Besides, everyone likes to feel powerful, and passing on an important job lead to someone is a way of showing one's power.

Never give someone as a reference without checking with him or her first. And try to keep in touch with people whom you plan to use as references. A call out of the blue after five years of no contact may not produce as glowing a reference as a call that is simply part of your routine of keeping up with old business friends.

Call any employment agencies or headhunters who have ever expressed an interest in you. Call suppliers, clients, old managers, the person you met at a party last week who had some interesting business ideas.

When you talk to these people, just mention that you are beginning to look around. Note that there is no rush, that you have not mentioned this to anyone with whom you currently work and do not plan to, and that you would like to hear if anything interesting turns up. Be polite and low key about your request for help.

News of most executive-level jobs is passed by word of mouth before they are listed in advertisements, but this is no reason to leave any stone unturned in the search. Read the ads in newspapers and trade journals and papers regularly. (Read them, however, at home or very discreetly at the office; it is surprising how often a sudden interest in the trade journal with the best ads will tip off others to your plans.)

Whenever you can, shoot higher than your current job level in using contacts. Just as you can improve your tennis game when you play with a slightly better player, you can find tips about higher-level jobs from someone with a more prestigious position.

## USING EXECUTIVE PLACEMENT SERVICES

The key to using executive placement services is to do just that—use them. Executive recruitment services fall into two general categories. One kind takes a sum of money from you in return for marketing you to companies. The fee ranges from several hundred dollars to several thousand dollars. While many of these agencies are reputable, the fact is that they have already gotten their money and will have less of a stake in finding employment for you. If you use a company like this, or any recruitment company, for that matter, be sure you have checked its reputation very carefully before you enlist its services in your behalf.

The second kind of recruitment company takes its fee from the company that eventually hires you. Needless to say, this company has more of a stake in finding work for you. Such recruitment organizations work at all levels of business; some place people only in the $60,000-plus salary range; other executive recruitment firms start with a salary range as low as $12,000, and some have no minimum salary.

There is another way in which this type of firm can be selective. In the more elite firms, referrals are always made through contacts. If you want to establish a contact with one of these firms, make a few discreet inquiries among acquaintances to see who has used such a recruitment agency and would be willing to let you use his or her name when you call. Once you have the name of someone who is known to the agency, call him or her, introduce yourself, and ask if you can drop a résumé in the mail or make an appointment to talk. (Occasionally one of these agencies will obtain your name and will contact you to see if you are interested in changing jobs. Even if you decline, make a note for future reference of the person to whom you spoke as well as the name of the agency.)

Executive recruitment agencies tend to devote more time and effort to candidates who are qualified for high-paying executive positions. At the lower salary levels, there is a point of diminishing returns in the amount of time they can invest. This is something any executive should be aware of. One way to counter diminishing interest is to make it clear that you are using more than one recruitment service and that you are actively looking on your own.

There is a tendency among executive recruitment agencies, as among other types of employment agencies, to offer a client a job that may not exactly match his or her needs or interests. Such offers need only be politely declined, although one interesting counterploy helps to keep an agency interested when you must decline a job that has been suggested. Say that you have a counteroffer involving more money or a position that is much closer to what you want. If the service is highly interested in selling you and stands to gain a good-size fee from doing so, it will work a little harder and faster to place you.

In dealing with executive recruitment agencies, play fair and polite but play with your self-interest in mind, and they will frequently be of help to you as you climb to the top.

## SETTING UP AN INTERVIEW

Once you have sent out initial feelers and answered a few ads, making appointments for interviews is the next step. In obtaining an interview, always go directly to the person with the power to hire. This is usually your prospective supervisor—a supervisor being, by loose definition, the person who can get you a promotion or a raise and who can hire and fire you. Especially at the executive level, it is important to avoid the personnel office of a company. Going through personnel is a giveaway that you lack contacts or are not aggressive enough to pick up the phone and get through to the person who *can* hire you.

A skilled interviewer will let you tell him or her what you know about the firm, so never go to an interview without first having done some homework. You need to know something about the company's history, its profit picture, its image, and its future plans. A word of warning, though: All this information should come from public sources. Even if your best friend or old college roommate works there and has personally introduced you, never admit to knowing anything about the inner politics or workings of a company during a job interview.

## DRESSING FOR THE INTERVIEW

Always dress appropriately for an interview, even though this means different things in different cities, companies, and professions. As a rule of thumb, plan to dress as you would if you were going to work—only slightly more conservatively. A woman who might ordinarily wear a silk shirt and linen skirt to work might want to add a jacket. A man who wears a suit should pick his best-looking and most conservative one for a job interview. All professions have unspoken dress codes, however, as do individual companies. For example, if you want a job in a hot Madison Avenue advertising company, your efforts may well be facilitated by showing up for the interview in a mauve shirt and a wild tie.

Whatever you do, do not dress casually for an interview. Under no circumstances should you wear jeans or corduroys—even if they are what you would wear daily were you to get the job. One of the unwritten rules of the interview is that the prospective employee must appear immaculate and totally pulled together for the interview. If the weather is bad, wear boots and change to clean shoes when you arrive at the company for the interview. If you discover a loose button on a coat as you are heading out the door for the interview, put on another coat. A lost button, unshined shoes in need of reheeling, or dirty or broken fingernails all can and will be held against you when you are seeking a job. They will be seen as reflections of your ability to do your work satisfactorily.

## THE ETIQUETTE OF THE INTERVIEW

When job hunting, it is important to display the fact that you know how to behave among civilized company. After all, the entire ritual of job hunting is designed to show that you understand the etiquette of the world of work. Here are some tips that will help you on any job interview.

1. Try to make a good impression on everyone with whom you come in contact, especially the secretary or receptionist who greets you. The person who interviews you may well ask his or her opinion of you, or he or she may even decide to offer an unsolicited opinion, particularly if you were not overly polite.

2. You must arrive on time. There is simply no excuse you can offer, short of a national disaster, for being late for an interview to obtain a job that you seemingly want very much.

3. Make the first move to shake hands, or be prepared to make the first move. Until recently, etiquette books recommended that the prospective employee wait for an interviewer to offer his or her hand, but today's aggressive job seekers do better to extend their hand first, regardless of the interviewer's sex. It is always a gracious gesture to make toward another person, and it can also be taken as a sign that you have leadership qualities.

4. If you have some time in the reception area before the interview begins, ask if you may hang up your coat. You will look more at ease if you go into the interview with as little extra baggage as possible. If you are ushered into the interviewer's office immediately, wait until he or she asks if you want to remove your coat and indicates where to put it.

5. Men remove hats when they enter a building, and women keep their hats on. Gloves should be removed by either sex before shaking hands with someone, particularly if they are of the bulky winter variety.

6. Unless you are greeted with a very obvious power tactic, such as a long, ongoing phone conversation or a long wait in someone's office, do not sit down until you are asked to do so.

7. Do not smoke or chew gum or, for that matter, accept candy,

even if it is offered. Any of these activities will detract from
your effectiveness as a speaker.

8. Whether to call someone by a first name can pose a problem
in a job interview. Generally, don't use first names unless the
interviewer indicates that this is his or her preference. Even
then, be slow to use them if you are young or are being hired
at a relatively low level. If you are being hired at an executive
level, though, then you should be more comfortable using first
names in an interview.

   If the interviewer is a woman, call her "Ms." or "Miss,"
but don't make a point of asking her which she prefers. That
has been worked to death and isn't a good conversation
starter.

9. Once you are seated, don't fidget. Sit up straight without
seeming stiff and look directly at the interviewer.

10. Listen intently. When ready to answer a question, it is sometimes effective to take a moment or two to ponder the answer.
You will appear thoughtful and your answers will seem more
meaningful and less as if they have been prepared in advance,
which, of course, they have been.

11. Exhibit self-confidence, but be careful not to turn the interview into an ego trip. The person interviewing you is trying to
determine one thing—how much use you will be to his or her
company. Remember this and try to keep your answers to any
questions pertinent.

12. Look for signals that the interview is ending and make a
graceful exit. The interviewer may say "It has been especially
pleasant talking with you," or "We will be in touch with you,"
or he or she may simply rise. Thank him or her, shake hands,
and if you feel the interview has gone well, ask whether you
can call soon or when a decision can be expected.

   If the interview has gone so well that you feel you are a
prime candidate for the job, you may graciously express your
interest and desire to work for the company, but be careful
not to overdo any flattery. A flashy display of false flattery as

you exit may only give the person interviewing you second thoughts.

## TOUGH INTERVIEW TACTICS

Most interviewers have some sort of strategy. Their most important goal, of course, is to evaluate what you can do for the company. On another level, though, an interviewer will be testing how aggressive you are, how you handle stress, how high your anxiety level is, how you handle an awkward situation, and, most important, how well you will fit in and how valuable you will be.

Almost everyone has heard stories of interviewers' deliberately entrapping interviewees. The most famous of these is the version of the interviewer who offers a cigarette to an unsuspecting person who accepts it and then has to flounder for an ashtray—for there is none in the room. Actually, it would be nice if all such tactics were so obvious. Unfortunately, the more important the job you are seeking, the subtler the tests you must undergo.

If you really want to know what is going on in an interview, an excellent book on the subject is *The Evaluation Interview* by R. A. Fear and R. J. Chiron (New York: McGraw-Hill, 1990). This book discusses in detail such matters as seeming to take the interviewee into one's confidence as a means of getting him or her to open up and confess things he or she would not ordinarily divulge; staring piercingly; raising the eyebrows; or using other body language that will make the interviewee so ill at ease that he or she may begin to chatter—and in the course of chattering divulge information that is best not revealed.

Several other good books on this subject are worth reading if you want to bone up on the psychological tactics that can and will be used against you; check the local library for them. In this book we are concerned with the etiquette of countertactics to these techniques.

### Being Ignored or Kept Waiting

What appears to be a case of bad manners exhibited on the part of the person who is going to interview you may actually be a test of your patience. If so, good manners should help you prevail. If an interviewer keeps you waiting, take the nearest chair (in his or her office, if that is where you have been asked to sit), pull out a magazine or a crossword puzzle, and start to work. If you opt for reading, avoid a serious trade journal and stick instead with something such as *Time* or *Newsweek*. After all, there is no need to overdo this ploy, which has the effect of presenting you as a self-possessed and hard-to-ruffle person.

Do the same thing if an interviewer is engaged in what appears to be a lengthy phone call. (First, though, allow him or her a few minutes on the phone in case this is not a ploy.) It is polite to show no signs of having overheard a conversation, even if it occurs two feet away from you. Unless you are asked to, in fact, do not participate in any miscellaneous conversations that interrupt the interview. Your advice will be needed only after you are hired.

### Handling Personal, Financial, and Illegal Questions

You do not have to answer personal or financial questions, but your best bet is to have a tactful reply ready for the interviewer who *does* ask. Generally, these questions are put to you in loose terms: "I suppose your divorce was an upsetting experience?" or "Wow, with interest rates the way they are, I can imagine what you got held up for when you bought that house." In response to questions like these, which the interviewer knows he or she has no business asking, your best bet is to laugh and say something vague, such as "Well, yes, I suppose so" or "Well, possibly that was the case." If you carry it off, the ultimate way to deflect a personal question that you don't wish to answer is to smile and say nothing.

More difficult to handle are questions that are clearly illegal. It is illegal to ask about your ethnic origins, your religion, your age, your marital status, or your plans for childbearing, but this doesn't stop certain interviewers from asking. Job seekers should realize, though, that such questions can be—and often are—a double bind. People who ask them care about such matters, and you will be in trouble whether you choose to answer the question or to dodge it.

Sometimes you can gently remind the interviewer that he or she shouldn't be asking a certain question. In some situations saying "I wonder if you realize that is an illegal question" is enough to put the issue to rest. Doing so is a gentle way of putting the interviewer on notice that you know your rights. Still, in certain circumstances even saying this much will cost you the job. And if you are offered the job, you must consider whether you will be able to do well in an environment that obviously harbors prejudice over your age, sex, marital status, religion, or ethnic origins. No matter how much you need a job, it's probably better to decline employment where you will clearly be subject to prejudice. Fortunately, there are a growing number of sophisticated, open-minded companies that welcome diversity. These companies would never dream of asking an illegal question during an interview.

## Answering Open-Ended Questions

In any job interview, you should be prepared to handle open-ended questions. They are a favorite tactic of the interviewer seeking to put you so much at ease that you succumb to saying things you might not otherwise divulge. A comment such as "My, you are young to have accomplished so much" has far more beneath the surface than meets the eye and requires a carefully planned answer. To acknowledge such a comment too modestly and quietly shows a lack of aggressiveness, and to answer it at great length may open the way for you to say a lot of things about your achievements that you never meant to say. Try something such as: "Thank you, I'm glad you feel that way. Actually, I think what helped me most was my ability to . . ." Go on and describe one strong trait about yourself and then wrap up your answer.

Open-ended questions are often used to start someone talking about a problem area, such as a poor work record, an extended period of unemployment, a personality clash with a boss, a reason for leaving a job, or an explanation for being fired. Fortunately, you know more about the flaws of your record than anyone else does, so go into an interview with a ready answer to use in reply to such questions.

For example, an interviewer might say "I suppose you were upset over being fired?" or "I assume that you enjoyed your six-month break from work?" In the former case, explain without rancor what the problem was that led to your firing, minimizing it as much as possible and making yourself look good. Never lie about what happened, and never show bitterness toward others you have worked for. You might, for example, consider saying: "I felt bad that there was a personality clash. I've thought a lot about what precipitated it, and I feel it was basically a difference of opinion in management techniques. I suppose my fault was in wanting to move forward too fast . . ."

With the latter question, explain what you did during a period of unemployment that makes you a more useful employee—perhaps you took a special course on entertaining clients at home at Harvard Business School, researched a book on modern management methods, or wrote articles for business journals. Make it clear that you were not sleeping late or job hunting sporadically, you were seriously job hunting while also keeping busy with an important project.

## Countering the Ultimate Tactic

Occasionally you may encounter out-and-out rudeness in an interview. Be careful; it may only be a test. The appropriate reaction—if you think you want to work for people who behave this way—is no reaction at all. Just continue displaying good manners and hope that the boor who is not displaying his or hers is only making a small-scale power play and is not always so rude.

## PLAYING DOWN HUMOR

Humor doesn't work well in a job interview, contrary to what many people believe. For starters, it's a mistake to be flip about anything that may be a potential problem for you or for your prospective employer—the fact, for example, that you were fired from your last job or have been out of work for a year. These aren't laughing matters, and an attempt to treat them as such will not work in your favor.

It's also a mistake to think that a job interview that turns out to be lots of fun and laughs (and virtually no real substance) was successful. In fact, it was probably just the opposite. You were wooed into revealing a side of yourself—a goofy one—that may well cost you a job you want. The job interviewer who was quick to share the laughs with you was also taking your measure, and while he or she may have found you charming, chances are that you were deemed too lightweight and irresponsible for the job.

Furthermore, the use of humor is one of the rare things that you and not the interviewer can control. The savvy job interviewer doesn't make wisecracks or tell jokes during an interview. If the interviewer tells a joke, by all means laugh, but then wait for the next question. Don't tell a joke back. Young executives often fall victim to the trap of thinking that an interview that was full of laughter will actually turn into a job. They rarely do.

## PLAYING UP CONNECTIONS

If you need to learn to play down humor on a job interview, you also need to know that it's okay to play up connections, or at least it's okay to use them. Connections are part of the way the business world goes round. They help to establish that you belong—or, in the case of a job interview, could belong. They don't necessarily get you the job (although in many instances they do), but they certainly can open doors for you.

Connections are when you went to the same school as the interviewer, or when you grew up in the same neighborhood (or part of the country), or when you have a personal tie to someone at a place where you would like to work. Connections are when you like the same sport or enjoy the same weekend leisure activities. They are any common thread that will endear you to the job interviewer or the company.

How you use connections has much to do with how valuable they will be to you. The best ones are used with subtlety. The fact that your résumé indicates you were a member of a club at college that the interviewer (or company president) was also a member of is enough. You may never actually talk about the tie.

Or the association may be mentioned when you make your initial contact. Sometimes it comes up during the interview. If it does, acknowledge the tie but don't trade on it presumptuously. Never say anything that might indicate that you expect to be given a job because of your connections. Even if this is exactly the case, why alienate people over this?

## ACTING LIKE A TEAM PLAYER

One important task for any interviewer will be to take your measure as a team player. When you hear questions about teamwork, it is important to speak well of your colleagues and of the company you currently work for. Specific comments and compliments about the company you are hoping to go to work for are also a good way to convey the impression that you will be a loyal team player. You might, for example, comment that the interviewer's company has always been well known to you for its early innovations in team organization, or that it is known to most outsiders as a company that is good to its employees. Ask questions about the corporate structure that show you will welcome the opportunity to work with others closely. Describe team projects or other examples of cooperative work projects that you have been involved with in the past.

## SHOWING OFF PERSONAL STRENGTHS

One of the things you must accomplish in any job interview is to show off your strengths in a way that is actually rather aggressive. A certain degree of aggressiveness impresses prospective employers and is expected of job applicants. It can be tricky to show aggression, however, without also appearing arrogant or smug. Fortunately, a touch of graciousness can help you achieve exactly the right balance between aggression and humility. A way to do this, for example, is to say: "I like to think that I'm good at organizing people so they will work well together." Adding "I like to think" and other similar qualifiers softens the fact that you are building up yourself.

A kind of forthrightness that would not necessarily play well socially may be exactly what is called for in a job interview. In a social situation, for instance, when you are complimented, the polite response is a simple thank you. When complimented in a job interview, though, it's okay to say thank you and add a reaffirming statement, such as: "I like to think that I'm good at working with new customers. I've worked hard to develop that skill." Adding the extra refining statement that in effect builds you up is exactly what is called for.

## Talking About Problem Areas

There may be some problem areas in your job history that emerge during the interview. Stay calm when the subject is brought up. One female senior executive had to explain why her career was cut short at a bank when she got a superior who simply did not like women and who made it obvious that he would do nothing to promote her career. She resigned to look for another job full time. When she was confronted with this seemingly rash move, she had a ready answer that served her well:

> Frankly, it became obvious from the new executive vice president's treatment of me and the other women working under him that he was not favorably disposed to women in business. While I tried not to let it bother me personally, it eventually caused several other women and me to look for new positions.
>
> Since a key promotion that I had been working toward steadily for eleven years was obviously not going to be in the offing, and since I had saved enough to support myself, I decided to resign and devote myself full time to looking for a new, more challenging position.

This woman made her point so well—and she also had to explain why she was not given a good reference by the executive vice president—that she soon had three very tempting offers in banking.

Sometimes the problem area is more personal, as when you have to explain that you have been living in a substance-abuse facility for the past six months or that you can never or rarely work overtime because you are a divorced parent with a small child.

The trick in a job interview is to minimize your weaknesses while continuing to emphasize your strengths. When explaining about your alcohol problem, you might say:

> I had to admit that my drinking was out of control, which is more then many people can do. I then took steps to remedy the situation, and I believe I have emerged a stronger, better person for having done this. I've learned a lot about myself in the past few months.

A working parent with a small child should be prepared with a statement to explain his or her inability to work late in the following way:

> Because I have a three-year-old whom I'm raising alone, I won't be able to give the amount of overtime to the job that I would like. I do view this as a temporary situation, and I am confident that I can more than make up with efficiency what I lack in overtime hours. Juggling parenthood and work has taught me nothing if not how to be efficient.

If you do have a problem that could affect your performance on the job, the best thing to do is to discuss it openly and honestly. Better to explore what is expected of you—and what you can deliver—now, before you take the job, than to find out later that you have not made a good match.

## Telling Little Lies—When and How

Job hunting invariably requires some white lies or maybe even gray lies, since they are not told to salve anyone's ego but rather as a maneuver to get you what you want. One lie you will have to tell is about the amount of money you are making (assuming that you are looking to receive a substantial increase). Another white lie or two may have to be told to the people with whom you currently work, for example, when you miss a day of work to go on an interview.

Let us consider the latter instance first. Secrecy at work may be of the utmost importance to your current job security. Employers don't like to think that their employees are out looking for another job, and in some instances you could lose your current job if your job-hunting efforts became known.

The best strategy when job hunting, then, is to keep a low profile and be very discreet. Discuss your efforts, if at all, only with colleagues whom you can trust absolutely.

When you must take time off work for a job interview, especially one where you must travel out of town, the only solution may be to tell a white lie and say that you are doing something else. Feign a dentist's appointment or claim that your college roommate is getting married if you have to be gone for several days. Best of all, of course, if you can get away with it, is simply to take a personal or vacation day and not offer any explanation.

## Settling Salary

The other lie you will probably tell is about your salary. Executives who hire and executive recruitment agencies all admit that lying about one's current salary is a common practice, although less so at some times than at others. The amount you exaggerate by varies with your salary range and with the kind of contract you have with a prospective employer. Employees in the lower executive ranks, earning from $25,000 to $50,000, generally add 10 to 15 percent; executives in the upper echelon may tack on an extra 20 to 30 percent.

An executive recruitment agency may increase a salary by more than an individual would. Once an agency represents a client, there is little likelihood that a prospective employer will do anything to double-check a salary. Also, executive recruitment agencies know the salary range a company is willing to pay, which makes it even easier to exaggerate a prospective employee's salary.

There is only one time when you are liable to be caught exaggerating a salary, and that is when you are unemployed. If you are still employed, it is a courtesy for the prospective employer not to check on you there. This means he or she will call only references who would have no idea what you are now earning. Furthermore, many companies today refuse to release salary information or any other personal information about employees, past and present.

Best of all, of course, is to maneuver yourself into a more honest and enviable position where you do not have to state your current salary, but rather can say that you will need $35,000 or $48,000 or something in the "high 40s."

Be bold and state your salary needs when the discussion on money starts. If the interviewer was going to offer substantially less, he or she may well go to someone higher in the corporation to check on the possibility of meeting your salary requirements if you have become a desirable prospect. Another reason to state your salary demands up front is that once the interviewer has announced a range far below what you can accept, it may be impossible to negotiate a compromise very far upward.

Some people who have perfectly good common sense in all other areas of their careers lament the need to lie to a current or prospective employer. A truly ambitious person, however, usually knows it is the best way to get what he or she wants and to protect personal career interests.

## Beyond Salary: Talking Benefits

Go into the final interview with a clear idea of what you want, what you would like to have, and what you will give up if need be. Above all, plan to be flexible. A company may offer a privilege you never thought of getting that will outweigh the one you did think of asking for.

There is an etiquette to asking for benefits at the hiring stage. Mention those that you have received through your former employer and those that you think you will need to do the job well. Any *business* excuse for needing a benefit will do. You cannot ask a firm to pick up a country club membership tab because your spouse likes to play golf and won't be happy about relocating unless assured of a place to play. You *can* say that you need a country club membership because of the business contacts it will provide you. You *can* mention that you play tennis several times a week with an important client and would like a company membership so that you can return the client's invitations.

If the company is eager for you to relocate fairly soon, this gives you an easy opening to mention any problems you are going to have selling your house or finding housing in a new community. A wise prospective employer will read between the lines and offer whatever he or she can. Make sure, too, that the company will pay moving expenses, although this has become a standard executive benefit. Whether you will need a car is usually readily agreed upon by both parties.

Sometimes you can do a little jockeying over physical position within a company during the hiring process. Usually this is necessary only in huge corporations, where office sizes and types are less than desirable even at middle-management levels. When you are shown the facilities, usually during the final interview and before you sit down to work out the final arrangements, your new employer often will indicate where you will be working. If you are not offered an office that is sufficiently large for you to work in, consider mentioning this later when the two of you sit down together. But whatever you do, don't say you need a large private office because you had one before. Give a valid business reason why you need one, something such as "I've never worked in an open area before, and since I handle many of my sales calls by phone, I was wondering whether it would be possible to have an office that offers more privacy." Before mentioning this, though, you should realize that where you sit initially is not nearly so important as where you sit a few months later after you have had a promotion and have begun to prove yourself to the company. Then, too, companies either realize the value of privacy for employees or they don't, and arguing over office space may appear petty to a prospective employer who doesn't see the need for privacy. The executive hiring you also may be powerless, in a large company, to do anything about your office. In short, it is frequently not worth it to make a point of physical surroundings.

## POSTINTERVIEW ETIQUETTE

One very small gesture guaranteed to win anyone extra points is to follow up an interview with a thank-you note. Since this is still basically a business situation, the note may be typed and should be written on your business letterhead—your personal one, that is, not the one of the company you currently work for. Thank the person for taking the time to see you and perhaps add a kind comment or two about the company and how you hope to be hearing from them soon. Try not to write more than one paragraph, or the note may begin to look either pandering or social.

## WAITING TO START A NEW JOB

Once you have worked out the details of a new job and set a starting date (and asked for confirmation of everything by letter), the interview will end. You have nothing official to do for your new employer until the day you start.

An especially gracious gesture on the part of the executive doing the hiring, however, is to maintain some contact during this period. A lunch might be arranged to introduce a new executive to colleagues, or a purely social celebration dinner might be planned. Nothing starts off a new employer-employee relationship on a better footing than making the new employee feel that the company is truly pleased to have hired him or her.

## RESIGNING GRACIOUSLY

There is an art to resigning graciously, and in these days of executive job hopping, it is one that merits careful mastery. Leaving one company to go to work for another is never a completely permanent severance. You may return to work there someday, and frequently you will find yourself using former supervisors as references. Therefore, it pays to leave in everyone's good graces, which is not always an easy feat, since the mere act of resignation often implies that there is something you don't like about a company or a supervisor.

## Giving Your Supervisor the News

Once you have accepted an offer to go to work for another firm, make sure that you are the person who delivers the news to your supervisor. It is a courtesy that you owe him or her. If your supervisor is going to be unavailable for a few days, explain to your new employer that you would appreciate having any formal announcement held up until you have told your current employer. Then don't leak the news to anyone; it always gets out, and your supervisor will hear it one way or another before he or she sets foot in the office again.

If your supervisor is out of town for an extended period of time, you can either resign to his or her superior or try to contact your supervisor by phone. Generally your supervisor will appreciate your making the effort to contact him or her; many have shown hurt feelings when passed over in a resignation by an employee.

## Planning to Take Your Leave

When you are making arrangements with your future employer, request whatever amount of time you will need to wrap up any assignments you are working on for your current employer. This does not mean, however, that you must think in terms of finishing assignments, for once you have resigned, you will find you are a lame duck. Think, instead, of tying up loose ends and transferring your work to someone else, or of organizing your work properly so that it can be easily transferred to someone else.

Unless you are very close to being irreplaceable, two to three weeks' notice is usually sufficient. Companies don't encourage even an executive who has resigned with the best possible feelings to stay much longer than that. Then, too, the time between your resignation and your actual departure is a fairly emotional one that is best not prolonged. Pack your briefcase, tell your colleagues how much you have enjoyed working with them, and leave.

## Giving and Attending Farewell Celebrations

As a rule your colleagues or employees will plan luncheons and other festivities to say good-bye. An especially gracious gesture is to plan something for your colleagues and those who have worked for you.

By all means, you should ask anyone who has especially helped you or has been a mentor to you to lunch or dinner. While this is a time to terminate some relationships, it is also a time to strengthen friendships and even business relationships that you wish to continue. Turning the tables with some entertaining is an excellent way to do this and to say thank you.

## Maintaining Ties

Make an effort to keep up any business or personal ties you value after you leave, for the day will surely come when you will need references for your next job, and the task of supplying references usually falls to the person who employed you several years back.

# 16

# Hiring and Firing

Most of us view the job-hunting process from an intensely personal perspective, namely, from that of the job hunter. Yet for every person seeking a job, there is an executive with the power to hire and fire. In fact, hiring and firing is one of the most important aspects of an executive's job. The kind of staff that an executive is able to garner shapes a company's image internally and externally. Hiring and firing is so important that before a change master comes in from outside to restructure a company such as IBM or Hughes Aircraft, he or she typically spends time reviewing the résumés of management to see whether it is strong enough for the transition it will be required to undergo—and presumably to decide who should stay and who should go. At some point in his or her career, every manager assumes some responsibility for hiring and firing. And there is an art to doing each well.

## FIRING WITH COMPASSION

Too often, when employees are going to be laid off, the news ricochets through a company before an announcement comes from management. In the worst cases, the rumor mill gets hold of an individual firing before the employee learns that he or she is about to be let go.

Even hiring, normally a happy occasion, can be mishandled in a way that leaves a trail of irretrievably wounded feelings. Consider the excited young executive who had just landed the job of his dreams. The only problem was that he was leaving what *had* been the job of his dreams, and he wanted above all else to preserve good relations with his soon-to-be-former boss. Imagine his dismay then when his new superior lunched with a friend who worked in the same place as the young man and indiscreetly announced the new hiring. The news filtered back to his supervisor before he could resign. The damage to their relationship was irreparable. The young man felt bad that he hadn't resigned earlier, but the real villain was the tactless manager who let the news slip prematurely.

Needless to say, one of the most important aspects of hiring and firing is to do so without embarrassing snafus. Here are a few hints to help you accomplish this.

1. Keep all transactions confidential. If you decide to hire someone, that is between the two of you. If you interview someone and decide not to hire, that is still between the two of you.

   The same thing applies to firing. Nothing is more painful to everyone in an office than to know that someone is about to be fired. If you plan to dismiss someone for any reason, keep silent until you have told the person being dismissed. Afterward, discuss the matter as little as possible. You may need to reassure your staff or bolster morale if there are mass firings or layoffs, but there is never any reason to discuss the details of an individual case.

2. Do all the hiring and firing yourself, in person. It is a courtesy to the person involved, a kind way to end a relationship and a gracious way to begin one.

3. When dismissing someone, show respect for his or her feelings and opinions. After all, the ability to take away someone's job is the ultimate sign of power; it is more potent than giving raises, benefits, and promotions, and it can become an ego trip

for you if you are not careful. Leave the person's ego intact if at all possible. It is perfectly acceptable to point out why the person is being fired, but it is not okay to hammer home the point so the person walks away destroyed. The time to hammer home an employee's faults, if at all, is when you are warning an employee that his or her behavior is unacceptable and may result in a firing if not corrected.

4. Before firing someone, give plenty of warning. This is necessary not only in these litigious times but also moral. If someone is not doing a job well or the right way, he or she deserves warning before being fired.

5. When someone is not being fired for cause but rather because the company is making cutbacks, be sure this is absolutely clear. Tell the employee that he has done nothing wrong, and that you will be happy to recommend him or her for other jobs. It is especially gracious to say that you very much regret having to lose such a good employee.

6. Do not promise someone a recommendation that you will not be able to deliver. Mention, if asked, that the person might better seek a recommendation elsewhere. If at all possible, though, try to give someone a good recommendation, even if you have fired him or her. What you disliked may not offend another employer so badly. If you must say something unflattering, couch it tactfully and surround it with the person's good points.

## When the Decision Is Not to Hire

If you decide that a certain interviewee is not what you are seeking after all, you owe it to the person to tell him or her yourself. Techniques such as suddenly becoming unavailable or leaving the talks dangling indefinitely or saying that your company won't be hiring right now after all, when you know you intend to hire someone else, are cowardly and rude.

Telephone the person or invite him or her to your office to say that you have decided not to offer the job. Avoid going into details that might hurt the person's ego unnecessarily, but give as honest an answer as you can. Instead of saying "I don't think your personality will work in our company," you might say "I feel that you might find yourself in conflict with the person for whom you would have to work. You are very different people, with different management techniques, and would clash sooner or later. Your management techniques are excellent, but I would rather see you put them to work somewhere where they will be truly appreciated. Because of this, I have decided not to offer you this position. I hope you will understand."

If the person is obviously under- or overqualified, this is one of the easiest things of all to explain and hurts no one's feelings.

## WHEN YOU MAKE AN OFFER

One of the truly pleasant tasks of an executive is to tell someone he or she is going to be hired for a job.

If you are going to offer a position to someone, call or write the person and ask when he or she can come in to see you. At this stage of negotiations, you both will know what is going to happen. Making the job offer is the least important aspect of this interview; the real purpose of the interview is to hammer out the financial arrangements.

Sometimes an offer is formally made in a letter and reinforced with a friendly phone call, which may be followed by a brief waiting period while the prospective employee makes his or her decision about whether to accept the job. When the job has been accepted, the meeting to talk out arrangements is set up.

# A Final Word

A n executive is someone with the power to *execute*, a verb that
means to *administer* as well as to *discharge, electrocute, behead,* or
*hang.* And although the latter may be harsh terms, they are
how some employees feel when they work for executives who do not
respect them or the work they do. Unfortunately, poor management
styles are rife, and poor managers are far more common these days
than sympathetic, supportive ones.

This need not be the case, nor does it work in the best interests of
business. The best managers know from the start or soon learn that
they get the most efficient and productive work from employees who
perform in a cooperative and, dare we say it, a well-mannered,
workplace.

Admittedly, creating a cordial, respectful workplace takes more
effort than doing the opposite. After all, unless given encouragement
to go in another direction, people tend to be naturally competitive at
work. Anyone can snarl at employees and create a threatening, overly
competitive workplace. It takes real finesse, time, and attention to
nurture employees and consistently to treat everyone who works for
you with genuine respect.

Manners, of course, are an important key to creating a pleasant work environment for everyone from the lowest clerk to the CEO. People work more efficiently if they know what is expected of them not only professionally but also socially. Executives play an important role in setting the tone for an entire company. In a world that is fiercely competitive, executive etiquette is the veneer that keeps the workplace civilized.

# Index